BASIC SOCIOLOGY

C. EMORY BURTON

Contributing Editor
Frank Mensel

authorHOUSE®

AuthorHouse™
1663 Liberty Drive, Suite 200
Bloomington, IN 47403
www.authorhouse.com
Phone: 1-800-839-8640

First published by AuthorHouse   4/6/2009

ISBN: 978-1-4389-5652-7 (sc)

Printed in the United States of America
Bloomington, Indiana

This book is printed on acid-free paper.

Preface

The purpose of an introductory text should be to awaken in its readers an appreciation of its subject matter, which in this case is sociology. Many students assume that sociology is an esoteric discipline removed from their everyday interests and concerns. Others confuse it with social work or even psychology. The introductory text should awaken students to the broad and yet very practical range of subjects in the field. Hopefully, many will be motivated to continue their study of the subject by going more deeply into readings or by taking additional courses in the field.

This book was planned with the intent of providing a concise overview of the major elements in sociology, while selecting several important and interesting themes for deeper exploration. These themes include life in contemporary Japan, the effect of television on children, poverty in the United States, and domestic violence. An effort has been made to keep the text affordable for the average student.

While the focus of most of the material is on the United States, there is considerable emphasis on the interdependence of all countries, and this is particularly evident in chapters 3 (culture), 7 (community), 12 (religion), and 13 (social change and globalization). While there is no chapter on gender, that topic is covered in the chapters on culture, socialization, and family. Population is treated in chapters on community and social change. A glossary contains 178 terms, with 67 of them marked with an asterisk (*) as being especially important.

A great deal of credit for the book goes to Frank Mensel, the former chairman of the Board of Trustees of the American Student Association of Community Colleges, who is listed as a contributing editor. Mr. Mensel inspired the work, wrote a large part of one chapter, and edited the entire manuscript.

William Hornyak of El Centro College, Dallas, cooperated with Dr. Burton in planning the book, and made a contribution to the chapter on socialization. Darrel Wilbanks took many photographs for the work, eleven of which were used. Mr. Wilbanks took all the photographs except those for chapters 2, 8 and 13. Joanne Raye added some information about life in contemporary Japan, and technical help was provided by Allen Mabry and Paul Burton.

Comments on the book are welcomed, and may be sent to the author at Emory234@sbcglobal.net.

Table of Contents

Introduction

Sociology means watching people and figuring out why they do what they do. It helps us see what goes on behind the scenes, and how deeply our society and the groups we belong to influence us. Why do different racial groups have different experiences in life? Why do women experience the world in a different way from men? Why are there different social classes in our country? Why are there homeless people? How are we affected by major social issues such as globalization, immigration, and urbanization?

One mistake beginning students often make is to assume that sociology deals with such obvious subject matter that careful study is not required; it is simply common sense. This is incorrect for at least two reasons: there are critical terms that must be learned if one is to appreciate the insights of sociology, and careful study will often uncover truths that contradict common sense (Macionis 2004: 4).

The effort required to become familiar with sociology can have many rewards. One can understand his or her social world better; elements of social life, such as family and culture, can be understood in a new way; and one can gain insights into himself or herself. It can be a fascinating journey.

Why might one consider majoring in sociology? One answer is that the field is so broad that it provides an excellent general education. Most companies want employees with a good general education and good communication skills, and (with a few exceptions) don't care what your major is. Sociology has relevance to anything involving people in groups, whether that is education, law, government, religion, marketing, public relations, or health care. Sociology concerns all of social life, and is a good major for those who have broad interests.

Students often ask, "What can I do with a degree in sociology?" As one teacher answered, "Almost anything" (Henslin 2007: 332). It can be your passport to most types of work in society. Most sociologists teach in colleges and universities. Applied sociologists work in a variety of areas from counseling people, studying how diseases are transmitted among social groups, studying how children's programs actually work, studying statistics for public agencies such as the Health Department, relating lack of prenatal care to behavioral problems in school, and many other types of jobs.

White Rock Marathon, Dallas, Texas.

Chapter 1: WHAT IS SOCIOLOGY?

There are a number of acceptable definitions of sociology, but basically it refers to the systematic study of society and social interaction. "Society" refers to people who interact in a defined territory and share a culture. "Social interaction" refers to the process by which people act and react in relation to others.

It is important to appreciate that sociology includes a broad range of subjects. Some everyday interactions sociology deals with include dating patterns, the behavior of people in a restaurant, the formation of "cliques" in high school, and the development of a gang on a city street. Sociology is also concerned about globalization, urbanization, immigration, and social changes that affect the lives of many or all of the people in society.

Sociology is one of the social sciences, the others being psychology, political science, anthropology, and economics. (History has been considered a social science, but is now generally listed with the humanities.) Probably the closest field to sociology is cultural anthropology. Traditionally anthropology deals with ancient or less developed societies, but also considers modern ones. The two fields overlap in the areas of cultural and social organization.

Another field sometimes confused with sociology is psychology, the study of behavior, especially in such areas as thinking, learning, perception, emotions, and motives. The emphasis in psychology is on the individual, while the emphasis in sociology is on the social context, but the two fields can overlap.

Some beginning students confuse sociology and social work. The latter field is a profession for helping people. It draws upon knowledge from all social sciences, including sociology. Sociologists do not usually try to intervene in the social world. Rather, they attempt to provide knowledge for those who do intervene (Turner 2006: 26).

Some sociologists limit their efforts to analyzing society and publishing their work in books and sociological journals. Others feel an obligation to use their insights to make society a better place by changing it in significant ways and work for social reforms.

Sociologists are currently engaged in evaluating programs in more than 100 countries around the world. Most of the programs they evaluate are creations of governmental agencies. They include social insurance, welfare services, health care, educational services, housing assistance, and crime prevention efforts (Dentler 2002: 195).

There is a field known as applied sociology, which uses sociology to solve social problems (Macionis 2004: 5). An example would be the Supreme Court decision of 1954 which outlawed racial segregation in public schools. (The court considered research from sociologists in its decision.) Sociology can be applied to many areas such as crime, illegal drugs, teen pregnancy, health care, and slum housing. But there are those who believe applied sociology is not enough to actually change society.

Variables

One common term used in sociology, as well as in other social sciences, is *variable*. A variable is a trait or characteristic that can vary (change) from one person to another. *Gender* is a variable that can vary between *male* and *female*. *Age* is a variable than can vary between *young, middle-aged, old,* and so on. (The categories of a variable are technically *attributes*.) Being familiar with a number of common variables is useful for a number of reasons.

The following 13 common variables are not necessarily the most important ones, but they help illustrate the type of analysis done in sociology. These variables are gender, age, race, religion, residence (inner city, suburb, small town, etc.), language spoken, education (years completed in school), religion (if any), employment (whether one is employed or not, and if not, is the unemployment voluntary or involuntary), occupation (assuming one has one), income, possessions (house, land, stocks, etc.), memberships (in various groups or organizations), and family (single, married, divorced, etc.).

A simple device to remember these variables is to construct two words vertically with each letter representing one of the variables. The words are *program* and *relief,* as shown below:

way to remember the variables

PROGRAM:	Possessions
	Race
	Occupation
	Gender
	Residence
	Age
	Memberships
RELIEF:	Religion
	Employment
	Language
	Income
	Education
	Family

One advantage of becoming familiar with these variables is that one gains some idea of the range of topics sociology considers. The point is not so much the qualities adhering to an individual, but the way these traits relate to the social world. Some in this list, such as memberships, occupation, and family, are clearly related to other people, but actually *all* of them are. Take *gender,* which might seem to be a highly personal matter. Does the fact that one is male or female influence the way one relates to other people? Of course it does, and thus gender, like all the others, is actually a social variable.

Of course there are many other variables. People's beliefs (favoring or not favoring gun control, for example) and behavior (how frequently one attends religious services) may be variables. One could consider all of these to relate to individual people, but other variables relate to the social order, such as rate of urbanization or rate of immigration. Sociology deals with all of these and others.

Becoming familiar with these variables can help one answer some sociological questions. Suppose one is asked what types of people in our society are more vulnerable to poverty. By looking over the list of variables listed above, one can infer several traits that might suggest being poor. (Obviously, one with low income and few possessions would be poor, but that's not very illuminating.) Females and non-white persons are somewhat more vulnerable to poverty. One who is unemployed or employed in a low-wage industry is more likely to be poor than someone who earns higher wages. A resident of an inner city or an isolated rural area may be more vulnerable than someone from an affluent area. A non-English speaking person, someone with little education, and a single parent (especially a female) would be more likely to be poor.

⚔ One thing that sociologists do is to try to *relate* variables to each other and to other variables. _*Education*_ is related to _*income*_ in that a person with a good education is likely to have a higher income than one without that education. (That is not always true, of course.) Is *gender* related to *occupation*? If it is observed that women have trouble getting higher-level positions and are not promoted as readily as men, the answer is clearly yes.

One important variable is _social class position_. The study of social class, known as _social stratification,_ is one of the most important subdivisions of sociology (see chapter 8). By utilizing some of the variables listed above, it may be inferred that a higher-status person, or member of the upper class, would have a prestigious occupation with high income and significant possessions, have a good education (at least a college degree), belong to some important organizations, live at a prestigious address, and perhaps come from a respected family.

Two additional terms are important in understanding sociology. One is *institutions (or social institutions)* and the other is *social structure.* Institutions may be defined as established patterns of action and thought that organize important social activities. They exist to answer some of the recurring problems of life. The following examples should make this clear.

One important requisite in any society is education, particularly for children and young people. It may be possible to get an education on one's own, such as by reading, watching educational programs on television, talking to informed people, and the like. But society recognizes a specific way of becoming educated, and that is why it sets up schools, colleges, trade schools, universities, and the like. (While a particular college is an institution in a sense, sociology tends to look at the broader function of education itself as an institution.)

Sports are a major enterprise in many countries, including the United States. You may remember, as a child, getting together with a dozen or more other children and playing baseball or softball. The group would find a vacant lot, put down something like garbage can lids for bases, estimate where the foul lines were, choose up sides and play the game. There might be only two or three bats and just one ball, so while the enterprise would be considered a sport, it would be too casual and unorganized to be considered an institution.

Consider what happens when the community decides to organize the activity. A group of boys might form a team, find a sponsor who would help provide uniforms, hire umpires, and provide an actual stadium to play the games. There would be an arranged schedule with other teams and something like a Little League is organized. When something becomes organized enough to be an established part of the society, we can consider it an institution.

Take the case of a young man who claims to be the best tennis player in the United States. If asked to justify that, he replies that he has played many people around the country and has never lost a match. Given that tennis—a part of sports—is highly structured, such a claim would not be taken seriously by most people. Does he have a ranking by the United States Tennis Association? Has he won a tournament such as the United States Open or the U. S. Clay Court Championship? Only if he can answer these questions affirmatively would his claim be taken seriously.

An important issue in this country is health care. One might conceive of health care as an individual matter. One who is sick or injured might take care of this need through self-treatment, resort to herbal remedies, ask friends what they have done for a similar condition, and the like. But there is a standard way of dealing with health needs: one consults a physician or clinic, perhaps is given a prescription to be filled at a pharmacy, and in some cases is sent to a hospital. Because there is a generally understood way to deal with health issues, health care is considered an *institution*.

Other common institutions include economics (the way a society deals with the production and distribution of goods), politics (government and its officials), family, and religion. Family is considered an institution because while it is possible to bear and raise children outside of marriage, the society (specifically, the state) takes an interest in the marriage by setting up important laws to regulate it. Religion is often involved in marriage and family as well.

An individual might consider himself or herself religious in that he or she practices personal meditation and attempts to be influenced by religious ideas. But in a society of any size, organized religious groups such as churches, synagogues, temples, and mosques will develop. These groups may well have membership lists and a specific program, and so religion has become institutionalized.

Another term important in sociology is *social structure*, which may be defined as the framework that surrounds us, consisting of the relationships of people and groups to one another, which give direction and set limits on behavior. While this may seem complex, the basic idea is that much of our lives are constrained by forces in the larger social world. While we may think our thoughts and actions are purely our own, they are heavily influenced by the culture and the social world in which we live. (See chapter 5.)

You may see that the last two terms are closely related. An institution is simply a highly structured way to accommodate a social need. The more organized an activity is, the more structured and predictable it is, the more it is likely to be thought of as an institution. To a large extent, it is this socially structured world of institutions that sociology concerns itself with.

C. Wright Mills (1916-1962) wrote that the task of sociology was to realize that individual circumstances are inextricably linked to the structure of society. He called this linkage *the sociological imagination*. This involves moving away from thinking in terms of the individual and his or her problem, focusing rather on the social, economic, and historical circumstances that produce the problem. It acknowledges that at some level our experiences are shaped by macro-level forces (Harper and Leicht 2007: 11).

A simple example is the plight of an individual looking for work during a serious recession or depression. If the economy is not producing enough jobs, and if layoffs or outsourcing are proceeding at a rapid pace, this person may well have difficulty obtaining a job, or at least one that he has been anticipating. The sociological imagination reminds him or her that the problem may not lie in his or her efforts, but in the social situation of that time.

Or take a 60-year old widow, still attractive, who would like to re-marry. The problem she may find is that there is a distinct shortage of attractive, eligible men in her age group. Women outlive men by several years, and the society is more likely to approve a man's marrying a woman several years younger than he, rather than the reverse. She may be forced to look for a man 70 or older as a potential husband.

Using the sociological imagination, "one can shift from the examination of a single family to national budgets, from a poor person to national welfare policies, from an unemployed person to the societal shift from manufacturing to a service/knowledge economy, from a single mother with a sick child to the high cost of health care for the uninsured, and from a homeless family to the lack of affordable housing" (Eitzen and Zinn 2007: 6).

A Global Perspective

Thirty years ago, one might take a sociology course and limit one's concerns to the United States, or whatever country the student happened to live in. Only in the study of culture would one be likely to consider the ways of life of other societies. Because of what is known as *globalization*—the study of the larger world and our society's place in it-- such an approach is seldom taken now. The fact is that what happens in any country is strongly related to what goes on in the larger world. (See chapter 13.)

The events of September 11, 2001, should remind us that we are a part of a global world. The fact that many of the products we consume are made, in part or in whole, in other countries is another reminder. The lives of people around the world are intertwined; social relationships do not stop at national borders. One country's problems— unemployment, drug abuse, pollution, AIDS, inequality—are part of a larger global situation. What appear to be local events are shaped by events taking place in other countries. And multinational corporations are significant forces in structuring social relationships that transcend national boundaries (Ferrante 2006: 25).

To save space, this book will focus on the United States, assuming almost all its readers will be from that country. Chapter 3 on culture will include several cross-national comparisons, however, and later chapters will make reference to important global concerns such as immigration and economic globalization.

The Development of Sociology

Most sociology textbooks state that sociology emerged as a scholarly discipline in the late 19th century. While that is technically correct (the word "sociology" was coined by a Frenchman named Auguste Comte in the 1850s), it is misleading. The ancient Greeks had much to say about the society in which they lived, as did some of the Hebrew prophets. The great Greek philosopher Socrates became known for asking questions about the world, and getting people to examine the ideas they had taken for granted (Charon 2007: 12).

In the Enlightenment, the philosophical movement of the 18th century that emphasized the use of reason, the stage was being set for the scientific study of the world, including society. Names such as Descartes, Locke, and Kant were important in this general development. One of these philosophers, Charles Montesquieu, helped set the stage for sociological thinking. He felt that society should be treated as a "thing." (While Montesquieu is best known for his theory of the separation of powers, which was the basis for the U. S. Constitution, he also sought to explain human laws and social institutions.) (Turner 2006: 13)

Some significant world events helped lead to the development of sociology. Two of these were major revolutions in France and the United States. Perhaps even more important was the Industrial Revolution of the late eighteenth and early nineteenth centuries. The Industrial Revolution was the move from human (and animal) labor to the use of machines. People turned to external sources of power as in oil or steam. Machines began to take over the skills of the worker and numerous factories developed. The growth of railroads and steamships symbolized this development. As you might guess, the Industrial Revolution had a huge impact on the way people lived their lives.

The person generally considered the founder of sociology was a Frenchman, Auguste Comte (1798-1857). Profoundly influenced by the French Revolution, Comte moved to Paris and began to reflect on what holds society together. Why do we have (in most cases) stable social order instead of anarchy and chaos? To answer this and other questions, Comte concluded that the correct way to answer would be to apply the scientific method to social life. While Comte wanted to call this new field "social physics," he settled on the term *sociology,* "the study of society."

Comte believed that, rather than simply reflecting on society and the world, or following traditional explanations, sociology should be considered a scientific discipline, as much as astronomy and physics. He thought scholars could discover general laws that could explain the operation of the social universe. These laws would be tested using systematic methods. Further, he believed that sociology should be used for reform of human life. Comte's reputation declined later in his life and his conclusions have been subject to great debate, but his formative role in the discipline is accepted (Turner 2006).

For many years, when sociology textbooks discussed influential early thinkers in the field, they were limited to men. But women have also been important, and perhaps the most important 19th-century woman was Harriet Martineau (1802-1876). She was first known for translating much of Comte's work into English, but she became an important intellectual in her own right.

Martineau viewed the social world as composed of cultural values, beliefs, and norms (rules), that she called *morals* (that term would not be used in that sense today). She believed that these values and beliefs directed individual behavior and provided guidance for associations among individuals. The culture (way of life) of a group of people never wholly accounts for people's behavior because there is always a difference between what one is supposed to do and what one actually does. Hence social structures are always changing (Turner 2006: 12-13).

Another contribution of Martineau is in making observations about people and variables. She visited the United States and tried to view the country in all its diversity. Instead of just visiting the cultural centers and talking to the country's leaders, she made a point of observing all kinds of people, including slaves, prisoners, factory workers, and farmers. She tried to compare the actual workings of the society with the principles on which the country was founded.

The most important 19th-century thinker who influenced sociology was Karl Marx (1818-1883). He was born in Germany but spent much of his time in London, writing in collaboration with Friederich Engels. He is widely considered as the inspiration for communism (though that was a later application of his ideas), but it would be a serious mistake to conclude that his work is unimportant since communism has declined. In addition to his recognition in sociology, Marx is considered an important intellectual in history, philosophy, economics, and political science. At least some understanding of the thought of Marx is essential for any educated person.

Marx believed that society is characterized by persistent *conflict,* or struggle between major groupings in the society. While conflict can exist on a number of levels, Marx stressed *economic* conflict, that is, the struggle between those with large resources and power in the society and those economically deprived. He argued that the rulers of society, the people who owned the factories, land, and machinery, used their position of power to exploit (take advantage of) the workers. Thus there were two major classes, the bourgeoisie (the capitalists who owned or controlled most things) and the proletariat (the mass of workers who owned little or nothing). For Marx, one's economic status determined his or her social class.

Today conflict theory is a major perspective in sociology (see chapter 2), stressing the struggle between two or more groups. But conflict is not limited to economic conflict, that between rich and poor, or between employers and employers (stressed by Marx), but between middle class and working class, blacks and whites, males and females, conservatives and liberals, rural dwellers and urban dwellers, and so on. Marx pointed out that conflict is what leads to social change.

Marx felt that the conflict between rich and poor (to oversimplify it somewhat) was a tenuous situation; it could not go on forever. What should happen (and Marx considered this inevitable) is that the workers would become aware of their disadvantaged position and unite against their oppressors, resulting in a classless society. This has been an enormously influential idea in the twentieth century, especially in such Latin American countries where the masses of people have felt exploited (Henslin 2007: 4-5; Turner 2006: 17-18).

Some areas of sociology where Marx has been influential include political sociology, social stratification (an analysis of social class, see chapter 8), social movements, and social change (see chapter 13). Further, sociologists who want to expose inequality and resist the domination of one segment of society by another have found inspiration in Marx. "Marxian theory remains an insightful explanation of the technical and economic forces that generate tensions and change in capitalist societies" (Harper and Leicht 2007: 17).

Two later thinkers are generally considered the most important of the early sociologists (Marx, as we have seen, was influential in several areas), namely Emile Durkheim and Max Weber.

Durkheim (1858-1917), the great French sociologist, thought the essential question of sociology was how to explain the integration of society—what would hold it together--as it became larger and more complex. His answer has been important for all later sociologists.

By integration, or solidarity, Durkheim meant the extent to which members of a society are united by shared values. If one can visualize a community, such as a small town, where people take pride in their community, are active in local organizations, generally agree on major issues, often have parades or other celebrations, and where few people are moving out of the community, we could say it has high social integration. This is the major factor that Durkheim explored.

There are two ways a community could have high integration. The first would be brought about by commonality, in that the people were very similar in such areas as social class, interests, and occupation. They felt close to the other residents and so a type of integration would be likely to ensue. Durkheim called this kind of integration *mechanical solidarity*.

The other way a community (even a large city) might be integrated results when the members of the community specialize in various pursuits. This works to the benefit of the community as a whole, because there will probably be somebody around to take care of specific needs that will arise. If one is sick, there are doctors and hospitals. If one needs home repairs, someone who specializes in that area will be available. If one needs psychological help, a trained counselor will probably be around. If one enjoys sports, there will be sports teams and other opportunities to watch or participate in. Thus the community as a whole benefits when many people specialize. Durkheim called this kind of integration *organic solidarity*.

Durkheim was also a fine researcher, and conducted a famous study of suicide. Suicide was commonly viewed as an individualistic act, more appropriately studied by psychology than sociology. But, after careful analysis, Durkheim found that people were more likely to commit suicide because of a lack of close attachment to other people or groups. The isolated individual without close family or friends was much more likely to take his own life than someone integrated into groups (Macionis 2004: 3).

Durkheim stressed how elements of the social world fulfilled one or more needs of society. This approach has been called *functionalism*, a major perspective in sociology (see chapter 2). For example, schools perform the important function of training children and young people to be productive members of the society, and that of course is functional (useful) to the society as a whole. The various social institutions—family, education, politics, religion, health care—all contribute to the smooth functions of society, at least according to this perspective.

A conclusion Durkheim reached, which is important to sociology, is that *human behavior cannot be understood simply in individualistic terms; we must always examine the social forces that affect people's lives* (Henslin 2007: 5, emphasis in original). There is a social basis to much of individual behavior. Examples of social forces would be the crime rate, unemployment rate, and the divorce rate.

Max Weber (1864-1920), the brilliant German sociologist, had a wide range of interests. He was familiar with Marx's ideas about inequality, power, and social change, but sought to modify them. He would agree with Marx that economic status is important in one's social class position, but he argued that other factors are important as well. For example, one may have *prestige* that is not totally dependent on one's financial worth. An honored person in the community might be looked up to without being wealthy. Then someone could have *power* (influence) without much money.

Weber was very interested in the changes that were taking place over time in most societies. He saw the changes from the *traditional* society, where things were done simply because they had always been done that way, to a *rational* society, in which people gave some thought as to what was the most efficient way to accomplish a goal. Weber referred to this shift as *rationalization*.

A simple example might be gift-giving at Christmas, a widespread tradition in the United States and other countries. A problem with this traditional practice is that one may well not know what the other person wants or needs, or what size or color of the gift would be appropriate. Many people receive gifts they never use or take back to the store. A more rational approach might be to go shopping with the person, to make sure he or she likes what you are buying, to give gift certificates, or perhaps not to give gifts at all.

Weber extended this analysis to modern bureaucracy, which might be defined as a system of organization with clear lines of authority, intended to emphasize efficiency. Weber remains one of the seminal thinkers on this important subject. While he recognized that bureaucratic structures were necessary and probably inevitable, he also saw that something of personal freedom was lost in their extension.

In his most famous book, *The Protestant Ethic and the Spirit of Capitalism,* Weber analyzed why capitalism emerged in some countries and not others. He set forward the theory that Protestantism, with its more individualistic thought, provided more fertile ground for the growth of capitalism than Catholicism. The values of Protestantism produced a cultural ethic that sanctified work and world achievement, encouraged frugality, and discouraged consumption. This influential theory is still being discussed and debated today (Turner 2006: 18-20; Henslin 2007: 5-6; Harper and Leicht 2007: 19).

Sociology was slower to become accepted in the United States. The first department of sociology was established at the University of Kansas in 1890, a century after the first public university was opened in Chapel Hill, North Carolina. The University of Chicago, which was to become the best-known school of sociology in this country, began in 1892. Atlanta University, at the time an all-black school, adopted it in 1897. Harvard University did not make it a department until 1930 and the University of California at Berkeley in the 1950s. Today sociology is a standard course in most major colleges and universities.

An important American theorist was George Herbert Mead, a philosopher at the University of Chicago. Mead was quite different from such sociologists as Durkheim and Weber because of his "micro" approach to sociology. A "micro" approach emphasizes small-scale patterns of society, that is, it focuses on a relatively few people at a time. The school of thought Mead began is known as *symbolic interaction.*

For Mead, humans are born into a society and must adapt to ongoing patterns of social organization. Children must acquire those capacities that allow them to cooperate with others. They do so by learning to communicate with conventional symbols (things which people attach

13

meanings to) such as a smile, a gesture, or an object. A child learns to take the *role* of another; for example, a child can take care of younger siblings by taking on the role of a mother or father.

Mead was concerned with how people develop a *self*, an identity that arises as we see ourselves as others see us. Mead argued, in a way now generally accepted, that we are not *born* with a self. On the contrary, one's self arises in social interaction. Mead's ideas are extremely important for the field of socialization, or the process of learning the ways of one's culture (see chapter 3). Although he thought of himself as a philosopher, Mead is considered to be the most important American sociologist of the first half of the twentieth century (Turner 2006: 21).

The civil rights movement in the mid and late twentieth century made significant changes in American society. This has brought to the forefront a black sociologist of that century, W. E. B. DuBois (1868-1963). After earning his doctorate at Harvard, he studied with Max Weber at the University of Berlin. Returning to the United States, he wrote and worked as an activist all his life. A group he began, the Niagra movement, merged with some white liberals and became the National Association for the Advancement of Colored People.

DuBois looked at what he called 'the strange meaning of being black in twentieth-century America." He emphasized the need to understand the lives of African Americans, specifically how they see the world and how this perception is different from that of whites. At first, he was optimistic about the future of black people in this country, but he later lost hope. (DuBois died in 1963, the same year Dr. Martin Luther King, Jr., delivered his famous "I Have a Dream" speech at the March on Washington.)

DuBois' influence was in establishing a type of sociology that focused on patterns of discrimination and oppression, not only of blacks but all ethnic groups subject to prejudice and discrimination. These issues are still extremely important for many sociologists (Turner 2006: 23-26). (For more on race, see chapter 9).

Clearly sociology is a very broad field, interested not only in small-scale events like the interaction among a few people, but in broad movements and changes that affect people in society. Studying it can not only illuminate our social world, but help us understand ourselves.

(For more on these theorists, see Turner et al 1995: for Comte, 13-46; for Marx, 102-167; for Durkheim, 284-340; and for Weber, 168-232.)

Summary

The study of sociology is concerned with people in their interactions with each other and with the larger society. It delves beneath the surface to explain why people act as they do. To study society carefully requires critical examination following generally accepted rules. Contrary to the beliefs of some, sociology is much more than common sense.

Sociology is one of the social sciences, the others being psychology, anthropology, economics, and political science. It is probably closer to cultural anthropology than to any of the others, but overlaps with all of them, especially psychology. That field focuses on the individual while sociology focuses on the group. Social work, though related to sociology, is a profession that seeks to help people.

Studying sociology is integral to an excellent general education, and appropriate for those with broad interests. A degree in this field can be helpful for careers in education, government, law, marketing, public relations, human resources, and other areas.

There are differences among sociologists. Some investigate the small-scale interactions among a relatively few people; others study the larger issues that affect the entire society. Some are content to analyze society and publish their findings. Others believe one of the purposes of sociology is to reform society. Applied sociology is the attempt to use it to solve social problems.

Understanding variables, traits or characteristics that can vary, is helpful in understanding what sociology deals with. A list of 13 variables was given as useful to know, though there are many others. It is also important to understand how variables are related to each other and to other variables.

While the attempt to reflect on society goes back at least to the ancient Greeks, it is generally understood to have emerged in the late nineteenth century as a response to important changes in the world, particularly the Industrial Revolution. Auguste Comte is considered the founder of the discipline.

Harriet Martineau wrote about culture, the beliefs and values of a people, and noted that people do not always behave in ways appropriate to their own culture. She made an important study of the United States and made it a point to talk to people in all walks of life to ensure an objective analysis of the country.

Karl Marx, the most important thinker we consider, wrote about the importance of conflict, a struggle among various groups. He believed that the people at the top, the rulers or owners, exploited the workers at the bottom. Marx's concerns about the disadvantaged people at the bottom of society have been highly influential.

Emile Durkheim, the great French sociologist, was concerned about social integration or solidarity of a community or society, meaning the extent to which the members shared social values. He found that one way they could have high integration is to specialize in various pursuits, contributing to the functioning of the community as a whole. His work on suicide showed that isolated people were more likely to commit suicide than those more integrated into the community.

Max Weber, a brilliant German sociologist, had a variety of interests. He thought that prestige and power, as well as economic status, were important in determining social class position. He wrote a great deal abut the move from traditional behavior to more rationalistic behavior, resulting in modern bureaucracy. In a famous book, he tried to show that Protestantism was more likely to lead to capitalism than Catholicism.

Sociology was slower to become accepted in the United States, but by the early twentieth century it was being taught at most colleges. An important early American sociologist was George Herbert Mead, who wrote about the development of the "self," that identity that was based on the way one is treated by other people. He emphasized one's relationship to the symbolic world, marked by facial expressions, gestures, and objects. Mead is considered one of the founders of the perspective known as symbolic interaction.

W. E. B. Dubois was a pioneering black sociologist who did important work in the area of race relations, particularly the black experience in America. Although DuBois, who was an activist for civil rights his entire life, became disillusioned about racial progress in this country, his work laid important groundwork for later studies in the area of racial discrimination.

Sociology can be an exciting study of the world and its peoples. It looks beneath the surface of much of social life to the structures and institutions which guide our lives. It can highlight social problems and help point to ways they can be solved. And it can help all of us become active participants in society (Macionis 2004: 5).

References

Charon, Joel M. 2007. **Ten Questions: A Sociological Perspective,** sixth edition (Belmont, California: Thompson/Wadsworth).

Dentler, Robert, 2002. **Practicing Sociology: Selected Fields** (Westport, Connecticut: Praeger).

Eitzen, D. Stanley, and Maxine Baca Zinn. 2007. **In Conflict and Order: Understanding Society,** eleventh edition (Boston: Allyn and Bacon).

Ferrante, Joan. 2006. **Sociology: A Global Perspective,** sixth edition (Belmont, California: Thompson/Wadsworth).

Harper, Charles L., and Kevin T. Leicht. 2007. **Exploring Social Change: America and the World,** fifth edition (Upper Saddle River, New Jersey: Pearson Education).

Henslin, James M. 2007. **Sociology: A Down-to-Earth Approach, Core Concepts,** second edition (Boston: Allyn and Bacon).

Macionis, John J. 2004. **Sociology, the Basics,** seventh edition (Upper Saddle River, New Jersey: Prentice-Hall).

Turner, Jonathan H. 2006. **Sociology** (Upper Saddle River, New Jersey: Prentice-Hall).

Turner, Jonathan H., Leonard Beeghley, and Charles H. Powers. 1995. **The Emergence of Sociological Theory,** third edition (Belmont, California: Wadsworth).

The great German sociologist Max Weber

Chapter 2: THEORY AND METHODS

We have seen that sociologists are interested in people and their relationships in the social world. So do they simply collect information about people and society in a random way? If they did, the result would be a huge set of unconnected items. Ways must be found to organize and hopefully to explain the information they have at their disposal. Therefore, theory is indispensable.

A *theory* is a set of related statements about how some parts of the world fit together and how they work. Theory refers to how one explains things in a way that enables us to make sense of particular facts and events. It shows how two or more facts are related to one another (Macionis 2005: 10). Theory is the *analytical* or *explanatory* aspect of sociology, as it is in every science. Ideally, theories receive consistent support that produces carefully conducted research.

Social scientific theory seeks to determine the logical and persistent patterns of regularity in social life. A scientific theory is an abstract explanatory scheme that is potentially open to disconfirmation by evidence. It assumes that life is regular, not totally chaotic or random. You may have noticed a pattern in the traffic in a city: traffic picks up noticeably every morning from about 7:00 to 9:00, eases off significantly, then becomes more congested around 4:00 to 7:00 P. M., Monday through Friday. This is a *pattern.*

Architects tend to make more money than unskilled laborers. Men ordinarily earn more than women, and whites more than blacks. Couples who marry at a very young age are more likely to divorce than those who marry later. The violent crime rate will be higher in a large city than in a small town. Even though there are exceptions to all these generalizations, the patterns still exist.

Most theorists no longer pursue purely abstract ideas, but are looking at real problems: globalization, identity, risk, trust, civil society, democracy, and so on. Theory is coming closer to addressing real social problems experienced by common people as opposed to the professional concerns of sociologists (Alexander et al. 2004: 259-260).

Theory is a word often employed in everyday life, though not in the same sense as it would be in a social science. A fan may have a theory about football, perhaps believing that the team with the best defense will win the Super Bowl. One may believe that the baseball team with the best pitching will win the World Series. One may have a theory that a recently-married couple will divorce within a year. (These are not full theories in the way they are used in sociology, but they illustrate the type of thing theory does.)

In sociology, there are several theoretical *perspectives* (ways of looking at society) that guide the studies of scholars. It is like a framework that can be used to think about what is going on around us. These are much broader than the informal theories mentioned in the previous paragraph. Three of these deserve to be discussed, remembering that there are many more theories than are mentioned here. (For some additional theories, particularly concerning children, see chapter 4.)

Symbolic Interactionism

This perspective is the most recent of the three, but it might be helpful to begin with it. It is the only one of the major perspectives that takes a *micro* approach to social reality. A "micro" approach is one that analyzes small-scale patterns of society; its emphasis is on a relatively few people considered at one point in time. (Sometimes, of course, this approach has implications for the macro world.) Those who prefer this perspective do not deny that there are other aspects of society that are important (such as urbanization, immigration, or globalization), but they believe localized interactionism is the most meaningful way to analyze the social world.

Society, according to this perspective, is a product of the everyday interactions of its members. Society lives because of the ongoing interaction among people—the exchange of goods, information, feelings, and the like. Social order and social change result from all the immense variety of repeated interactions among individuals and groups.

The emphasis in this perspective is on how people interpret and respond to what they and others are doing in everyday interaction, that is, how they experience and define what they and others are doing, and how they influence others (and are influenced by them). The emphasis is not so much on the behavior that takes place, but how the people involved *view* and *interpret* that behavior. Max Weber said we should focus not only on overt behavior and events, but on how they are interpreted, defined, and shaped by cultural meanings (Harper and Leicht 2007: 56).

This approach is called "symbolic" because it seeks to explain the everyday symbols people use in relating to others. A *symbol* is something to which people attach meanings and use to communicate with others. It could be a material object, like a ring or a trophy, but it could also be a look, a gesture, or any form of verbal or non-verbal communication that implies a meaning beyond itself.

Without symbols we would have no aunts or uncles, employers or teachers—or even brothers or sisters. Symbols define for us what relationships are. We would not know to whom we owe respect and obligations or from whom we can expect privileges—the stuff that our relationships are made of (Henslin 2007: 11).

The extent to which our daily lives are filled with symbols is not fully recognized. Someone might make your day with a word of appreciation or a hug. Someone might ruin your day with a perceived dirty look or word or some snub. If another driver on the street honks his horn at you, that action needs to be interpreted, perhaps as a rebuke (you pulled into his lane) but possibly a greeting (a friend recognized you).

What is the symbolic meaning of a kiss? The answer is that it depends on the social context. A kiss might be a friendly "good night" between people who have been on a date. It might be an innocent greeting, as when the talk show host kisses a female guest on the cheek. Or it might be an aggressive gesture that is preliminary to a sexual assault. It has to be interpreted in its symbolic context.

Everyday conversation is filled with symbolic language. (Language itself, of course, is symbolic since the words stand for realities beyond themselves.) If someone mentions that he has gotten a raise at work, that he and his significant other have moved into a new and larger home, and that they are planning a three-week trip to Europe, these disclosures may well symbolize their presumed material success in life.

Another term discussed in the interactionist perspective is *self*, which may be defined as our identity, or the ability to see ourselves as others see us (or at least as we *think* others see us). The main point sociology makes about this is that no one is born with a self; the self develops out of social interaction. A person treated well with much encouragement will probably develop a high sense of self; one mistreated and constantly denigrated will probably have a low sense of self.

The development of the self is explored in some depth in the branch of sociology known as *socialization* (see chapter 4), which may be defined as the process of developing and learning the values and norms (rules) of society. Consideration is given to parents and family, the school, the peer group, the mass media, and other individuals and groups who influence one's development.

One of the founders of this school of thought was Charles Horton Cooley (1864-1929), who coined the term *primary groups,* intimate groups that shape our development (the family is a good example). Another was George Herbert Mead, mentioned in chapter 1. Mead stressed that children learn to take the *role* of another person, that is, to understand how someone else feels and thinks and to anticipate how that person will act. (Mead's ideas are discussed further in chapter 4.) One of Mead's students, Herbert Blumer, became an advocate of Mead's ideas for over 50 years (Turner 2006: 21).

A weakness of this approach is that symbolic interactionists have difficulty in examining the large-scale movements and trends that exist in any society, such as urbanization and immigration. According to some scholars, symbolic interactionists cannot account for social structures and processes that are larger than the individuals interacting within them (Ferrante 2006: 51).

Through symbolic interaction we coordinate our actions with those of other people. We can make plans for future behavior through symbolic interaction. Symbolic interactionists analyze how our behaviors depend on the ways we define ourselves and others. If you are fascinated with the way people and small groups of people relate to each other, you will appreciate the insights of symbolic interactionists.

A Functional Perspective

Unlike symbolic interactionism, the remaining two theoretical perspectives are *macro* in nature, meaning they focus on large-scale patterns of society. Rather than emphasizing the everyday relations between a few people, they consider large patterns and institutions, such as urbanization (the development of cities), economic changes, immigration, and globalization.

The *functionalist* perspective emphasizes the order and stability that exists in most societies; in fact, this approach has been called the *order* perspective. This approach examines the social universe as a system of interconnected parts. The parts are then analyzed in terms of their functions, or consequences, for the larger system. For example, education is important for any society because its members need to become trained in whatever the society deems important.

In chapter 1 we discussed *institutions* that make up any society, such as economics, politics, education, sports, healthcare, and law enforcement. A functionalist perspective analyzes these functions in terms of how well (or how poorly) they are contributing to the overall stability of the society. Further, this approach notes how the various institutions are related to each other; a problem in one institution will likely be reflected in problems elsewhere.

An example might be problems in education. If the public schools are not successfully educating young people, the effects will be noticed throughout the society. The business world may find a short supply of educated employees to replace those who retire or die. Poverty will probably increase because people lack the education necessary to obtain good jobs.

A dramatic example of how problems in one institution can affect the entire society occurred in the Great Depression of the 1930s. Unemployment reached 25 percent and the economic downturn led to an increase in bankruptcies, homelessness, and other negative consequences. The family, schools, religion, and healthcare suffered setbacks. No institution in the country was unaffected by this decade-long depression. The nation had similar experience with the recession of 2008-2009.

One of the first proponents of functionalism was the sociologist Herbert Spencer (1820-1903). He developed a theory of human social organization and presented a wide range of historical data to support his views. According to Spencer, large, complex societies develop interdependencies among their components. Society has evolved from simpler to more complex forms much as the biological world does. Various elements of a society are analyzed in terms of how they help a society to survive—that is, the *functions* that they serve for the larger society (Turner 2006: 15).

Of the thinkers considered in the previous chapter, Emile Durkheim is the most important representative of functionalism. Durkheim's concern was with social integration or stability. Unlike Spencer, however, Durkheim emphasized the importance of common ideas as an integrating force. He recognized cultural symbols (values, beliefs, language, ideologies, etc.) as important for the integration of society. Religion, for example, can support the society by validating important moral values.

Analogies can be used to explain functionalism. An automobile has many parts, such as the battery, spark plugs, and carburetor, which contribute to the smooth starting and running of the automobile. If not working properly, the car may not start or may run poorly. This is comparable to a society with different parts (institutions), all of which have functions to enable the society to run smoothly.

A more common analogy is that of the human body. The various parts, such as the heart, lungs, bladder, and liver, must function properly if the person is to be healthy. If one of the important parts is not healthy, the whole body will suffer. Similarly, if one of the institutions of society is not working well, the entire society will be affected.

A recent American sociologist, Robert Merton, developed the idea of functionalism. Merton recognized that some functions, which he called *manifest* functions, were the obvious and intended ones. For example, schools have the manifest function of educating and training people so they can function in the society. But there are also those Merton called *latent* functions, which are unintended or less obvious. Schools serve as a baby sitter for children; they provide jobs for many people (teachers, administrators, etc.); and they provide a setting for activities like sports and plays.

Does functionalism imply that everything always goes well in a society? Actually it does not, because of the concept of *dysfunction*, a negative impact on the larger society when an institution is not working well. Obviously, the economic downturn during the Great Depression was a dysfunctional aspect of American society in the 1930s. If public schools are not providing the education needed for children, the dysfunctional effect will be felt.

While functionalists do not suggest that everything always goes well, a legitimate critique of the position is that it often sees society as too well integrated. It tends to ignore conflict, disagreement, and major differences. During the civil rights controversy of the 1960s, it would have been difficult to analyze what was going on from a functionalist perspective. Or, functionalism might have trouble analyzing the relationships between the Israelis and the Palestinians today.

Despite these weaknesses, functionalism has an appeal because it forces us to look at the social universe, or any part of it, as a systemic whole whose constituent elements operate in ways that have consequences for this whole (Turner 2006: 44).

A Conflict Perspective

A conflict perspective, which emerged in the 1960s, is an important alternative to functionalist theories. It agrees with functionalism in taking a *macro* position, that is, it focuses on the large-scale features of the society. The disagreement is that conflict theory sees any social structure as rife with tension and social conflict or struggle.

Conflict, according to this view, is the central dynamic of human relations. A major reason that conflict is so widespread is due to the social *inequality* that may be found in any society. While many conflict theorists stress economic inequality, particularly between the rich and the poor, inequality may take a number of forms, such as tension between the races, between males and females, between the old and the young, and the like.

The various forms of inequality may, and sometimes do, erupt into many diverse forms of conflict, such as violence, crime, riots, protests, demonstrations, and strikes. The potential for social conflict may be felt in many different areas, such as strained interactions with ethnic groups, or resentments against the power of parents, teachers, and employers (Turner 2006: 47), or hostility against immigrants.

Conflict theory argues that *the inherent scarcity of certain goods and values* is the source of strains and contradictions in social systems. Thus inequality is the source of conflict (Harper and Leicht 2007: 50; emphasis in original).

Some students assume that conflict theorists *prefer* a world in conflict to one that is orderly and stable, but that is not the point. Conflict theorists point out that the conflict *does* exist, and so it makes sense to recognize it. Even a society that has no open conflict such as strikes and demonstrations will have conflict simmering beneath the surface. Therefore conflict is a basic contingency of social life and should be recognized.

The most important conflict theorist was Karl Marx, whose views were examined in chapter 1. His emphasis was the struggle between the people at the top (we might say the rich, though Marx would say the owners or rulers) and the struggling workers below them. Marx would say that the rulers exploit the workers because, though the workers do most of the actual work, the rulers escape with the vast majority of the rewards.

Conflict theory asks the question, "Who *benefits* from existing social arrangements?" The question is not whether or not the society appears orderly, but whether some are profiting at the expense of others. If the rich are benefiting at the expense of the poor, whites at the expense of blacks, the upper class at the expense of the lower classes, or males at the expense of females, a conflict situation exists.

A more recent adaptation of conflict theory is known as *critical* theory, claiming that theory should be used to emancipate people from oppression. Proponents of this approach seek to call attention to inequalities, to analyze the processes that result in inequalities, and to propose ways to eliminate inequalities and the domination associated with them, especially in the areas of gender, ethnicity, and social class (Turner 2006: 47-48).

While conflict thought has rightly called attention to the various dissensions and struggles in society, it could be criticized in that it tends to ignore stability, cooperation, and order in society. Some of the more developed societies have developed a relatively cohesive pattern of interaction which conflict theorists sometimes do not recognize.

Research Methods

The social world is highly diverse: one may be interested in studying a small group such as a fraternity or sorority or an athletic team; one may wish to study the relations between management and labor; or one may be interested in large-scale events such as immigration. How does one go about this—what *steps* are to be taken and what *methods* of research would be appropriate to study whatever one is interested in?

Research methods refer to specific strategies used to gather and analyze data. As a generalization, scientific theory deals with the logical aspect of science; research methods deal with the observational aspect;

and statistics offer a device for comparing what is logically expected with what is actually observed (Babbie 1989: 17).

While some students assume that research methods are highly abstract and removed from everyday life, the truth is that almost everyone does some research from time to time. The high school student who looks up information about several different colleges is engaged in a type of research. Someone who finds a recipe for a favorite dish, then substitutes a similar ingredient for the proposed one, is doing a type of research. A person who is dating three or four people may well be comparing them as potential life partners, and that is research of a sort.

Most students are interested in the social problems that affect us-- crime, poverty, environmental pollution, and others. But these problems cannot be solved until we understand how they come about and persist. "Social science research offers a way of examining and understanding the operation of human social affairs. It provides points of view and technical procedures that uncover things that would otherwise escape our awareness" (Babbie 1989: xxvi).

Some students are overwhelmed with the thought of mastering research methods all at once. The thought of learning and applying statistical models to various forms of research can be daunting. But for the beginning student, it is sufficient to be familiar with two things: first, and most important, know the major steps in the research process. Second, be able to name several actual methods commonly used in research and gain a rough understanding of each one.

The major steps in the research process are important not only in sociology but in all of the social sciences. To overlook these steps is to risk sloppy or at least misleading research. However, in actual research some of these steps might run together, or one or two might be omitted altogether (Henslin 2007: 21-22; Berger 2001: 15).

1. Select a topic. It is perfectly acceptable to simply choose a topic you are interested in; it doesn't have to be a world-shaking issue.
2. Define the problem. In most cases, this means to narrow the topic. "Crime" or "poverty" cannot be analyzed in one research project. "The effect of televised violence on children" is better, though even that topic probably should be narrowed.

3. Review the literature. This means reading the material that has already been published on this subject. Unless this is a doctoral dissertation, a sampling of some of the major findings on the subject may suffice.

4. Formulating a hypothesis. A *hypothesis* is a statement of what you expect to find according to what you have read. It states the relationships that can be examined empirically. Most hypotheses take the form, "If A, then B," for example, "If children watch significant amounts of violence on television, they will be more aggressive in real life." The hypothesis may or may not be confirmed in your study. (In some studies, especially that done by participant observation, there will be no hypothesis.)

5. Choosing a research method. There are several methods available to social scientists in performing research. One should choose the method that appears most likely to answer the research question. This step is also called a *research design*. Several of these are named on the coming pages.

6. Collect the data. *Data* simply means recorded information. Some care should be taken to ensure that the data you collect is relevant for your purpose.

7. Analyzing the results. If a hypothesis was used, this would be the place to test it, to see if it had been confirmed. (Of course a study may contain more than one hypothesis, and some contain none at all.)

8. Share the results. For the professional sociologist, this usually means publishing the results in a professional journal such as *The American Sociological Review;* or the written report might be presented at a professional meeting of social scientists. For the college student, sharing the results might mean writing a term paper to be presented to the instructor and possibly to other class members.

Step 5 invokes the choice of a particular method, in what is called a research design. Serious research will have an *empirical* character, that is, it will seek to analyze data obtained in the real world, rather than simply speculating on something that seems reasonable. It is important for the student to be able to name several of the most commonly-used methods, which follow.

1. Surveys. Surveys collect data by having people answer a series of questions. Surveys are sometimes called *polls*: most of us are familiar with the Gallup, Harris, and Roper polls, which present information about people in a given country or other locale. Surveys may be taken to examine *behavior* or *opinions*. In addition to national surveys, surveys may be taken of employees in a company, members of a particular college, and the like.

It is sometimes asked how a national poll can accurately reflect the behavior or opinions of the country as a whole, since only a few thousand people are actually surveyed. The answer is that if a good *sample* segment of the larger group, known as the *population*, is obtained, reliable results may be claimed for the people as a whole. A good sample is one that is unbiased, that is, it is representative of the population (the larger group in which we have an interest).

Surveys are of two types. If we ask questions of people and record their answers ourselves, these are called *interviews*. If we distribute questions to the people and ask them to answer the questions themselves, these are *questionnaires*. Interviews may be done face-to-face, or by some other means, such as the telephone.

Surveys are the most common method employed by sociologists, not because they are necessarily the best method, but because they make possible the gathering of a significant amount of data at one time, they are quickly administered, and they are appropriate for the application of statistics. However, they can be vulnerable to bias on the part of the researcher or the respondents.

A *correlation* is said to exist between two variables if one of them is likely—or less likely—to occur when the other variable occurs. There is a correlation between early marriage and likelihood of divorce, for example. The two variables *wealth* and *attending college* are correlated: the richer the family, the more likely their child is to go to college (Berger 2001: 21). Correlation does not prove causation, however: that two variables are correlated does not establish that one is causing the other. In the social sciences, "causes" are always inference, not things that are self-evident from any given set of observations (Harper and Leicht 2007: 5).

Most analysis of survey data (and certain other types of data as well) are conducted with computers, which, as we all know, have been revolutionizing most areas of modern social life. Most computers can perform intricate computations and provide sophisticated presentations of the results. The computer can be programmed to examine several variables simultaneously and to compute a variety of statistics (Babbie 1989: 356).

The next two methods are forms of *observation*, which means observing and recording, in a systematic and unbiased manner, what people do. It is usually done in a naturalistic setting, such as at home, in a workplace, or on a public street, but it is also possible to carry out observation in a *laboratory*, a specific place (usually a room) designated for such studies (Berger 2001: 20-21).

2. Detached (non-participatant) observation. This refers to observing a group of people while remaining apart from the group you are studying. If an observer watched a first-grade classroom through a one-way mirror, that would be detached observation. An advantage of this is that the observer would be unlikely to influence the behavior of the group he or she is studying.

3. Participant observation. Like the previous method, this involves observing a group of people, but in this case one is a part of the group he or she is studying. One may already be a member of the group, or one may join the group in order to study it more closely. This method is also known as *fieldwork*. All of us use fieldwork all the time. "We do field research whenever we observe or participate in social behavior and try to understand it, whether at a corner tavern, in a doctor's waiting room, on an airplane, or anywhere" (Babbie 1989: 261).

Some of the most interesting studies in sociology have used participant observation. Observers have studied homeless people (by living with them for a time), truck drivers, those in the military, athletic teams, religious cults, and any number of people who might not have been well studied by any other method. Anthropologists have often used this method as a way of learning about people in other cultures. An advantage of observational studies is that the observer is examining the real world, not just the answers that people have given to questions.

4. The Experiment. This investigation is designed to untangle cause from effect. The idea in an experiment is to test the effect of

something on some aspect of the social world, usually people's responses to a particular stimulus or situation. Typically, people gather in a laboratory (mentioned above) designed for this purpose. Experiments involve taking action and observing the consequences of that action (Babbie 1989: 212). This method is most common in psychology but is well known in sociology as well.

In the *classical* experiment, there are two matched groups of subjects: an experimental group, which is exposed to the situation of interest, and a control group, a similar group that is not exposed to the situation. One may then be able to draw relevant conclusions. An example may clarify this.

Suppose one wanted to determine if filmed violence increases aggression in children. One possible way is to set up an experiment by obtaining two groups of children as much alike as possible. For example, one might have seven boys and five girls in one group, seven boys and five girls in the other. There might be three nonwhites in each group. Their ages should be approximately the same, and so on.

Once the groups have been set, the first group, known as the experimental group, would watch some violence on film. The others, known as the control group, would watch a neutral (nonviolent) film. Then the children would be watched carefully by trained observers as they played together. If the children who watched the violence behave in a clearly more aggressive manner, that would be evidence that it was the violent material they watched that led to their aggressive behavior.

Many experiments do not take the classical form, but can still have some relevant insights. A famous experiment from the 1970s was conducted by Philip Zimbardo, who asked for male student volunteers from his college (Stanford University). He divided the men into twelve "prisoners" and twelve "guards," using the basement of one of the college buildings as the "prison." Physical violence was outlawed, but the guards were free to improvise in various ways. The guards wore uniforms, carried nightsticks, handcuffs and whistles, and wore reflecting glasses. The prisoners were forced to follow orders from the guards.

Taking the role of guards, the students in this role were abusing their power and treating the prisoners badly. The prisoners began to develop emotional problems, and soon the experiment had to be terminated because the guards had gotten out of control and because the prisoners were suffering both physical and emotional abuse (Turner 2006: 169-170). While such an experiment would not be permitted today for ethical reasons, the study was illuminating in showing the power of roles in groups.

5. The Case Study. A case study is an intensive examination of a single individual (or a small unit, such as a family) over a period of time. Edwin Sutherland, a famous criminologist, made a case study of a lifelong thief and wrote a book, *The Professional Thief,* detailing his findings. Case studies provide a wealth of detail, and are rich in possible insights. The complexity of a human life is easier to comprehend through the rich qualitative, or descriptive, information of a case study than a study involving sheer numbers (Berger 2001: 26). A weakness of the case study is that the nature of the method limits the study to one or a few people.

6. Existing Data, also known as secondary analysis. This particular method is not considered original research, but it seeks to utilize data that has already been gathered by others. Most students are familiar with something like this in writing a term paper. The library, the internet, a Chamber of Commerce, the Census Bureau, and many other agencies have a wealth of data that can be utilized in research.

7. Unobtrusive Measures. This after-the-fact method seeks to gain information from data observed *after* the behavior has occurred. One can then make inferences about what must have taken place. If parents of an adolescent leave him or her alone for a week-end, then on their return find the house littered with beer cans, cigarette butts and other incriminating evidence, they may assume some sort of party has taken place without their knowledge. Newspaper reporters have been known to go through the garbage cans of a famous person to see if they can find something of interest. While this may not appear to be a major research method, sometimes it may be the only way to determine what happened on a given occasion.

To find out what exhibits are the most popular at a museum, one might check the wear and tear on the floor in front of various exhibits; those where the tiles have been worn down the most are probably the most popular. To get a sense of the most popular radio stations, you could arrange with an auto mechanic to check the radio dial settings for cars brought in for repair (Babbie 1989: 292).

8. Other Methods. People's letters and diaries (used with their permission, of course) can reveal important information about the person's behavior and often about the society in which he or she lived. Comparative studies will compare a subject in different cultures; an example would be a comparison of healthcare in the United States and Canada. Newspaper accounts and other historical data provide a source of research. Visual studies, which can range from photographs to videotapes, are a growing method in the social sciences. The ubiquity of the video camera has meant that crimes and other important behavior are often captured on film.

Social scientists use a sufficiently large sample of observations. The *replication* (duplication) of inquiry provides another safeguard. This means a study can be repeated, either by the original investigator(s) or by others, checking to see if the same results are produced each time (Babbie 1989: 6).

Applied research refers to specific research projects with policy implications. This kind of research could be conducted for a city government, a business firm, or a political aspirant. Market research, in connection with consumer preferences and practices, for example, is a common form of applied research. It is predicated on a need for specific facts and findings with policy implications (Babbie 1989: 34).

The conduct of good research can be an interesting and exciting endeavor. Those doing it may gain a feeling of closeness to the people being studied in a way not possible by simply reading about them. They may have the satisfaction in knowing that they have made at least a small contribution to the world's store of knowledge.

Even if you never conduct a complex research project, you will find yourself continually confronted with the research of others, and it will be important to know how to assess what you read. To interpret the claims of advertising or of politicians is one example. If you incorporate the scientific outlook in your life, you will be logical, observe accurately, and be rigorous in relating what you observe to what you understand.

Summary

The analytical or explanatory nature of sociology is known as *theory.* Theory is essential if we are to explain and understand the mass of data available to us.

There are three major theoretical perspectives in sociology. Symbolic Interactionism seeks to analyze a relatively few people at a time, paying close attention to the *symbols* they use in everyday life. Functionalism is concerned with the way the various institutions of the society work together in promoting order and stability in society. Conflict thought analyzes the conflicts or struggles that go on among the competing interests in society.

Research is essential if sociology is to make progress in understanding a rapidly-changing world. In conducting serious research, the eight steps in the research process, from selecting a topic, choosing a research method, collecting and analyzing the data, to publishing the results, should be followed.

The major methods used in sociology are the survey or poll, which can utilize either an interview or questionnaire; an observation of a group of people, which could be either participant or detached (non-participant) observation; the experiment; and existing data. Other less frequently used methods include the case study, unobtrusive measures, visual methods (film and videotape), and the analysis of historical materials such as newspapers or diaries.

References

Alexander, Jeffrey C., Gary T. Marx, and Christine L. Williams (editors). 2004. **Self, Social Structure, and Beliefs: Explorations in Sociology** (Berkeley: University of California Press).

Babbie, Earl. 1989. *The Practice of Social Research,* fifth edition (Belmont, California: Wadsworth).

Berger, Kathleen Stassen. 2001. **The Developing Person Through the Life Span**, fifth edition (New York: Worth).

Ferrante, Joan. 2006. *Sociology: A Global Perspective,* sixth edition (Thomson-Wadsworth).

Harper, Charles L., and Kevin T. Leicht. 2007. **Exploring Social Change: America and the World**, fifth edition (Upper Saddle River, New Jersey: Pearson Education).

Henslin, James M. 2007. *Sociology: A Down-to-Earth Approach: Core Concepts* (Boston: Allyn and Bacon).

Macionis, John J. 2204. *Sociology: The Basics,* seventh edition (Upper Saddle River, New Jersey: Prentice-Hall).

Turner, Jonathan. 2006. *Sociology* (Upper Saddle River, New Jersey: Prentice-Hall).

Assi Plaza, Dallas.

Chapter 3: CULTURE

Those who have traveled extensively are aware of the significant differences among various societies in the world. Languages spoken, mode of transportation, style of dress, music, sports, preferred foods, table manners, and many other areas of life differ from one society to another and often within a given society.

Culture refers to the total way of life of a group of people, their shared customs and practices. It is an overall design or blueprint for living, the shared understandings that people use to coordinate their activities. Culture is *a distinctive way of life of a group of people*. It enables the individual to adjust to the problems of living.

Newborns have no language, no values or morality, no ideas about religion, war, money, love, or use of space: they acquire these things. Culture penetrates its members at an early age and quickly becomes part of their assumptions about what normal behavior is. It is the lens through which people perceive and evaluate what is going on around them (Henslin 2007; 37).

> Culture propagates our taken-for-granted truths, a set of assumptions generally accepted without serious question. A given culture...may emphasize progress or place great importance on tradition. It may be committed to the individual or the collective. Culture will tell us to value freedom, materialism, family, or art. It will teach us to work hard, take it easy, compete, cooperate, exploit others, or love others. Culture is a broadly general guide to how people are supposed to behave in a given organization (Charon 2007: 119).

Culture does not mean *refinement*, as in fine wine, opera, and ballet. Social scientists prefer the term "culture" to refer to all elements of a society's way of life. It is not the people themselves (that is a group or a society). It is not the *study* of people's practices (that is sociology or anthropology). Nor is culture necessarily identical with the practices and beliefs of a nation: one nation may have two or more cultures.

While culture does not mean refinement, sociologists do distinguish between *high* culture, cultural patterns that distinguish a society's elite, and *popular* culture, cultural patterns that are widespread among a society's population (Macionis 2004: 46). Symphony orchestras and fine art would be among the former, football among the latter.

Another distinction is that between *ideal* culture, that which is worth aspiring to, and *real* culture, that which people actually follow (Henslin 2007: 56). Democracy is an ideal value in American life, but in its actual (real) expression it is approximate and incomplete.

Culture includes both material and nonmaterial elements. Examples of the former are automobiles, television sets, computers, cell phones, and shopping malls. Examples of nonmaterial culture, also known as symbolic culture, are beliefs, values, language, and symbols. The material and nonmaterial elements shape each other.

Technology is the organization of information and knowledge about how to control and manipulate the environment. New technology has a significant impact on social life, especially computers, satellites, and the electronic media. Technology sets the framework for a group's nonmaterial culture. If a group's technology changes, so do people's ways of thinking and how they relate to each other (Henslin 2007: 58).

Human emotions, bodily sensations that we experience in relationships with other people, are expressed very differently in various cultures. There are rules that specify appropriate ways to deal with emotions such as sympathy, grief, guilt, jealousy, or embarrassment. For example, in America same-sex friends are supposed to like one another but not feel anything like romantic love (Ferrante 2006: 88).

Cultures vary in terms of the way people control anger, express anger, and how to feel sorry, guilty, or happy about our anger. We even learn when anger is "useful" or "harmful" to our goals (Charon 2007: 42).

Laughter is heavily influenced by culture. What is funny in one culture may not be in another; jokes are notoriously difficult to translate into another language. And laughter occurs not only when people are amused: it can be an expression of emotions such as anxiety, sadness, nervousness, happiness, or even despair (Ferrante 2006: 89).

Culture is *learned* behavior, that is, it is not instinctive or inborn. Babies are destined to learn the ways of the culture into which they are born and raised. Interactionists, discussed in chapter 2, point out that culture arises in symbolic interaction, learned from family, school, friends, and others. *Race* is not a determining factor in culture: two people of the same race, raised in different societies, may behave quite differently.

Sights, smells, and tastes are culturally determined. Dogs and snakes are defined as edible in some Asian countries, while most Americans would find this appalling. Americans are not born with a preference for hamburgers and hot dogs, any more than people in other countries are born with a preference for rice or fish. These tastes are learned in the process of growing up in a particular culture. "There is no such thing as a human nature independent of culture" (Jencks 2004: 6).

That behavior is learned distinguishes human culture from that of lower animals. Many animals, such as ants and bees, have a social life, but their behavior is presumed to be instinctive, that is, ants and bees carried on much the same activities a thousand years ago. Lower animals behave in fixed, species-specific ways. Humans are much better able than other animals to evaluate their ways and improve their cooperative endeavors.

The implication that animals lack culture has been challenged. Anthropologist Marvin Harris believes that chimpanzees have developed a rudimentary culture, and Japanese macaques have a variety of customs and institutions based on social learning. "Apes and monkeys have a few traditions, but humans have uncountable numbers of them" (Harris 1989: 63).

Some three million years ago, our distant human ancestors grasped cultural fundamentals such as the use of fire, tools, and weapons and were able to create simple shelters and fashion basic clothing. This made culture their primary strategy for survival. Humans developed the mental power to fashion the natural environment for themselves. Since then, they have made and remade their worlds in countless ways (Macionis 2004: 37).

Human culture is *cumulative,* meaning that it adds what it learns to that of previous generations. The knowledge we learn in our lives is not lost when we die but is passed down to others. Culture is passed to the next generation through what is known as *socialization* (see chapter 4).

Cultural transmission is the process by which one generation passes culture to the next. Cultural heritage contains countless symbols of those who came before. Thus the continuity of culture is ensured (Macionis 2004: 38).

The Elements of Culture

There are six elements to culture. These are beliefs, values, norms, sanctions, symbols, particularly language, and technology.

Beliefs are conceptions or shared ideas people accept as true. These may be based on tradition, common sense, scientific fact, religion, and so on. "Anyone who tries hard will make it," "marriage leads to a fulfilling life," are beliefs, whether or not they are true in every situation. Of course individuals in a given society will differ in their beliefs, but there is a core of generally accepted ideas that help shape the culture.

Values

Values are broad, abstract, shared standards of what is right, appropriate, worthwhile, and desirable. They set the general tone for social and cultural life. Examples of values are freedom, happiness, broadmindedness, cleanliness, obedience, and national security. Some values are more cherished and dominant. In most Asian countries, family, self-discipline, and respect for older people are dominant. Americans are more likely to value the individual, personal achievement, success, and freedom.

Cultural values are widely held beliefs that some activities, relationships, or goals are important to the community's well-being. What makes a person successful? What objects are worth owning? What activities are rewarding? To ascertain the values of a society, we can ask what preoccupies people, what gives the individual high status in the eyes of others, what people say is good, bad, desirable, what is rewarded or punished, and for what principles will the people fight.

Values are matters of preference, and it is impossible to prove that certain ones are the true ones for all to follow. They are not statements of fact but commitments to what we think life should be (Charon 2007: 155).

Sociologist Robin Williams listed several important American values which include personal achievement (doing well), work for its own sake, material comfort, moral concern and humanitarianism, efficiency and practicality, progress, material advancement, equality, freedom, democracy, and nationalism/patriotism (summarized in Macionis 2004: 38-40). Sometimes conflict develops among some of these values, as between equality and freedom.

Another example of conflict is the controversy over abortion. It involves not just disagreement over beliefs about motherhood, life, and conception but actual combat among organized groupings, and because beliefs are so strongly held (Kristen Luker, cited in Turner 2006: 83).

Certain American values might be added today: leisure (as seen in the emphasis on recreation), physical fitness, youthfulness, and a concern for the environment (Henslin 2007: 54).

Norms

Norms are written or unwritten rules that specify behavior appropriate to a particular social situation. Norms are based on values, but they are more concrete and specific. Common norms in America are washing hands before eating, leaving an appropriate tip for the waiter or waitress, and looking carefully before crossing the street. While many of the norms have been codified into law, such as laws against burglary, many others are simply a part of common understanding.

A common norm in public life is "first come, first served," applicable to numerous transactions. When a friend speaks to you, you are expected to make some kind of response. A couple who receives a number of wedding gifts is expected to acknowledge the gifts with a thank-you note, although there is no law on the matter.

There are two types of norms, *mores* and *folkways*. Mores, also called taboos, are norms that are considered highly necessary to society. A person does not murder another; adults do not have sex with their children. Transgressions of mores normally bring severe penalties. Almost all mores have become codified into law, such as laws against assault, murder, and espionage.

Folkways refer to less salient norms that apply to mundane aspects or details of daily life. Keeping one's lawn cut, dressing properly for an occasion, or eating with proper table manners are examples of folkways. Violations of these norms may bring criticism, but people are unlikely to become highly upset over their breach. Folkways play an important role in shaping the daily behavior of members of a culture.

In Korea, people eating do not pass items to one another, except to small children. People reach and stretch across one another and use chopsticks to lift food from serving bowls to rice bowls or to their mouths. The implication is that the family, not the individual, is the most important unit. Americans have clearly marked eating spaces, do not trespass into others' dining spaces, and use separate utensils to take food (Ferrante 2006: 78-80).

Various norms may change over time. American society has become more tolerant toward unmarried couples' living together than it was 30 years ago. Tipping a waiter or waitress ten percent was considered appropriate some years ago, whereas the norm in quality restaurants today has moved to 15 or 20 percent. Norms vary widely in their salience and in the ways they are enforced.

Sanctions are socially imposed rewards and punishments for conformity or nonconformity to norms. Formal sanctions, such as a fine, lawsuit, or jail term, are obvious. Sometimes the group is sanctioned for the misdeeds of an individual; if a football player commits an infraction, for example, the *team* is penalized. Controversy often occurs over the nature of formal sanctions, as in the current debate over capital punishment. Informal sanctions include a word of rebuke, ridicule, or ostracism. The power of informal sanctions to enforce conformity is not always appreciated.

Positive sanctions, or rewards, include a smile, a word of thanks, a pat on the back. More formal positive sanctions include a promotion, a medal, or other honor. (For more on norms and sanctions, see chapter 6.)

Symbols and Language

Symbols, discussed briefly in chapter 2, are objects, words, or gestures that can express or evoke meaning. A cross, a frown, a whistle, a flashing red light, or a raised fist are examples. Culture is filled with symbols, which can evoke meaningful responses. A national symbol such as a flag can awaken feelings of patriotism. Certain automobiles such as a Mercedes-Benz or a BMW may symbolize wealth; expensive and fashionable clothes may connote success. Virtually everything we experience, do, desire, and see is tied to symbols.

In the 1960s there was a move away from culture as customary behavior, to a stress upon culture as idea systems, or structures of symbolic meaning. Culture was viewed as a shared system of mental representations. Culture, as a structure made up of representations of reality, was understood to orient, direct, and organize action in systems by providing each with its own logic (Rapport and Overing 2000: 96-97).

Gestures are symbolic acts, shorthand ways to convey messages without using words. The meaning of a gesture may change completely from one culture to another, which can lead to misunderstanding and embarrassment (Henslin 2007: 41). Global travel provides endless opportunities for misunderstanding. General Motors discovered that its Nova did not sell well in Latin American countries: the word in Spanish means "No Go."

The most important symbols are found in *language*, a system of symbols that allows people to communicate. Many scholars believe language to be the key to culture. As we learn language, we learn about culture. Language is a thinking tool; to become fluent in a language means being able to think in that language. Words describe not only things but relationships. They are the primary means of capturing, communicating, discussing, and changing understandings to new citizens (children or immigrants). By means of language, ideas, knowledge, and attitudes pass to the next generation.

Language conveys important messages above and beyond the actual meaning of words. A *connotation* is a word or set of words that implies certain assumptions beyond their literal meaning. An *idiom* is a group of words that, when taken together, have a meaning different from the meaning of each word understood on its own. To speak of being "under the weather" does not mean what the actual words say, but indicates one is not feeling well (Ferrante 2006: 84).

Many words in American culture carry positive symbolic meaning. Patriotism, loyalty, freedom, mother, and family, are examples of such words. Other words, such as loafer, bastard, promiscuous, and traitor, carry negative meaning. Some innocent words may come to have negative connotations: "politician," for example, means simply someone working in the political sphere, but many view the term as a scheming person out for personal power.

The language of the Hopi Indians is different from English in the way it treats the notion of time. In English, time is a noun which can be modified: saved, lost, or wasted. For the Hopi, time is a verb and cannot be manipulated. Time simply flows and humans bend to its way (John B. Carroll, cited in Turner 2006: 73).

Technology

Technology refers to the information, techniques, and tools used by people to satisfy their varied needs and desires (Henslin 2007: 82). Material technology refers to knowledge of how to make and use things. Social technology is the knowledge about how to establish, maintain, and operate the technical aspects of social organization. Procedures for operating a corporation or a university are examples of this.

Diversity of Cultures

There is enormous diversity among the various cultures of the world. The sex drive is highly variable across cultures. Some cultures forbid sex after birth of a child for two to four years or more. This brings no apparent stress or unhappiness. Another group finds kissing disgusting. Most Asian cultures venerate old people much more than does the Western world. Arranged marriages have been common in many cultures, including some today. Polygamy, the marriage of one man to two or more women, has been common in many societies. (See chapter 11.)

Just about every imaginable idea or behavior is common somewhere in the world. The Japanese name intersections rather than streets, a practice that regularly confuses Americans. Baseball games in Japan end between 10:15 and 10:30 P. M., regardless of the score or the inning. Bathrooms lack toilet paper in much of rural Morocco (Macionis 2004: 51).

Differences between peoples can delight, puzzle, and disturb us. (S)ome people have many children, and others have few; some honor the elderly, and others push them aside; some are peaceful, others warlike; and people have thousands of distinctive religious beliefs as well as different ideas about what they consider polite and rude, beautiful and ugly, pleasant and repulsive. This amazing capacity for difference is a matter of human culture (Macionis 2004: 34-35).

In Mexico, to buy a car, one pays 50 percent down and the balance within a year. In China, friends hold hands regularly. A man from West Africa noted that in America, people who date seem to have to see each other every day. A man from Nepal was amazed at all the automobiles: in his country, he said, most people ride motorbikes, take the bus, or walk. A young woman from Germany was amazed at all the air conditioners, and felt as if she were freezing all the time. In Columbia, a young woman lives with her parents until she gets married. In Iran, women cover every part of their body except their hands and feet. If one loses his watch in Iran, he has about a 90 percent chance of getting it back; in America, a lost watch is pretty much thought to be gone (adapted from Ferrante 2006: 93-94).

Sociologists do speak of *cultural universals*, a value or norm found in every society. There are universal human activities (speech, music, storytelling, marriage, preparing food, funeral rites, etc.), but there is no universally accepted way of doing any of them. The specific customs differ from one group to another (Henslin 2007: 56).

Culture shock refers to the disorientation and stress found in an unfamiliar cultural setting. One undergoing culture shock must reorient him or herself to the new situation. Some customs that seem strange or even threatening to Americans seem normal and proper in other cultures. An American might experience culture shock when visiting Vietnam and finding dog on the menu in a restaurant, or when confronting denigration of women or female genital mutilation.

Many immigrants to America report culture shock when facing Western customs. Someone from India might find it puzzling that many Americans keep dogs and cats in their own home. It isn't necessary to go to another country to experience culture shock: someone who moves from rural Mississippi to San Francisco, for example, will see things rarely found in the Deep South.

Ethnocentrism

Most people grow up assuming that their own culture is right and proper and others inferior by comparison. Using one's culture as the standard for judging the worth of foreign ways is known as *ethnocentrism*. It is to take one's own group as the center of everything;

all others are scaled and rated with reference to it. When we look at other cultures, we tend to distinguish them according to how close they come to our own. Americans refer to China as "the far East," while the Chinese themselves refer to their country as the "Central Kingdom."

Ethnocentrism is the tendency to use what we have shared—values, ideas, norms---as a starting point for thinking about and judging other people. We tend to think in terms of what we have learned in interaction. It becomes easy to see alternate ideas, values, and actions as threats to what we feel loyalty to rather than simply qualities that are different from ours (Charon 2007: 159).

Ethnocentrism has been found in every culture. The Greeks called all non-Greeks "barbarians," and the Romans saw the world as divided into the civilization of Rome and the barbarian people. The medieval world divided people into heathen and Christian (Charon 2007: 151).

Even anthropologists, who study the cultures of the world, have sometimes assumed a kind of ethnocentrism. The idea of the superiority of Western culture, particularly its scientific success, became a potent yardstick through which anthropologists assessed the accomplishments of other cultures. It became easy to characterize other cultures as in contrast to our own. "Simple" technology became equated with simple minds (Rapport and Overing 2000: 99).

Some ethnocentrism is necessary if people are to be emotionally attached to a cultural system, contributing to the stability of the society. But it often promotes prejudice and attitudes of superiority. Something different from what we have always taken for granted may not be inferior. Many Americans who have traveled to Europe believe these countries have some advantages over America, as in their lower rates of violent crime, their superior public transportation, and their universal health care.

The opposite of ethnocentrism is *cultural relativism*, the examination of behaviors or ways of thinking in their cultural context, in terms of that society's values. It means refusing to judge another culture by the standards we have always known; it is an attempt to understand others, to appreciate their ways of life, and avoid superficial judgments. Culture must always be understood in the plural and judged only within its particular context (Rapport and Overing 2000: 92).

Endorsing cultural relativism, however, does not mean accepting every cultural practice as proper. One can be critical of human sacrifice, slavery, child prostitution, and female genital mutilation without being a bigot. The point is to keep an open mind and realize that all societies have valid ways of carrying out their routine activities.

Subcultures

Within most cultures, significant variations from the larger culture may be found, and these are known as *subcultures*, groups that possess distinctive traits that set them apart from the main culture. Subcultures may be based on ethnic, religious, age, dress, or behavioral criteria. Many of these are localized, such as Chinatown, Little Italy, a convent, a monastery, an Indian reservation, or a military base. Other groups are not necessarily segregated but share some things in common, such as artists, truck drivers, gays, rodeo cowboys, wilderness campers, professional athletes, or Hollywood actors.

Members of subcultures tend to interact with each other more than with people outside the group. They see the world through somewhat different symbolic glasses and behave differently. As subcultures develop, they tend to develop their own language, styles of behavior, and particular meeting places. The "language" of the bureaucrat, military officer, or folk-rock music star reflects their own ways, their own culture.

Cultural *diffusion* refers to the borrowing (stealing, purchasing, or copying) of ideas, products, and other things from other societies. Baseball has been borrowed by people in over 90 countries, and basketball by people in at least 75 countries (Ferrante 2006: 91). Much of American language, customs, family life, cooking styles, and ways of dealing with the joys and sorrows of life, have been borrowed from other cultures. This does not mean that one culture borrows everything from another; it borrows *selectively*, utilizing those items that fit in with the standards of its own culture.

In America, most clothing, furniture, clocks, newspapers, money, and even the English language are derived from other cultures (Ralph Linton, cited in Macionis 2004: 50). Japan has adopted not only capitalism but also Western forms of dress and music. In Mexico, the most popular piñatas are no longer donkeys but Mickey Mouse and Fred Flintstone (Paul Beckett, cited in Henslin 2007: 59).

Cultural change is inevitable. Your grandparents will recognize profound changes compared to the way of life they knew when growing up. Change is encouraged by invention, adopting new cultural elements such as the video camera, and discovery, recognizing something already in existence, like the athletic abilities of women (Macionis 2004: 50). (See chapter 13.)

Some parts of a cultural system change more quickly than others. Technology moves more quickly than the nonmaterial culture. William Ogburn used the term *cultural lag* to refer to the failure of the nonmaterial culture to keep up with material culture; humans are often more willing to adopt new techniques and tools than to change their cultural values and traditions. Today a woman can give birth to a child by using another woman's egg, which has been fertilized in a laboratory with the sperm of a total stranger. This can disrupt traditional notions of motherhood and fatherhood (Macionis 2004: 50).

Usually, people do not question the origin of the cultural values and norms they follow. Nor are they aware of alternatives. They tend to accept the ways they know as natural and normal. The ways they know become internalized, made a part of their mind-set. The culture that we learn becomes a part of our very being and comes to influence every aspect of our lives. It is impossible to escape the complex influences our culture has on us (Charon 2007: 43).

Theories About Culture

The three sociological theories introduced in chapter 2 have something to say about culture. Interactionism stresses that culture, especially in its symbolic aspects, arises out of everyday interaction with other people. Cultural symbols are created, sustained, or changed by interaction among people (Turner 2007: 80). We are able to enter new situations with some guidance as to what to expect.

Max Weber, a thinker discussed in chapter 2, emphasized that all people live in a world of meaning. To understand human action is to understand how people define their world, how they think about it. That thinking is anchored in a socially created culture (Charon 2007: 42).

Functionalism emphasizes the consequences of values for guiding people's actions and motivating them to participate in society. It views culture as a complex strategy for meeting human needs. Culture gives meaning to what we do and binds people together. Its ideas, values, and norms fit in relation to the particular group. Following Durkheim, functionalists believe that consensus over values is crucial to society (Turner 2006: 76). Sociologist Talcott Parsons believed that culture has a central role in ensuring the equilibrium of the overall system; it maintains cooperation and integration between persons (cited in Jencks 2004: 28).

Conflict theory sees a link between culture and inequality. Some people gain from culture at the expense of others. In most cultures, people are taught that the rich and powerful people have more energy and talent than others and therefore deserve their wealth and privilege. Cultures do not address human needs equally, according to this perspective, and allow some people to dominate others. Culture is largely a matter of habit, which drives them to repeat troubling patterns, such as racial prejudice and sex discrimination, in each new generation (Macionis 2004: 55-57).

Marx, the most important conflict theorist, maintained that people's values, norms, and beliefs are exaggerations of reality. Much of culture, he wrote, is ideology, or ideas that act to defend society as it exists, including its inequality of power and privilege. The ideas created by and for the powerful are taught to most people. Their purpose is to defend the inequality that exists (Charon 2007: 57-58).

Each perspective has something important to say about culture. Interactionists describe how culture is generally learned in everyday relationships. Functionalists point out how culture tends to bind people together, though they may overlook some negative consequences. Conflict theory highlights the negative aspects, but it understates the ways in which cultural patterns integrate members of a society.

Convergence in Cultures

Many of the same cultural patterns are now found the world over. English is rapidly becoming the second language of most of the world. Societies around the world now have more contact with one another than ever before, thanks to the flow of goods, information, and people.

There has never been more international trade, and consumer goods are flowing around the world.

By rapid expansion of the media, virtually every human on earth can potentially be exposed to the culture of others. Because of globalization, the economics of the world are increasingly interconnected. Symbols of a population can be lifted from their local context and presented to others. (See chapter 13.)

The media and globalization dramatically increase the circulation of cultural symbols. As a result, in the modern world people are exposed to far more culture than was ever possible in the past. Some observers refer to this as a cultural revolution (Turner 2006: 85-86).

Satellite-based communication enables people to experience the sights and sounds of events taking place thousands of miles away. Advancing transportation technology keeps the world moving faster. In most nations, significant numbers of people have been born elsewhere. The nations of the world are joined together into a global communications network

However, this trend is uneven. It is more pronounced in urban areas. Desperate poverty deprives people of even basic necessities. And people everywhere do not attach the same meanings to cultural elements. People look at the world through their own cultural lenses (adapted from Macionis 2004: 53).

While people are products of cultural experiences, they are not exact replicas. Two people born and raised in Detroit, even in the same part of the city, may reflect quite different attitudes and values. Cultural symbols are perceived and interpreted in discretely individual ways. There may remain great differences between the perceptions of different individuals (Rapport and Overing 2000: 27). People can accept and reject certain aspects of their culture at the same time. Nor are people passive agents of their culture. They can reject, manipulate, and create cultures.

The better we understand the workings of the surrounding culture, the better prepared we are to use the freedom it offers us.

A Closer Look: Modern Japan

As an illustration of the great varieties of culture around the world, modern Japan is worth a closer look. The country is slightly smaller than the state of California, but has a population of about 125 million, about 40 percent that of the United States. Japan is a mountainous country, with ranges through each of the four main islands. In addition to overall scenic beauty, the country has numerous volcanoes and frequent earthquakes. The climate resembles the eastern coast of the United States.

Few countries have changed as profoundly as Japan since World War II. The country has gone through a major transformation and in many respects has become like any other industrialized country. This was a result of conscious efforts to modernize the country after the Western model.

The daily lives of average people who live in urban areas of Japan are very similar to those in the United States. One difference is that they are much more likely to ride a bicycle or a crowded train to work than drive an automobile. At lunchtime they are more likely to eat at the employee dining hall, but sometimes they go out to nearby restaurants.

Members of the generation born after Japan became an affluent country think and behave differently from their elders who grew up during and immediately after the war. The older generation was brought up to respect the virtue of hard work, thrift, and responsibility to the group to which one belongs. The new generation is said to be individualistic and even irresponsible. The older generation seems puzzled by the younger generation's behavior.

Although changing, conceptions about the family remain the fundamental source of identification of individuals in the society. Family registration is required. A new household register is created when a marriage is reported. This register is just as important as the birth certificate is for an American citizen.

After World War II, the traditional family and marriage custom lost authority. Arranged marriages, once common in Japan, now comprise less than 10 percent of all marriages. The divorce rate is low but more accepted than in the past. The remarriage of older men and women is no longer uncommon. Many are putting off marriage until the late 20s and more people never marry. The birth rate is low.

The number of working women has increased steadily. Traditional thinking about gender roles is still strong among men, and while women have full opportunity in theory, they have a long way to go. There are far fewer women in important positions or public life than in the Western world.

Japan has long been known as a country inhabited by homogeneous ethnic groups with very similar cultures. In comparison with the United States, Japan is extremely homogeneous. Except for a small minority, the Japanese people believe they descended from ancestors who lived in the country from time immemorial.

In Japan today, many local cities have very modern city halls, libraries, theaters, schools, and other cultural centers. Tokyo is the political center of Japan and the center of her economy. Most of the big business corporations have headquarters in Tokyo, and the largest stock exchange market is there. The city also dominates the country's cultural life, and major universities are located there.

A Japanese speaker must constantly keep in mind his or her relative position to the other, which is determined by one's own social position, age, relationship, or other factors related to the particular circumstance.

In shaping Japanese thinking, Confucianism had a profound influence throughout the nation's history. This tradition encouraged principles of moral conduct, family ethics, social relationships, and the government. The emphasis was on the son's piety to his father, people's loyalty to rules, and the wife's faithfulness to her husband. (See chapter 12.)

For most Japanese today, formal religion involves rites and services more than religious doctrines or discipline. Yet people regard religious sentiment as important. Most of the people accept Shinto and Buddhism simultaneously. Typically, Japanese marry before a Shinto altar and are buried, after cremation, in a Buddhist funeral. Just about every family has an ancestral altar in the house.

Traditional Japanese music before the introduction of Western music is the *hogaku*, considered to be a precious cultural asset. Traditional folk songs are regarded as an important cultural legacy and are classified as hogaku. Many of these songs are sentimental and express the traditional values of common folks. Music involves many instruments.

Japanese painting was influenced by Chinese art with a Buddhist theme. The tradition of calligraphy, writing with brush and black ink, has a long history in Japan. Brush writing has been an important part of primary school education.

Yochien is an expensive private school of high quality, with uniformed students. As noted above, students engage in incredible arts projects. Graduation is considered a huge event.

Ceramics and pottery are widespread. The finest craftsmanship was dedicated to making tea bowls for the tea ceremony. *Ikebana*, flower arrangement not so much for decoration but as a form of creative art, has a long tradition in Japan. There are over 2,200 schools of ikebana.

Bonsai, originating in China, means potted and trained miniature trees or plants. They are made to look like they are growing in nature.

Chanoyu, known as "tea ceremony" in the Western world, is a form of art centering on serving and drinking tea. It is a refined art of entertainment for elegant social gatherings. The ceremony encompasses various arts and crafts such as ceramics for the bowls, paintings and calligraphy for hanging scrolls, flower arrangement, architecture, and landscape gardening. Chanoyu is associated with Buddhism.

Traditional theater used to be popular, but draws only a few people today. It is costly and requires some training on the part of the member to enjoy it. Still, ordinary people know something about traditional theater and the names of famous actors whose faces are familiar from television.

The cinema (motion pictures), particularly drama, is popular in Japan. The country has produced several prominent directors, including internationally-known Akira Kurosawa. There has been an explosive popularity of comic books and comic magazines since the 1970s. Over 50 comic magazines for youth and adults are published weekly or monthly. Cartoons and comic strips have become a major attraction in movie theaters and on TV.

The Japanese live in smaller houses with new designs. Few can afford to build in the traditional style. Highrise condominiums are now common. Air conditioning is common but most homes do not have central heating. The interior of the home is a combination of traditional Japanese concepts and modern Western style. A ritual tradition in Japan is a hot bath at the end of the day.

Japanese gardens incorporate natural slopes, rocks, sand, water, trees, and plants. A garden is meant to be a replica of the scenic beauty of nature or an imagined paradise. The Japanese love of natural beauty and their sensitivity to the changes of season are reflected in their gardens.

Meals in Japan range from traditional cuisine to more convenient Western-style fare. Young people seem to be weaning themselves from the rice-centered traditional meal. Increasing numbers of people eat fast food or ready-to-eat food sold in the basement section of department stores.

People prefer to get fresh food. Many people shop almost every day. Every neighborhood has one or more supermarkets, although they are much smaller than those in the U. S. Fish is the main dish in traditional Japanese cuisine; octopus and squid are popular.. Fish at supermarkets are already cleaned and cut into serving portions. The box lunch, sold everywhere, is the most common way of eating lunch.

Japanese enjoy a great variety of foods. The standard staple food is rice, as well as other grains or potatoes. A bowl of soup and other dishes are common. Meat and dairy products are increasingly popular among the younger generation. The Japanese enjoy seafood, beef, pork, chicken, eggs, soybean products, and vegetables.

Everyday Japanese clothing is just the same as in industrialized countries. The traditional Japanese clothing is no longer a part of everyday life and is reserved for special ceremonial occasions. Today people (usually women) in kimono are rarely seen on the streets except during holidays.

The Japanese celebrate a large number of holidays, and the most important is the New Year. There are parades, decorations about the house, gift giving, and a ceremony at home. The second biggest holiday is *Bon*, a Buddhist-mid-summer festival which involves a mass migration to family reunions at old homes in the countryside. This festival includes *Bon Adori*, which is a dance. The Doll Festival, in the third month, celebrates the growth of girls, who get elaborately manufactured dolls to be displayed at home. *Hanami*, cherry blossom viewing, symbolizes ultimate beauty. The Japanese love to picnic under cherry trees in full bloom.

Sumo and baseball are the most popular spectator sports in Japan. Sumo is a special type of wrestling of ancient origin. Sumo matches are filled with rituals. Baseball is played at a high level and Japanese players are being recruited by the major leagues in the United States.

People are very mindful of sending the right kind of gifts and spend a lot of time and money on customary gifts. The business card is used more extensively in Japan. It is a custom to bring souvenirs from places one has visited.

The Japanese express respect, apology and affection by bowing. The depth and duration of bowing vary depending on the situation and the relationship of the people involved. The handshake is sometimes used, but hugging among adults is almost non-existent. Bowing is the universal form of greeting in Japan (adapted from Kamachi 1999).

Summary

Culture refers to the total way of life of a group of people, their shared customs and practices. It includes material elements (such as automobiles) and nonmaterial elements (religious beliefs, other values). Culture is not innate but is learned in the process of living in a particular society.

There are six elements to culture: beliefs, concepts accepted as true; values, abstract principles as to what is worthy; norms, specific rules and guidelines for everyday behavior; sanctions, rewards or punishments for keeping or violating the norms; symbols, especially language; and technology, the information, techniques, and tools people use to satisfy their needs.

There is huge diversity among the various cultures of the world. Ideas and practices assumed to be normal by some people might be rejected by others. Variations in culture include whether a culture is warlike or peaceful, the respect or neglect given to the elderly, and attitudes toward material possessions. Just about every imaginable idea or behavior is common somewhere in the world. "A Closer Look" depicts aspects of the culture of modern Japan.

Ethnocentrism is the tendency to judge other cultures on the basis of one's own. This can have some positive effects, but it often tends to lead to prejudice and bigotry. Subcultures are groups who have distinct differences from those in the larger culture. They could include localized groups such as Chinatown, a monastery, or a military base, or they could denote those who are not segregated physically but who have certain things in common, such as actors, rodeo performers, gays, or professional athletes.

Symbolic interactionists stress how culture, particularly in its symbolic aspects, arises out of everyday interaction among people. It emphasizes how people define the situations of life and give meaning to everyday events. Functionalism points out the consequences of cultural values for overall stability in society, emphasizing the cooperation that results from cultural integration. Conflict theory believes that culture defends society as it is, promoting inequality and the domination of the powerful.

References

Charon, Joel M. 2007. **Ten Questions: A Sociological Perspective**, sixth edition (Belmont, California: Thomson-Wadsworth).

Ferrante, Joan. 2006. **Sociology, A Global Perspective**, sixth edition (Belmont, California: Thomson Wadsworth).

Henslin, James M. 2007. **Sociology, A Down-to-Earth Approach, Core Concepts,** second edition (Boston: Allyn and Bacon).

Harris, Marvin. 1989. **Our Kind** (New York: HarperCollins).

Jencks, Chris. 2004. **Culture,** second edition (New York: Routledge).

Kamachi, Noriko. 1999. **Culture and Customs of Japan** (Westport, Connecticut: Greenwood Press).

Macionis, John J. 2004. **Society, the Basics**, seventh edition (Upper Saddle River, New Jersey: Prentice Hall).

Rapport, Nigel, and Jeanna Overing. 2000. **Social and Cultural Anthropology: The Key Concepts** (London: Routledge).

Turner, Jonathan H. 2006. **Sociology** (Upper Saddle River, New Jersey: Pearson/Prentice Hall).

Church study group meets in home

Chapter 4: SOCIALIZATION

For a society to survive, its culture must be passed on both to new members, particularly children, and to immigrants who are new to the society. The process by which this occurs is called *socialization*: "the lifelong social experience by which individuals develop their human potential and learn culture" (Macionis 2004: 61). It refers to learning what is necessary to survive in one's society. No other animal is as dependent on socialization for survival as the human being.

The familiar verb "socialize" means to interact with others in an informal way. It suggests meeting with friends and having a good time talking, playing games, listening to music, or just catching up on the gossip and news of the day. This is somewhat different from the way the term is used in sociology; socialization is the *learning* process by which individuals incorporate the values and norms of their culture. Eating dinner with friends may contribute to the learning of the culture, but the sociological term is much broader.

Humans have to learn to get food, to build a shelter, make clothing, and handle other people. In fact, they must learn thousands of things if they are to survive in the particular society they live in. Humans live in a world where socialization is necessary for survival; that socialization is ongoing, lifelong, and broad in scope (Charon 2007: 32-33). The function of socialization is to produce integration, inclusion, consistency, and acceptance in members of society.

> Our talents, tastes, interests, values, personality traits, ideas, and morals are not qualities we have at birth but qualities we develop through socialization in the context of the family, the school, our peers, the community, and even the media (Charon 2007: 33).

Socialization may not determine all that we are, but its influence cannot be easily denied. Much of what each of us becomes can be traced to our interaction with others, and thus our individual qualities are in this sense really social ones. Sociologists emphasize how socialization influences our choices, abilities, interests, values, ideas, and perspectives—in short, the directions we take in our lives (Charon 2007: 35).

The infant, helpless at birth, is transformed into a human who can take part in society and its culture. Young children must be exposed to information that leads them to expect behavior, people, and objects to be cast in a certain way. They develop these expectations as they interact with others in their world. Through many exchanges with adults and others, children form views about objects and people. As they learn about the social group to which they belong, they begin to acquire basic skills (Ferrante 2006: 108). By this process, the culture passes from one generation to the next.

Through socialization children develop their *personality*, "a person's fairly consistent patterns of acting, thinking and feeling" (Macionis 2006: 61). This concept is stressed in psychology, but sociology is more likely to use the term *self*: "the part of an individual's personality composed of self-awareness and self-image" (Macionis 2004: 66). The concept of self is the awareness a person develops regarding the ability he or she has to see himself or herself as an object apart from others with distinguishing characteristics.

There is a window of opportunity for learning many of the basic skills and behaviors that are human and allow us to play roles in society. Human potentials must be activated within a certain timeframe, perhaps by age 10 or 11. If they are not activated, it will be difficult to acquire in full measure those capacities later (Turner 2006: 119).

Nature vs. Nurture

There has been controversy in the social sciences about the relative impact of *nature* and *nurture*. Nature refers to the genetic makeup or biological inheritance of the individual; nurture to the environment or learning experiences that make up the individual's life. A consensus has emerged that *both* influences are important. It is impossible to separate the influence of the two or to say that one is more forceful (Ferrante 2006: 114). All developmentalists agree that both nature and nurture interact to produce every specific trait: no characteristic develops as an exclusive response to either nature or nurture (Berger 2001: 52).

Charles Darwin concluded from his studies of evolution that the genetic potential of an organism enhanced its chances of survival in the world. For some, this concept implied that "instinctual behavior" was the primary force of survival for all organisms, including humans. To be sure, instinct has behavioral manifestations that help most organisms adapt to and survive in the environment, but it is questionable to use this concept to propose a reliance on biological explanations for the superiority of various groups of humans and the societies they develop.

As noted in the previous chapter, animals are governed by instincts, fixed traits that are inherited and shared by all members of a species. Birds build nests and migrate at the time set by instinct. When an attempt was made to apply the idea of instinct to humans, it did little to explain human behavior. It does not account for the wide variation of human behavior around the world.

The cerebral cortex, the thinking part of the brain, has at least 100 billion neurons or nerve cells. The number of interconnections is nearly infinite. This allows humans to organize, remember, communicate, understand, and create. They also learn the values, beliefs, norms, behavior, and language of whatever culture they are exposed to, and this is accomplished through social interaction (Ferrante 2006: 115).

Social scientists have been fascinated with studies of identical twins raised separately (Berger 2001: 80-81; Hamilton 1994). It is assumed the twins have an identical genetic makeup (their nature), so that any differences between them would presumably be due to their nurture. These studies are inconclusive: some studies have found twins who were raised in very different environments to be remarkably similar years later; other studies have revealed twins who were quite different, though their temperaments were similar. Sociology does not claim that genetics, or nature, is unimportant; it simply focuses on the actual experiences people have after birth.

Identical twins Jack and Oscar were separated as babies as their parents divorced and were raised in different environments. Oscar was raised by his grandmother, a strict Catholic. He learned to love Hitler and hate Jews. Jack was raised by his father, and learned loyalty to Jews and hatred of Hitler and the Nazis. The two brothers met briefly in 1954 and again in 1978. They had different attitudes towards the war and Jews, and their basic orientation towards life was different. Oscar was conservative, Jack more liberal. Oscar enjoyed leisure, while Jack was a workaholic.

At the same time, researchers also found that Oscar and Jack had both excelled at sports as children, but had difficulty with math. They both had the same rate of speech, both liked sweet liqueur and spicy foods, and they shared some unusual habits (Henslin 2007: 64).

The limits of certain physical and mental abilities are established by heredity, while basic orientations to life such as attitudes, are the result of the environment. For some parts of life, the blueprint is drawn by heredity, but even here the environment can redraw those lines (Henslin 2007: 64). The success of Tiger Woods at golf illustrates the importance of nurture, since his father introduced him to golf as soon as he could walk.

There have been cases of children raised in extreme isolation. One of the best known, as reported by sociologist Kingsley Davis, was Isabelle, who was raised by a deaf-mute mother in an attic, with a minimum of social interaction. She was discovered in 1938 at the age of 6 and was more like an animal than a human. She could not stand erect, speak, or communicate at all except by a few gestures and a strange croaking sound. She showed extreme fear and hostility towards strangers, especially men.

A program of training and nurture was introduced to Isabelle. Within a few months she could retell a story after hearing it; seven months later she had a vocabulary of 1500 to 2000 words and was asking complex questions. In about a year, she could write a few words, do simple addition, and retell stories after hearing them. She reached a normal level by the time she was eight and a half. In short, she covered in two years the stages of learning that ordinarily require six, and her IQ trebled in a year and a half.

Eighteen months after her discovery, she was a very bright, cheerful, energetic girl. She spoke well, walked and ran without trouble, and sang with gusto and accuracy. Her teachers said she participates in all school activities as normally as other children (Henslin 2007: 65). What Isabelle had lacked was socialization, meaningful interaction with other people.

Later sociologists added one important point to the study by Davis. Although Isabelle had spent her early childhood years in a dark room, shut off from the rest of her mother's family, she did spend most of this time with her deaf-mute mother. Davis and the staff who treated Isabelle assumed that being in a room with a deaf-mute is equivalent to a state of isolation. We now know, however, that deaf-mutes have rich symbolic capacities. Isabelle seems to have established an important and meaningful bond with another person (Ferrante 2006:115-116; Turner 2006: 119).

Children who received little attention in institutions suffered noticeable effects. Rene Spitz studied 91 infants who were raised by their parents during their first three to four months of life but were later placed in orphanages. At the time of their placement, the infants were physically and emotionally normal. At the orphanages they received adequate care with regard to their bodily needs, but little personal attention. The result was that the children were starved emotionally, resulting in such rapid physical and developmental deterioration that a significant number of the children died. Many were unable to stand, walk, or talk (cited in Ferrante 2006: 117).

All children need human contact, attention, and stimulation in order to develop normally. Being deprived of social interaction during one's formative years deprives individuals of their humanness. The makeup of the brain itself is altered by lack of human contact (Eitzen and Zinn 2007: 113).

Meaningful social contact with and stimulation from others are important at any age. Further, social interaction is essential to a developing sense of self, the conception of oneself as a certain kind of person. Social scientists agree with Mead that "it is impossible to conceive of a self arising outside of social experience" (cited in Ferrante 2006: 117).

Newborn infants have no sense of self-awareness. They are unable to distinguish between themselves and their surroundings. In time, especially with the use of language, the child begins to distinguish between "I" and "you" and "mine" and "yours"—signs of self-awareness (Eitzen and Zinn 2007: 115).

The emerging sense of self was demonstrated in a classic experiment. Babies looked in a mirror after a dot of rouge had been surreptitiously put on their noses. If the babies reacted to the mirror images by touching their own noses, they knew they were seeing their own faces. None of the babies under 12 months reacted to the mark as if it were on their own faces. Most of these between the ages of 15 and 24 months did react with self-awareness, perhaps by touching their own faces with an expression of curiosity and puzzlement (Berger 2001: 191-192).

Groups

By involvement in groups people develop personality. A *group* consists of people who regularly interact with one another (Henslin 2007: 101). Those who belong to a group assume an obligation to act according to the expectations of other members of their group. Self-identity revolves around group membership.

Sociologists have stressed the *primary* group as a major influence in socialization. As defined by Charles Horton Cooley, a primary group is one in which there is intimate, face-to-face interaction; it gives us an identity, a feeling of who we are (Henslin 2007: 134). Primary groups are important in forming the social nature and ideals of the individual. While the family is an obvious example of a primary group, other groups with closeness and intimacy, such as a group of close friends, would be as well.

People are influenced by other groups as well. A *reference* group is one that people use as guides in developing their attitudes and behavior. A devout Catholic might look to the Vatican for guidelines on belief and behavior; in that case, the Vatican would be a reference group for her. An *ingroup* refers to a group to which people feel closely attached, particularly when that attachment is founded on opposition to another group known as an outgroup (Ferrante 2006: 121). Often a strong loyalty will be felt to a group that feels threatened by an opposition group. (For much more on groups, see the next chapter.)

Gender Socialization

It has been well documented that boys and girls have somewhat different experiences in the process of socialization. Children learn gender expectations by observing others' behavior, such as the jokes or stories they hear about men and women and the portrayals of men and women in the media. Significant others may intentionally convey favored societal expectations to children. An undetermined, yet significant, array of male-female differences are products of the ways in which males and females are socialized (Ferrante 2006: 346; Crain 2000: 199).

Children frequently learn, through observation, the behavior of both genders. They usually perform only the behavior appropriate to their own gender because this has been reinforced in them (Crain 2000: 199-200). Many traditional cultures emphasize gender distinctions, and these are quickly evidenced in the patterns adopted by children. Almost every study of preschool children finds that boys are encouraged by their culture to take on different roles than girls (Berger 2001: 293).

By age 6, children have well-formed ideas and know which sex is better (their own). Shoes for preschoolers are often designed with such decorations as pink ribbons or blue footballs, and no child would dare wear the shoe meant for the other sex. Dress codes become rigidly enforced by the first grade. When they reach school age, a few children still may have a good friend of the other sex, but they rarely play with that friend when other children are around. Awareness that a person's sex is a biological characteristic that is not changed by clothing or activities develops gradually, not firmly until age 8 or so (Berger 2001: 288).

Parents, peers, and teachers tend to reward "gender appropriate" behavior. Parents praise their sons for not crying when hurt, for example, but caution their daughters about the hazards of rough play. This gender prejudice is strongest in the preschool years (Berger 2001: 292). Language stimulation differs by sex. Since girls are more responsive to language and mothers are usually more verbal than fathers, mother-daughter pairs will typically talk more and father-son pairs, less (Berger 2001: 295).

Boys are more inclined to engage in more assertive and aggressive activities, while girls are more likely to be involved in more gentle and verbal pursuits. By age 4, children are convinced that certain toys (such as dolls and trucks) and certain roles (such as nurses and soldiers) are appropriate for one gender but not the other (Berger 2001: 288). There is still some controversy as to whether these differences are innate, taught through socialization, or both. There can be little doubt, however, that socialization is an important part of the differences.

Gender-role stereotyping is evident in the décor of children's rooms and clothes and toys that match traditional color schemes as well as certain logos (a flower or an airplane). Most researchers believe the early influence of parents is determinative in this area. Girls have more dolls and domestic items whereas boys have more tools, sports equipment, and large and small vehicles in their rooms. Studies have documented more rigid stereotyped expectations of fathers compared to mothers (Wood, Desmarais, and Gugula 2002).

Barbie dolls have been marketed for more than 40 years and are available in 67 countries. An estimated 95 percent of girls between ages 3 and 11 in the United States have Barbie dolls. Executives at Mattel assume that the Barbie doll is a role model for the child. For boys, G. I. Joe became the first "action figure" toy on the market, being launched in 1964. It thrived for 12 years until 1976, when the line was canceled, then re- introduced in 1978. This toy is merely one in a long line of action figures that have been marketed to boys (Ferrante 2006: 347-348).

Theories of Socialization

Interactionist theory, dealing as it does with small groups, is well suited to analyze the process of socialization. This theory stresses that significant symbols and gestures allow us to interact with others. A *significant symbol* is a word, gesture, or other sign to convey a meaning from one person to another (Ferrante 2006: 126). We use symbols to communicate ideas, feelings, intention, and identities; to teach others what we know; to communicate to others and to cooperate with others; and to learn roles, ideas, values, norms, and morals. Symbols make possible the accumulation of knowledge possible (Charon 2007: 36-37).

Functionalists and conflict theorists, dealing as they do with macro subjects, have less to say on socialization. But in general, functionalists point out that smooth interactions among groups of people help promote the orderly workings of the society. Conflict theorists stress the problematic relations between the higher classes in society and the masses, and are more inclined to agree with Freud (discussed below) on the struggles between the individual and society.

George Herbert Mead, introduced in chapter 2, had much to say about socialization. He discussed the concept of a *self*, the ability to see ourselves as an *object* in each situation: we can be proud of ourselves, ashamed of ourselves, and so on. It is a given in sociology that *we are not born with a self;* the self develops through the eyes, words, and actions of others. Through interaction with significant others, a child first comes to be aware of the self (Charon 2007: 38). This development is a key part of socialization.

Mead posited two aspects to the self, what he called the "I" and the "me." The "I" is the spontaneous, autonomous, creative self capable of acting in unconventional or unexpected ways. The "I" takes chances and violates expectations. This could be expressed in creative artistry or in harmful deviant behavior. The "me" represents the social self, the self that has learned appropriate behavior. This self is more conventional, and takes into account or anticipates how others will respond (Ferrante 2006: 126).

In *role-taking,* according to Mead, the child steps outside the self and imagines its appearance from an outsider's perspective. Children acquire a sense of self when they become objects to themselves. All people have the ability to read the gestures of others and role-take with them. This way, they can take on the point of view of others, and coordinate their actions with theirs (Turner 2006: 120).

Mead described three stages the child passes through. The *preparatory* stage is marked by imitation: a boy might pretend to be shaving as he has seen his father do, even though is too young to be doing so. At this stage, children have almost no understanding of the behaviors that they are imitating. In doing so, children learn to function symbolically, that is, they learn that particular actions and words arouse predictable responses from others (Ferrante 2006: 127).

The *play* stage is voluntary or spontaneous activity, not subject to time constraints, given to amusement or relaxation. The child pretends to be significant others, people important in his or her life. The boy pretends to be his father, the girl her mother. If rules exist, they are developed by the children on their own and are not imposed on them by higher authorities (Ferrante 2006: 128). Mead would call this taking the *role* of another.

During childhood, play is the most productive and adaptive activity children undertake. Play is an ideal forum for learning specific social skills. Many of these skills are learned from play with peers, because only with age mates do children themselves assume responsibility for initiating and maintaining harmonious social interaction (Berger 2001: 279).

The *game* stage involves structured, organized activities with set rules and a projected outcome. The child has to learn to take the roles of all participants, and see how each position fits in relation to all other positions. In baseball, for example, if the batter hits a ground ball to the shortstop, the latter knows his role is to field the ball and throw it to the first baseman, who takes the throw while stepping on the base to retire the runner. More complicated games appear later, as in working for a large corporation.

The *generalized other,* a concept of Mead's, means a system of expected behavior, meanings, and viewpoints that transcend those of the people participating (Ferrante 2006: 129). The child learns to see things from another's perspective, and gains a sense of how others expect him or her to behave. A child might follow some instructions he or she recalls from a *particular* other (e. g., the mother) by not playing in the street. Eventually, the child heeds the voices he or she has incorporated from others—a parent, an older sibling, a grandmother, a teacher, even someone observed in the media—becoming Mead's *generalized* other.

Eventually children develop self-images from the way they are treated by others, or from the way they *perceive* they are treated. As they become sensitive to the appraisals they perceive others have of them, they develop a feeling between pride and shame. Those who are treated well will tend to develop a favorable self concept: they will tend to be self-confident, outgoing, happy. Those who think they are treated poorly will be timid or unhappy. Charles Cooley called this concept the *looking-glass self,* a self-image based on how people think others see them (Macionis 2004: 67; Eitzen and Zinn 2007: 115-116).

Behaviorist theory, also called learning theory, claims that all emotions and behaviors are learned through associations formed between stimuli (the environment) and responses. From social learning, or socialization, personality is molded as parents reinforce or permit a child's spontaneous behavior. John B. Watson, a proponent of this view, claimed that by the time the child is 3, parents have already determined whether the child is to grow into a happy or a fearful person (Berger 2001: 193).

In a famous proposal, Watson claimed that if he were given the supervision of a dozen healthy infants, he could take any one at random and train him to become any kind of specialist he might select—doctor, lawyer, artist, thief—regardless of his talents or penchants (cited in Crain 2000: 174). If Watson was right, nurture (socialization) is everything and genetics is meaningless, a claim most theorists reject.

Psychoanalytic theory, as developed by Sigmund Freud, interprets human development in terms of intrinsic drives and motives, many of which are irrational and unconscious, hidden from awareness These underlying forces are viewed as influencing every aspect of a person's thinking and behavior. This perspective also sees these drives and motives as providing the foundation for the universal stages of development that every human experiences (Berger 2001: 39).

Each stage that children go through includes its own potential conflicts between child and parent, such as toilet training. For Freud, how the child experiences and resolves these conflicts determines the person's lifelong personality and patterns of behavior. Many unconscious problems faced by adults have their roots in a childhood stage (Berger 2001: 39).

As noted above, Freud stressed *unconscious* motives for our behavior, publishing important work on the interpretation of dreams. Life is a constant struggle between the *id*, the base desires of the self, especially sexual, and the *superego*, the voice of society, formed as conscience. The *ego* is the part of the personality that seeks to reconcile the id and the superego.

Freud's work on personality development has been enormously influential, although to discuss it in detail would go beyond the scope of this chapter. While feminists and others are critical of much of Freud's work, his contributions are crucial in understanding the development of personality. (For a summary of Freud's views, see Crain 2000: 244-270).

Cognitive development refers to the way children think, reason, and learn. It focuses primarily on the structure and development of the individual's thought processes and understanding. This approach tries to determine how a person's thinking and the expectations that result from a particular understanding affect the development of attitudes, beliefs, and behavior (Berger 2001: 47).

The most important figure in cognitive theory is psychologist Jean Piaget. Piaget claimed that learning and reasoning form an important adaptive tool, and lead to more sophisticated reasoning. His concept of *active adaptation* refers to a biologically based tendency to adjust to and resolve environmental challenges. He believed that as that tool, learning and reasoning help people to meet and resolve environmental challenges. This unfolding must be accompanied by direct experiences with persons and objects (Ferrante 2006: 132; Berger 2001: 48). Piaget showed that children are active contributors to their own development, and must be developmentally ready if teaching is to be successful (Berk 2004: 13).

Piaget listed several stages most children pass through in this process. Each stage is characterized by an increasingly more sophisticated reasoning level. A child cannot proceed from one stage to another until he or she masters the reasoning challenges of earlier stages. The progression by stages toward increasingly sophisticated levels of reasoning is apparently universal, although the content of people's thinking varies across cultures (Ferrante 2006: 132-133). (A discussion of each stage would take us beyond the scope of this chapter. For a good discussion of Piaget, see Crain 2000: 110-146.)

The social psychologist Albert Bandura developed the concept of *social learning.* Individuals, he claimed, do not learn behaviors one at a time. They may observe a whole sequence or pattern of responses and imitate that pattern, and they may adopt it as their own. People both produce and are produced by their environment. Children observe the behavior of others and the feedback (positive or negative) for such behavior. This then serves as a guide for their actions as they model after others (Eitzen and Zinn 2007: 118).

In social situations, says Bandura, people often learn much more rapidly simply by observing the behavior of others. In Guatemala, for example, girls learn to weave almost exclusively by watching models. We learn not only from live models but from *symbolic* models, such as those we see on TV or read about in books. Prosocial behavior such as sharing and altruism can be readily influenced by exposure to the appropriate models (Crain 2000: 193-212).

Sociocultural theory seeks to explain the growth of individual knowledge, development, and competencies in terms of the guidance, support, and structure provided by the society. The theory emphasizes children's active role in human development (Corsaro 1997: 14). The child and his or her social surroundings join to provide direction to develop; participation in social life guides and energizes the child's mastery of new, culturally adaptive skills. This theory focuses on children's access to interaction with people more familiar with the culture (Berk 2004: 30). People are affected by society, but people also change society.

Human development, according to this viewpoint, is the result of dynamic interaction between developing cultures and their surrounding culture. Sociocultural theorists point to the many ways children learn from parents, teachers, and peers in their homes, schools, and neighborhoods. They also look to the ways in which instruction and learning are shaped by the beliefs and goals of the community (Berger 2001: 51-53).

Sociocultural theory is unique in viewing inner mental activity as profoundly social. The thoughts and imaginings that make us distinctly human are not independently constructed by the child, but are derived from his or her relations with other people. When a teacher says, "Put all the animals together and all the vehicles together," she teaches vital strategies for remembering (Berk 2004: 32-33).

A major pioneer of the sociocultural perspective was Lev Vygotsky, a psychologist from the former Soviet Union. The key principle for Vygotsky is the individual's internalization or appropriation of culture. Especially important to this process is language, which both encodes culture and is a tool for participating in culture. Vygotsky saw practical activities developing from the child's attempts to deal with everyday problems. The child always develops strategies in interaction with others. Human development is collective rather than individualistic (Corsaro 1997: 15).

Vygotsky was particularly interested in the cognitive competencies that developed among the very diverse people of the new (at that time) Soviet Union, such as the use of tools and the appropriate use of abstract words. He felt these competencies develop from interaction between novices and more skilled members of the society, acting as tutors or mentors. Vygotsky recognized that the skills, challenges, and opportunities involved in human development vary, depending on the values and structures of the society in question (Berger 2001: 54).

Adult Socialization

Socialization is a lifelong process; people never stop learning. People's experiences in new and varied social settings—work, family, education, community and neighborhood, religion, recreation, and so on—can subtly alter each basic component of personality. As we move into various new phases of life—and into new jobs, families, workplaces, communities, clubs, and organizations—our role playing style and cultural directives are the most likely to be altered (Turner 2006: 125, 131).

Resocialization

Resocialization is the process of learning new norms, values, attitudes, and behaviors (Henslin 2007: 85). It refers to being socialized all over again: discarding values and behaviors one has learned and taking up new ones. Resocialization occurs each time people learn something contrary to their previous experiences. A dramatic example would be "brainwashing" of prisoners of war. Another extreme example could be the college student who joins a religious commune, sells flowers on the street, and renounces his or her family. Less striking examples could be a man who becomes divorced, a woman who becomes a nun, or a person who enters psychotherapy.

Rarely is dramatic alteration of personality effective. More typically, attitudes, values, and beliefs change somewhat, but temporarily. Changes in self and motives are rarely long term and permanent. This is ample testimony to the strength and stability of human personality (Turner 2007: 126).

Agents of Socialization

Agents of socialization are people or groups that affect individual self-concept, attitudes, behaviors, or other orientations toward life (Henslin 2007: 78). To perpetuate its culture, society designates certain groups to socialize newcomers (children and immigrants). Many elements, internal and external to the child, work together as a dynamic system to affect children's thinking, feeling, and acting. Elements include the child's heredity and biological constitution; the people and objects in the child's everyday settings of home, childcare center, school, and neighborhood; community resources for child-rearing; and cultural values and customs related to child development and education (Berk 2004: 22).

Some agents of socialization could be clergymen, police officers, scout leaders, and neighbors. But the most important agents are the five singled out for special discussion below.

The Family

Around the world, the first group to impact the person is family. It is the most important socializing agent, especially during the first five years. A warm, supportive family environment usually produces happy, well behaved children. Family is also important for adolescents. "The parents equip the child with the information, etiquette, norms and values necessary to be a functioning member of society" (Eitzen and Zinn 2007: 119).

The family is an important primary group because it gives the individual his or her deepest and earliest experiences with relationships and because it gives newcomers their first exposure to the norms or rules of life. In addition, the family can serve to buffer its members against the effects of stressful events or negative circumstances, though it can also exacerbate these effects (Ferrante 2006: 120).

Parents are more than caregivers; they are also representatives of culture, and pass on the cultural traditions of a society, its language, core values and beliefs. Parents are the primary source of emotional support for the young. A child who experiences positive emotions from parents is more likely to develop a strong sense of trust in others and a strong self-conception (Turner 2006: 134).

Parents (and other adults) are vital conveyors of culture, through direct teaching of attitudes and values and through the imprint of culture on the activities they provide for children—conveying to the next generation the intellectual, scientific, aesthetic and moral achievements of our species. Parents help ensure that children acquire competencies that enable them to assume a responsible place in their society, and ultimately to participate in transmitting its values and practices to future generations (Berk 2004: 28).

The family nurtures children in five essential ways: it meets their basic needs by providing food, clothes, and shelter. It encourages learning and motivates education. It develops self-esteem, so that children know they are competent, loved, and appreciated. It nurtures peer friendship, providing the time, space, and opportunity needed to develop peer relationships. Finally, the family provides harmony and stability so children feel safe and secure with predictable family routines (Berger 2001: 367).

Despite much attention given to the impact of peers (discussed below), there is no conclusive evidence that the peer group has more influence than the family. Parenting practices have much to do with the children's competence at language and communication; sensitivity to others' feelings and needs; the capacity to get along with others within and beyond the family, beliefs, and attitudes (Berk 2004: 28).

Some observers, however, believe the family may not be as influential today as in the past. The reasons for this include a high rate of divorce and blended families, as well as the fact that other institutions, such as the school and recreation groups, have taken over some functions previously centered in the family. (For more on the family, see chapter 11.)

The School

For most children, the school is their first training in how they are expected to behave in impersonal groups. Here the child encounters the world of formal rules, and the impersonality of much social life in the modern world. It also may be the first time a child has encountered an authority figure outside the home. School teaches an individual how to play roles, express and control emotions, define self, and channel motivations in ways demanded by large organizations (Turner 2006: 135).

In school, the child breaks free from the closely supervised and limited arena of the young child. He or she can explore the wider world of neighborhood, community, and school. "They (children) experience new vulnerability, increasing competence, ongoing friendships, troubling rivalries, and deeper social understanding" (Berger 2001: 355).

Schools and teachers can play a significant role in the development of social, academic, and creative skills. School achievement can help all children, including those from seriously deprived backgrounds, to aspire beyond the limited horizons they may encounter in their daily lives. In good schools, achievement is within the grasp of almost every child because good schools are characterized by strong leadership, warm teachers, and high expectations about the achievements of the children (Berger 2001: 372).

Some researchers claim that regimented teaching not adjusted to the child's interests and capabilities undermines learning, motivation, and self-control. When children spend their time sitting, listening to teachers, and doing worksheets, they exhibit high levels of stress behaviors. In a follow-up, children who spent their kindergarten year in a highly teacher-directed classroom achieve more poorly that do age mates who come from kindergartens emphasizing play and hands-on, small-group projects (Berk 2004: 11-12).

Schools are likely to contribute to uniformity. Some observers have found a "hidden curriculum" which trains students to be patriotic, to believe in cultural values, to support existing institutions, and to obey laws. Schools teach expectations about appropriate skills, character traits, and attitudes that pay off, such as ambition and competitiveness (Eitzen and Zinn 2007: 119).

Schools do better with upper class and middle class children than they do with those from the working and lower class. One reason is expectations: teachers, like parents, are likely to expect more from the higher-status children, partly because they know the parents tend to expect success. They may help these children focus on their talents and interest in extracurricular activities.

Social learning theorists, such as Bandura, have argued that standard school practices such as ranking and competitive grading may make children feel inadequate. It would be better if children worked more cooperatively and could judge their work according to their own individual progress. Teachers need to feel self-efficacy as well (Crain 2000: 209).

A vivid experience in school, whether positive or negative, is likely to be remembered into adult life. The effect on a child of being punished unfairly, especially in front of other students may, for example, be profound. At the same time, when a child is praised for a project well done, it can increase his or her confidence and self-esteem.

(For useful guides for teachers, see Berk 2004: 248-250).

The Peer Group

The *peer group* is a social group whose members have interests, social position, and age in common (Macionis 2004: 70). Peers have the potential to enable the child to be independent from adult authorities. Peers teach social and group loyalties, and underscore the value of friendship and companionship among equals. Often distinctive subcultures may emerge among peer groups. Peers can have both positive and negative influences on the child and young person, but in general they tend to place more emphasis on popularity, social leadership, and athletic attainment than on character and scholarship.

Increasing contact with peers leads to an increasing sense of self-confidence. They can help children learn to resolve conflict, cooperate, form deep attachments beyond the family, and behave in ways that foster social harmony (Berk 2004: 28). In fact, some researchers think peers are the deciding influence on children, but others challenge this. Children become more dependent on each other, not only for companionship but for self-validation and advice. Peer relationships, unlike adult-child relationships, involve partners who must learn to negotiate, compromise, share, and defend themselves as equals (Berger 2001: 358).

Some researchers call the peer group the *society of children*, given the fact that children create their own subculture, which is firmly in place by age ten or so. It typically has its special norms, vocabulary, rituals, and rules of behavior that flourish without the approval, or even the knowledge, of adults. Activities such as hanging out at the mall, playing games in the playground, and having long, meandering phone conversations—do not involve adult participation (Berger 2001: 359).

Personal friendship is even more important. The understanding of friendship becomes increasingly abstract and complex. Children tend to choose friends whose interests, values, and backgrounds are similar to their own. From ages 3 to 13, close friendships increasingly involve children of the same sex, age, ethnicity, and social class. By age 10, children often have one "best" friend to whom they are quite loyal. The trend toward fewer but closer friends is followed by both sexes, but it is more apparent among girls (Berger 2001: 360).

Bandura believed that children tend to adopt the self-evaluative standards of peers rather than adults because children can more easily achieve the lower standards that peers set. Yet adults can encourage children to associate with high-achieving peers, and they can also expose children to models who are rewarded for adhering to high standards (Crain 2000: 202).

Organizations

At any time in life, particular individuals in groups, organizations, and communities can exert a significant influence on a person. A teacher, fellow worker, friend, or even a character presented in the media can influence each aspect of an individual's personality, although rarely to the extent that early interaction does in the family and early peer groups (Turner 2006: 134).

Most people in modern societies spend up to 40 hours per week in an organization, whether church, synagogue, athletic team, club, or neighborhood association. Such long-term and intense exposure to the culture and structure of an organization will exert considerable influence on personality (Turner 2006: 134-135).

The Mass Media

Often overlooked in socialization is the role of the mass media, forms of communication that are widespread in our culture, such as movies, mass-circulation magazines, and television. "In the United States, the mass media have an enormous effect on our attitudes and behavior" (Macionis 2004: 71). Not to be overlooked in more recent years are the computer, particularly the Internet and such activities as video games and text messaging.

Most people in modern societies are exposed to the media for several hours each day. If video games and virtual tours on the Internet are added to TV, radio, newspapers, magazines, and movies, the exposure to the media could be greater for many individuals than actual interaction with real people. It seems clear that media exposure can reinforce existing behavioral propensities. They present images of how people should play roles, deal with and express emotions, present and see self, while at the same time communicating particular values, beliefs, and norms (Turner 2006: 136).

Social learning theorists, such as Bandura, have shown that behavior is influenced not only by personal or life models, but also by those presented in the mass media. Film models, in particular, seem to exert a powerful impact, and one major implication is that television, which many children watch for hours on end, is shaping young lives. Social learning theorists have been especially concerned with the effects of televised violence on children and have found that it can increase children's aggressiveness in their daily lives. The findings are complex but substantial enough to warrant public concern (Crain 2000: 208-209; Shimanovsky and Lewis 2006).

A Closer Look: Television and Children

Today's world is a visually-oriented one. The average American 9-12 years of age attends 980 hours of school in a year's time and watches 1,340 hours of television. Studies in the U. S. and the United Kingdom have found that children may spend four or five hours a day watching some form of electronic media (Oates and Blades 2005). A recent report found that 90 percent of 2-year olds regularly watch TV, DVDs or videos, and one third of 3 to 6-year olds have a TV in their bedroom (Kuchment and Gillham 2008). This suggests that television is a potent influence on the beliefs, attitudes, values and behavior of those raised with it.

On the one hand, television has great positive potential for learning and development. It can impart mental skills. It can transmit knowledge and cognitive skills to the young child. It can increase our exposure to diverse cultures and provoke discussion of current issues (Macionis 2004: 73). However, it seems most effective when used as an addition to a teacher than as a replacement.

Commercial television at its best offers outstanding drama, music, documentaries, and skilled coverage of major events. Children are likely to possess richer vocabularies, though often only with a superficial comprehension of what the words mean. Recent research found that watching appropriate children's shows was linked with increased vocabulary in kids ages 6 months to 2 ½ years (Kuchment and Gillham 2008).

According to a study by Huston and Wright, children watching the video screen suffer the following effects: It takes time from active, interactive, and imaginative play. It sends faulty messages about nutrition. It provides sexist, racist, and ageist stereotypes. It undermines sympathy for emotional pain, in its bold, quick actions.

And it undercuts attributes, skills, and values that lead to prosocial activity (cited in Berger 2001: 281).

The nation's psychologists reported in 1996 that watching TV can lead to anti-social behavior, obesity, gender and racial stereotyping, bad grades and a lack of esteem for families. The psychologists found that commercial TV was least beneficial for the people who need it and use it the most—children, the elderly, minorities, and women (Macionis 2004: 71-72).

In a review of studies on TV viewing and academic achievement, Thompson and Austin found in most a significant negative relationship, especially with those who watched more than 10 hours of TV a week. "The research appears to be saying that high levels of unsupervised mindless television viewing, especially when done in lieu of daily reading or other academic stimulation, can have the potential to exert harmful effects on achievement" (Thompson and Austin 2003).

True learning has an active nature (reading a book, playing the guitar). People are more involved when they expend effort. Television, though, is a passive medium. A series of studies has shown that addiction to TV stifles creative imagination. One study exposed 250 gifted elementary students to three weeks of intensive viewing. They found a marked drop in all forms of creative abilities except verbal skill.

The major concern about the influence of TV on children has been in the area of violence. It has been estimated that children will view more than 30,000 violent deaths, and 40,000 attempted murders, by the time they turn 18 (Hamilton 1994). Because of a dramatic increase in special effects, death is made to appear intensely realistic. It has been found that children as old as seven or eight cannot easily determine whether TV violence is real, making it more anxiety-provoking (Hamilton 1994).

Numerous studies have substantiated that TV leads to aggressive behavior by children and teenagers. Children often disapproved of the aggression shown on TV yet still acted aggressively. Leonard Eron, the former head of the American Psychological Association's Commission on Violence and Youth, said, "The evidence is overwhelming" that TV viewing is linked to aggression (cited in Berger 2001: 281). This is not to assert, however, that TV is the major cause of violent behavior.

Other causes, particularly poverty, may be more critical (Macionis 2004: 122-123).

In an important series of studies, Jerome and Dorothy Singer followed children from age 4 to age 9. In general, they found that heavy TV viewing, beginning in the preschool years, is significantly associated with aggressive behavior, restlessness, and belief in a "mean and scary world" in elementary school. Television produces endless models of resolving conflicts through physical force; even "good guys" have to fight for their rights (Macionis 2004: 71). In a follow-up study years later, heavy viewers turned out to be more aggressive and were more likely to have been arrested (Hamilton 1994).

Studies have suggested that the viewer learns aggressive behavior and becomes desensitized to such expression (Shimanovsky and Lewis 2006). The American Medical Association states that watching crime and horror programs can produce callousness to the pain of others and a diminishing of sympathy and compassion. Viewers of persistent violence on TV believe the world is a hostile and unpleasant place. They are also less trustful of their fellow citizens.

Video games, if anything, are worse: they are more violent, more sexist, more racist. They desensitize viewers to violence in real life, making physical aggression more normal. Young video game players, by virtue of their age, are still in the process of developing an identity of worldview, and so are more receptive to media influence (Shimanovsky and Lewis 2006). Children exposed to substantial amounts of video violence are more likely than others to be bullies, more likely to retaliate physically to any perceived attack, more likely to be passive victims, and more likely to be onlookers rather than mediators when other children fight (Berger 2001: 281).

There is evidence that television watching leads to materialistic values. Eitzen and Zinn (2007: 122) claim that children are bombarded with materialism and consumerism. Many children say they would like to be rich and famous and appear on television. And television seems to encourage children and young people to attach more importance to appearance in general and clothes in particular. In the commercials, highly sophisticated techniques manipulate viewers into wanting the products.

Children's psychological immaturity as viewers and consumers leaves them more vulnerable to advertising influences. Children under the age of 7 are particularly vulnerable to advertising on television. Children may be led to buy products they do not need and spend money they do not have. Commercials emphasize snack foods with little emphasis on more healthy food. The high child obesity rate in the United States traces in part to persuasive food advertising. Children may view social and religious events (such as Christmas) in purely commercial terms (Oates and Blades 2005). An often overlooked point is that commercial messages are often more violent than actual programs (Shimanovsky and Lewis 2006).

Television in steady doses may encourage stereotyped opinions. In one study, children thought that no woman worked, professional people had all the power, doctors were handsome, policemen were brutal, artists were temperamental and lawyers were clever. Though there has been some improvement, minorities and old people are often stereotyped (Eitzen and Zinn 2007: 121-122; Crain 2000: 209).

In a study of prime-time dramas and comedies on the major networks, it found that older adults, children, females, and Latino characters were underrepresented, whereas middle-aged, male, and white characters were overrepresented. Latino characters were rated significantly less positively than all other groups (Harwood and Anderson 2002).

Experts suggest that parents prescreen as much as possible to make sure the show is teaching their child the same values they have. Limit screen time to one hour per day, discuss TV shows and games with your kids after they've viewed them, and read daily with them for at least 20 minutes (Kuchment and Gillham 2008).

The damaging effects of television on children may not be intrinsic to the medium but grow out of the way it is used. Television can be a passive, deadening activity if adults do not guide their children's viewing and teach them to watch critically and to learn from what they watch. Responsible parents must be involved in monitoring the quality and quantity of television their children watch. Children should be guided away from violent and adult-oriented programs and be encouraged to watch worthwhile shows (Berger 2001: 281; Macionis 2004: 71-73; Eitzen and Zinn 2007: 122-123).

References

Berger, Kathleen Stassen. 2001. **The Developing Person Through the Life Span**, fifth edition (New York: Worth Publishers).

Berk, Laura E. 2004. **Awakening Children's Minds: How Parents and Teachers Can Make a Difference** (Oxford: Oxford University Press).

Charon, Joel M. 2007. **Ten Questions, a Sociological Perspective**, sixth edition (Belmont, California: Thomson Wadsworth).

Corsaro, William R. 1997. **The Sociology of Childhood** (Pine Forge, CA: Pine Forge Press).

Crain, William. 2000. **Theories of Development: Concepts and Applications**, fourth edition (Upper Saddle River, New Jersey: Prentice Hall).

Eitzen, D. Stanley, and Maxine Baca Zinn. 2007. **In Conflict and Order: Understanding Society**, eleventh edition (Boston: Allyn and Bacon).

Ferrante, Joan. 2006. **Sociology, A Global Perspective**, sixth edition (Belmont, California: Thomson Wadsworth).

Harwood, Jake, and Karen Anderson. 2002. "The Presence and Portrayal of Social Groups on Prime-Time Television" (**Consumer Reports**, Vol. 15).

Henslin, James M. 2007. **Sociology, a Down-to-Earth Approach, Core Concepts**, second edition (Boston, Massachusetts: Allyn and Bacon).

Hamilton, Robert A. 1994. "Television Violence—What Influence on Young Minds?" Pp. 82-84 in **Human Development 94/95** (Guilford, Connecticut: Dushkin Publishing Group).

Kuchment, Anna, and Christina Gillham. 2008. "Kids: To TV or Not TV." **Newsweek** (February 18).

Macionis, John J. 2004. **Society, The Basics,** seventh edition (Upper Saddle River, New Jersey: Prentice Hall).

Oates, Barrie Gunter Caroline, and Mark Blades. 2005. **Advertising to Children on TV: Content, Impact, and Regulation** (Mahwah, New Jersey: Lawrence Erbaum Associates).

Shimanovsky, Michael, and Barbara Jo Lewis. 2006. "Influence Exerted on the Child Viewer When Exposed to Violent Imagery in Television and Print Advertising" (**Journal of Evolutionary Psychology**, Vol. 29).

Thompson, Franklin T., and William P. Austin. 2003. "Television viewing and academic achievement revisited" (**Education**, Vol. 124).

Turner, Jonathan H. 2006. **Sociology** (Upper Saddle River, New Jersey: Prentice Hall).

Wood, Eileen, Serge Desmarais, Gugula. 2002. "The impact of parenting experience on gender" (**Sex Roles: A Journal of Research**).

Children in a public park, Dallas.

Chapter 5: SOCIAL INTERACTION AND SOCIAL STRUCTURE

Except for a hermit or someone in a coma, almost all people interact with others every day. Most people pass others on the street or in a shopping mall, they meet with friends and acquaintances to eat or engage in other activity, and they attend meetings where they come into contact with others. Even the person who rarely leaves his or her home will likely interact with others by way of the telephone, email, or text messaging.

"We live our entire lives interacting and embedded in society" (Charon 2007: 39). Constantly social actors, people impress others, communicate with others, escape others, try to influence others, display affection to others, play music or create art for others, and so on. Almost everything they do has an element of the social—it takes other people into account. They do things together: cooperate, discuss, argue, teach, engage in conflict, play, make love, play tennis, or rear children.

Human beings cannot survive without other human beings. Humans have very few instincts and certainly will not survive in the wilderness without the assistance of other humans. Humans must interact with others to survive. It takes interaction with others who have been socialized in the ways of society to learn this process of survival. Interaction is the unique contact each person has with others. Interaction allows each person to recognize that he or she is impacted and influenced by others, and can be recognized as having an impact and influence on others around them.

Interaction is also present in a larger area, such as a neighborhood. Sidewalks, stores, streetcorners, playgrounds, and hundreds of other places provide occasions for people to interact with one another. One can see a pattern of crisscrossing interaction among people within the area. Their interaction with people from that area is more intense than it is with those outside the area (Charon 2007: 53).

Sociologists have written some fascinating accounts about the lives of streetcorner men, lower-class individuals who spend much time on the streets of large cities. Their lifestyle appears disorganized, as if they were simply coming and going randomly. The studies show, however, that they are influenced by the norms and beliefs of society. This is seen in their following the rules or "codes" for getting along; survival strategies; how they divide up money, wine, money, or whatever resources they have; their relationships with girlfriends, family, and friends; where they spend their time and what they do there (Henslin 2007: 96).

Social interaction is the process by which people act and react in relation to others (Macionis 2004: 85). It refers to the situation in which at least two people communicate and respond through language and symbolic gestures that may affect each other's behavior and thinking. People typically define, interpret, and attach meaning to each encounter they have. Social interaction enables people to create the reality they perceive.

Social Status

Status is a social position an individual occupies (Macionis 2004: 86). People occupy many statuses at the same time. One may be a son, grandson, nephew, husband, and father all at the same time, and one may be a computer scientist, employee, co-worker, a Catholic, and a member of a bowling league as well. Further, statuses change over the life course. As one gets married or divorced, graduates from college and takes on a new job, and as one eventually retires, his or her status changes.

Usually (but not always), one status implies that of another. Examples are husband-wife, parent-child, brother-sister, employee-employer, student-teacher, salesman-customer, and doctor-patient. In sociology, status does not necessarily refer to prestige: the owner of a restaurant may have higher prestige than the waitress, but both occupy a specific status.

An *ascribed* status is involuntary; it is either inherited at birth or conferred later in life. Examples of an ascribed status are gender, race, age, or family status (son, daughter, niece, nephew, etc.). An *achieved* status is voluntary, something one earns or accomplishes. One may become a student, a friend, or a minister. The term does not imply prestige: both a college president and a bank robber are achieved statuses (Henslin 2007: 99. For a fuller discussion, see chapter 8).

Status symbols are signs that identify a status. They take many forms: a tuxedo, a wedding ring, a uniform, or a badge: their intent is that others will recognize a status from the symbol. People use status symbols to announce statuses to others and to help smooth interactions in daily life (Henslin 2007: 100).

Roles

A *role*, one of the most important terms in sociology, means the behavior expected in a particular status. The difference between status and role is that one *occupies* a status, but one *plays* a role. Sometimes the word "hats" is used to signify different roles a person is playing, as in, "Our speaker tonight is an attorney, but he is wearing a different hat as he speaks to us on photography."

Guidelines for what is "appropriate" apply in most roles. Because of socialization, people usually *want* to do what their roles indicate is important. Roles lay out what is expected of people. As individuals throughout society perform their roles, those roles mesh together to form *society* (Henslin 2007: 101).

A person who occupies the status of a student will be expected to attend class, complete assignments, and pass examinations. These expectations are his or her *role*. Note that the role exists in theory even if the student never attends class or fulfills any of the other requirements. Society insists that people play their roles correctly. To do otherwise is to risk being judged by other people as abnormal, incompetent, or immature (Eitzen and Zinn 2007: 30).

The particular emphasis or interpretation that people give their roles, their "style," is known as *role performance*. A son or daughter may play the role of ideal son or daughter, being respectful, coming home at the exact hour requested, and so on. Or a son or daughter may behave in a way markedly different (Henslin 2007: 111).

One interesting characteristic of roles is that people tend to become the roles they play. Those who play a certain role long enough may become incorporated into that self-concept (Henslin 2007: 111). Chapter two discussed a famous experiment by Zimbardo where college students took on the roles of prison guards and inmates, and before long they were actually experiencing the role they had been assigned. Actors romantically involved in a long-running play have been known to actually fall in love with each other. People who have played the role of Jesus have found that they became more kind and unselfish in real life.

A well-known concept in sociology, attributed to W. A. Thomas, is known as the *Thomas theorem*: situations that are defined as real are real in their consequences (Macionis 2004: 90). If two young people believe they are in love (though the maturity of the love might be questioned), they will probably act on that belief. This can create a self-fulfilling prophecy: if enough people believe that the country is headed for a depression, their actions, such as withdrawing all their money from banks, could indeed bring about a depression.

Much problematic behavior may be defined as the failure to properly fulfill one's role. If a subordinate continually reviews the performance of his superior, and makes ready suggestions about how his superior could improve, he may not understand the proper role of a subordinate. An auditor who overlooks major discrepancies in the account of a corporation has not adequately fulfilled his or her role. If a man makes a pass at the teenage babysitter as he is taking her home, he is acting inappropriately in terms of his role.

Role strain refers to a tension between roles connected to a single status (Macionis 2004: 87). A mother tries to enforce certain rules for her child, while at the same time acting as a warm and loving parent, but sometimes there is ambiguity in performing these roles. A college professor may be expected to publish books and papers in her profession, but that could interfere with her role as a good teacher. (Notice that in these examples, there is only one status—mother or college professor—about which the strain exists.)

Role conflict is a tension between roles corresponding to two or more statuses (Macionis 2004: 87). Since almost all people occupy many statuses, there is ample opportunity for conflict to occur between two or more of them. A college student who is employed forty hours a week could experience stress in trying to fulfill both roles. A mother who works long hours outside the home may lack the time she desires with her family.

Role exit is the process by which people disengage from important social roles. A nun who leaves the convent to return to conventional life, an athlete who is cut from his team because of an injury, a person experiencing a divorce, or a person who retires after many years on the job are undergoing role exit. One researcher, in studying various types of role exit, found that in some cases a role had become so intertwined with the individual's self-concept that leaving it threatened the person's identity (cited in Henslin 2007: 112).

The social construction of reality is the process by which people creatively shape reality through social interaction (Macionis 2004: 89). People negotiate reality through their exchanges with other people. Through interaction with others, individuals *construct* reality; they learn ways of interpreting their experiences in life. A man and women who have been dating may have different expectations: one party may see the relationship as a prelude to a long-term commitment, while the other views it only as an opportunity to enjoy evenings together. Through negotiation, they may resolve the difference by coming to a mutual understanding.

A similar idea is called *definition of the situation*: the definition or interpretation of a particular situation people find themselves in, as just illustrated by the dating couple. A college professor may be delivering what he considers an inspiring lecture that could actually result in changed lives among his students, but some of the students could barely be listening and simply wishing the class would end so they could eat lunch.

The perspective known as symbolic interaction holds that the most significant part of life in society is social interaction, especially the symbols people use. People's actions are usually meant to communicate something to others, who try to understand the meaning of the action. It is not so much what happens to people, but how they interpret and make sense of it.

One application of this approach is people's use of personal space. All have a "personal bubble" to protect. Except for intimates, most people keep others out of this space. Most people try not to touch or be touched by the people next to them in line. The amount of space people need varies by culture: South Americans like to be close to each other when they converse (Henslin 2007: 108).

Dramaturgy

Within the perspective known as symbolic interaction there is a perspective called *dramaturgy*, which claims that social life is like a drama or a stage play (Henslin 2007: 111). Since actors take on roles, much of what was said about roles (above) is relevant to this approach. The socialization of children involves learning how to perform on a stage. We have ideas of how we want others to think of us, and we use our roles in everyday life to communicate those ideas. In sociology, an *actor* is simply a person who engages in behavior seen or heard by others; an *audience* is the people viewing or listening to that behavior.

Even "lines," the script learned by actors, has its analogy in everyday life. Few people memorize the exact words they plan to say for a given occasion (unless it is an important presentation or a proposal), but most people adapt to what is expected. If one person accidentally bumps into another, he is likely to say, "Excuse me." When someone is introduced to a stranger, he or she is likely to say, "It's good to meet you," or words to that effect.

Impression management is the process by which people manage their dress, words, and gestures to fit the impression or image they are trying to project (Ferrante 2006: 157). A young girl going on her first date may spend some time choosing her outfit and fixing her hair. Someone going on a job interview will likely dress appropriately and seek to be on his or her best behavior. While this could be seen as an attempt to manipulate others, impression management can be a constructive feature of social life because smooth interactions depend on everyone's behaving in socially expected ways.

All people have *front stages* on which to perform assigned roles. Here people take care to create and maintain the images and behavior an audience has come to expect.

Everyday life is filled with front stages. A front stage would be where the teacher lectures, or the minister preaches. When young people go out with friends, the scene represents a front stage. In dramaturgical terms, the front stage is wherever one delivers his lines (Henslin 2007: 111).

The *back stages* are places out of an audience's sight where individuals can do things that would be inappropriate or unexpected on the front stage (Ferrante 2006: 159). When one closes the bathroom or bedroom door, he or she has entered a back stage. For a waitress, the back stage is the kitchen where she goes to pick up the meal. In this area she might yell at a fellow employee, or even eat a french fry off the customer's plate.

The front stage would be the dining area where the customers are seated, where she will likely be on her best behavior.

Props, another term from the theater, decorate the person. For a teacher, these might be books and lecture notes; for a nurse or a policeman, it could be a uniform. Props, which are similar to *status symbols* discussed earlier, tell us how we should react. Some people use expensive automobiles or rare wine to convey messages about themselves (Henslin 2007: 113).

Interaction in everyday life

Emotions, or feelings, are an important dimension of everyday life. Often what people do is less important than how they feel about it. Paul Elkins reports that people everywhere express six basic emotions: happiness, sadness, fear, anger, disgust, and surprise (cited in Macionis 2004: 97). Moreover, people everywhere use much the same facial expressions to display these emotions. The purpose of emotions is social: supporting group life. Emotions are powerful forces that allow people to overcome their individualism and forge connections with others.

Culture plays an important role in emotional expression; it defines what *triggers* an emotion, and culture provides rules for the *display* of emotions. Some societies encourage the expression of emotions, whereas others belittle emotion and expect members to suppress their feelings. Many cultures expect women to show emotion while considering emotional expression by men as a sign of weakness. In some cultures this pattern is less pronounced or even reversed (Macionis 2004: 97).

Certain gender differences in interaction have been observed. In a study of initial conversations between young men and women, Clark et al. (2004) found that women generally disclose more about themselves and disclose more intimate information than men. But under certain circumstances, especially conversations with same-sex strangers, men are more forthcoming than women. Women appear to be less forthcoming in early conversations with male partners. Women need to believe that the recipient is discreet, trustworthy, sincere, and honest.

When men saw that their female partners talked more than they did, the women's social attractiveness was enhanced. Men believed that the more they discussed, the more favorably their partners viewed them. There is some evidence that both men and women assume that more positive impressions are formed by their partners when the man contributes more to the conversation. Most young men do not prefer to dominate introductory conversations with young women.

Another study found that men and women differ on numerous nonverbal behaviors. Women smile and gaze more, lean forward more, approach others more closely, and touch self more than men. The tendency of women to smile more than men was greater when the situation suggested anxiety or tension. The difference is greatest in face-to-face interaction and dwindles when individuals are assessed in nonsocial situations. Women appeared to sit more with an erect posture, leaned forward more, and raised their eyebrows more than men did (Hall et al. 2001).

Communication using body movements, gestures, and facial expressions is known as *nonverbal communication* (Macionis 2004: 93). There are many settings where people interact without saying a word. As people stand in line at the grocery store, share an elevator ride, or walk through a crowded mall, they make adjustments in their behavior to the close presence of others. A pat on the back, a hug, a smile, a frown or even silence may communicate important feelings.

Some researchers claim that the nonverbal parts of a message carry more weight than verbal messages when these two conflict. Females have been found to value nonverbal behavior more than males, and females are better "decoders" of nonverbal behavior than males. Communication among college students found that females engage in more nonverbal behavior than males. They were more likely to look their partner straight in the eye and to nod their heads when their partner spoke. Females who want to dissuade an aggressor display high rates of nonverbal rejection behavior such as yawning, frowning, and pocketing the hands (McQuinty et al. 2003).

One study observed pedestrians passing on the street. A common practice is to acknowledge the presence of others with a brief glance and then look away to show that they are not concerned about the other person and want to respect the individual's privacy. People would smile more at an opposite-sex person than a same-sex person. The study underscored the power of a smile in precipitating positive recognition in pedestrian passings (Patterson and Tubbs 2005).

Students in a classroom were told not to listen or cooperate with the other students. Their non-cooperation was much more nonverbal than verbal: students would turn their body away, play with their pen, bounce their knee up and down, and doodle. The importance of eye contact for communication in Western cultures was stressed, inasmuch as poor eye contact was noted most often in the non-cooperative behavior. In some Eastern cultures, however, eye contact is interpreted as aggression (Schwebel and Schwebel 2002).

Social Structure

Social structure refers to the typical patterns of a group, such as its usual relationships between men and women or students and teacher (Henslin 2007: 97). People learn their behavior and attitudes from their location in the social structure and they act accordingly. The positions people hold (their statuses) are powerfully important in their thinking. They see the world from the position they are in. A position gives one an angle on reality that is unique to that position (Charon 2007: 126).

As people interact over time, they establish relationships, they position and rank themselves in relation to one another, and they learn and enact roles. Structure refers to regularities in the relationships between actors in the interaction. Structure organizes people's actions in relation to one another (Charon 2007: 59).

Lives always exist within groups, formal organizations, communities, and society. They are spent in a world of social norms (rules, morals, customs) and social patterns (established systems of inequality, types of families and schools, etc.), and a larger social organization (Charon 2007: 40).

Groups

A *group*, discussed in chapter 4, consists of people who regularly interact with one another. Ordinarily, members of a group share similar values, norms, and expectations. To belong to a group is to yield to others the right to make certain decisions about one's behavior. Those who belong to a group assume an obligation to act according to the expectations of other members of that group (Henslin 2007: 101).

Secondary groups are those people belong to but on a less intimate and more formal basis. Schools, neighborhood associations, work groups, or athletic teams are probably secondary groups. (It is possible for a secondary group to become a primary one: members of a basketball team, for example, might see each other off court so that a type of intimacy develops.)

A *reference* group is "a social group that serves as a point of reference in making evaluations and decisions" (Macionis 2004: 111). Individuals use such groups as a guide in developing their values, attitudes, behavior, and self-image. People look to reference groups when unsure of what to do. Reference groups could also be the groups individuals would like to belong to, even though they may not at the time. A college student who would like to become a lawyer might consider the American Bar Association a reference group. A group of high school students who played basketball might take the San Antonio Spurs as their reference group.

Sociologists use the term *ingroup* to describe a group with which people identify and to which they feel closely attached, particularly when that attachment is founded on opposition to or even hatred for another group known as an outgroup (Ferrante 2006: 121). An *outgroup* is a group of individuals toward which members of an ingroup feel a sense of separateness or opposition. Such groups might be based on race, religion, social class, residence, or other criteria. Obviously, one person's ingroup is another person's outgroup.

Research was conducted on children at 44 elementary schools and nurseries throughout Northern Ireland. The children were shown pictures and objects such as Irish and British flags, Protestant and Catholic parades, and different soccer teams' uniforms. The research found that girls and boys from the Protestant and Catholic sides of Northern Ireland absorbed their communities' prejudice by age 5. They expressed preference for the symbols that represented their side. And they made comments suggesting that they like their own people while looking with deep suspicion on the outgroup (cited in Eitzen and Zinn 2007: 111).

One student recalls that, when he was about eight, he and his family moved to a new subdivision. For some unknown reason, two groups formed according to street. Members of each group pulled pranks on the other, such as throwing eggs and rocks at the other's houses. Later the student became good friends with two boys in the "outgroup" he used to torment. "None of us knows why we ever disliked each other" (cited in Ferrante 2006: 122).

Social Networks

Social networks are clusters of people who associate together, or simply *links* between people (Henslin 2007: 138). Social networks can be envisioned as lines that extend outward from a given person, gradually encompassing more and more people. Usually, a network includes people we *know of*--or who *know of us*—but with whom we interact rarely if at all. It is like a web that expands outward, often reaching great distances and including large numbers of people (Macionis 2004:114-115).

Social networks exist among individuals (on the micro level), and also among groups, organizations, communities, and nations. Sociologists have used network analysis to cast new light on interpersonal behavior, family and kinship systems, social cohesion, social mobility, power and political organization, and the covert control mechanisms that exist in free market economics (Harper and Leicht 2007: 246-247).

Recent interest in social networks has arisen from the popularization of *social capital*, which has emerged as a business competence, receiving wide attention in business journals and popular literature. Social capital refers to the advantages individuals possess by being connected to others. This advantage is created by a person's location in the structure of network relationships. Social capital "explains how people do better because they are somehow better connected with other people" (R. S. Burt, cited in Burton 2007: 2).

Organizations

Organizations are coordinating mechanisms created by people to achieve stated goals or objectives (Ferrante 2006: 181). They bring together people, resources, and technology in such a way as to achieve a goal. The goal may be to maintain order (a police department), to grow or process food (PepsiCo), to produce goods (Sony), or to provide a service (a hospital).

Organizations continue to exist even as their members die, quit, retire, or get fired. When an organization such as a church or a college has its one-hundredth anniversary, the likelihood that any original member of that organization will be present is extremely remote. Yet the organization celebrates the occasion with great pride.

The sociologist who wrote extensively about organizations and bureaucracy was Max Weber, introduced in chapter 2. Weber's concern was with the nature of organizations in society and the justifications for the evolution and existence of particular forms. His genius lay in relating these patterns of authority to religious beliefs, power, and status. Weber pointed out that certain groups within organizations have the right to coordinate, control, and direct, because they have achieved legitimacy in society at large (Hinings and Greenwood 2002).

Organizations are neither uniformly benign in their effects, nor separable from the larger sociocultural context. Aldrich says, "the concentration of power in organizations contributes not only to the attainment of large-scale goals, but also to some of the most troublesome actions affecting us" (cited in Hinings and Greenwood 2002). Organizations have the ability to influence public decision-making. They gain professional access to politicians and have the capacity to mobilize consequences of significance. In the Enron scandal, the actions of several types of groups affected people and organizations in substantial ways. (See bureaucracy, below.)

Multinational Corporations

Multinational corporations are enterprises that own or control production and service facilities in countries other than the one in which their headquarters are located (Ferrante 2006: 182). The United Nations estimates that at least 35,000 multinationals operate worldwide. Many of them are based in the United States, Japan, and Western Europe. They operate in foreign countries for many reasons, including a cheaper labor force, the availability of raw materials, and low-cost service to consumers outside the country.

Intense controversy has surrounded multinational corporations. Their supporters claim that they are agents of progress: they raise standards of living, yield higher productivity, increase employment opportunities, transfer technology, and promote cultural understanding. By employing hundreds of thousands of workers, they help the local community.

Critics of multinationals argue that they exploit people and resources to manufacture products inexpensively. They take advantage of a cheap and desperately poor labor force, lenient environmental regulations, and sometimes nonexistent worker safety standards, show insufficient concern for local conditions, and thus contribute to major social problems (Ferrante 2006: 182).

Social Institutions

Social institutions, mentioned in chapter 1, are social arrangements that channel behavior in prescribed ways in the important areas of social life (Eitzen and Zinn 2007: 42). Institutions are the ways society develops to meet its basic needs. Each institution has its own groups, statuses, values, and norms. Major institutions include marriage, family, education, economics, politics, sports, social control, the military, and health care.

People learn to follow institutional ways. It is common to work eight hours a day for five days every week. There is nothing normal or natural about this pattern, but it is the institutionalized expectation. Likewise with marriage, it is expected that a couple will marry and set up a conjugal household. Polygamy or group marriage is not an option. People vote, attend party caucuses, and make campaign contributions because these are various political institutions that society has developed.

Functionalists claim that social institutions perform vital functions for a society. Each society must replace members, socialize new members, produce and distribute goods and services, preserve order, and provide a sense of purpose. Those who follow a conflict perspective argue that powerful groups control society's institutions in order to maintain their own privileged positions of wealth and power (Henslin 2007: 104).

Bureaucracy

Weber described a tendency in modern society to create highly "bureaucratic" structures that were increasingly efficient, clearly ranked, and well managed. The positions created within these structures were formally laid out and listed both qualifications and responsibilities. Weber believed people would find the goals of efficiency and rationality important, even though the complexity of an organization grew consistently with size. He believed this trend would exist in every modern society (Charon 2007: 82-83).

Bureaucracy is a government characterized by specialization of functions, adherence to fixed rules, and a hierarchy of authority. The system is found not only in governments but in the armed forces, corporations, hospitals, courts, ministries, schools, and even churches. While the number of civilian federal employees has fluctuated since World War II, indirect federal employment has increased significantly through state or local governments or private firms funded by federal programs.

Weber was critical of the routine nature of bureaucracy, which could serve to hamper initiative. But he also underlined how important it is that administrators are socialized into an ethos of rule following, that is, they become governed by internalized codes of exemplary behavior, right or wrong, true or false. He viewed bureaucratic structure as a rationally designed tool deliberately structured in order to improve the ability to realize goals (Olsen 2006).

Weber argued that bureaucracy would be the dominant organizational form in the modern world. Its growth is the inevitable product of a long historical development toward the rationalization of human organization and cooperation. Weber viewed bureaucratic structure as a rationally designed tool, deliberately structured in order to improve the ability to realize goals. Bureaucracy can be seen as a rational tool for executing the commands of elected leaders. Thus it is an organizational apparatus for getting things done. Bureaucratic structure determines what authority and resources can be legitimately used how, when, where, and by whom (Olsen 2006).

Many people associate bureaucracy with a lack of initiative, excessive adherence to rules and routine, red tape, and inefficiency. Whether this is a fair criticism is an ongoing debate (see "A Closer Look," below). The concern over bureaucratic behavior stems from the increasingly important role that public administrators play in American governance. It is widely recognized that bureaucrats, as they interpret and apply legislated mandates, engage in policy making. Whether substantial bureaucratic involvement in governance can be reconciled with democratic ideas remains an issue (Dolan 2002).

A Closer Look: Can Bureaucracy be Effective?

With reference to American public administration, some scholars claim that acceptable and responsible conduct is far more common than generally believed. According to these writers, data reveal that the performance of bureaucracy is acceptable or satisfactory in most encounters with citizens (Goodsell 1994; Olsen 2006). Of course any large administrative apparatus has instances of inefficiency, maladministration, and abused power. But in America at least, these deficiencies occur within tolerable ranges. "Governmental administration in America may be regarded as generally competent and effective, if we look at it in a balanced way and in relation to what is possible" (Goodsell 1994: 3).

Investigators also found high levels of approval of bureaucratic services rendered at the town, city, county, state, and federal levels. In actual studies, despite a different public perception, bureaucrats are seen as usually helpful, honest, responsible, adaptable, efficient, dependable, fair, friendly, respectful, considerate, and courteous. Experience with federal bureaucracy was even more favorably perceived. This should confound those who insist that the federal government is "remote" from the citizenry and thus likely to render poorer service.

William T. Gormley, Jr., and Steven J. Balla's book, **Bureaucracy and Democracy: Accountability and Performance** (2004) offers a thoughtful and practical counterpoint to stereotyped assumptions. Examples highlight bureaucratic responsiveness, capacity for significant reform, and the use of discretion to improve conditions for individuals and organizations throughout society. Insights from several disciplines and from empirical research illuminate bureaucracy's complex external environment.

The book presents the pragmatic side of the bureaucratic problem-solving and the ability of many bureaucrats to make good decisions with limited time and information. Network theory emphasizes the role of relationships that are both within and outside of bureaucracy. This approach is useful in showing how public managers negotiate contracts, collaborate with nonprofit organizations, or act across departmental lines to implement policies and programs (Holser and Kloby 2006).

The United States government is unusual by world standards. It is a government subject to periodic review in relatively honest elections. It is a government massively constrained by law and Constitution. It is a government widely admired by foreigners for organizational innovation and technical prowess.

A common criticism of bureaucracy is its reliance on rules, presumably decreasing flexibility. Yet subjecting human conduct to rules has been portrayed as part of the processes of democratization and civilization. Rules tend to increase capacity for action and efficiency. They make it possible to coordinate many activities that make them consistent and reduce uncertainty. They enforce agreements and help avoid destructive conflict. Further, rules need not imply rigidity and inflexibility.

Bureaucracy has a role as the institutional custodian of democratic principles and procedural rationality. Bureaucratic rules contribute to democratic equality because they are relatively blind to the wealth and other resources of the citizens they serve. Bureaucracy is associated with low corruption, partly because a longer time horizon makes quick illicit returns less likely. Rules and service mesh to create trust in institutions of government, when implemented in an impartial and uncorrupt way. Bureaucratic autonomy is rooted in constitutional democracy and the principles of the separation of powers (Olsen 2006).

Goodsell (1994) shatters some stereotypes when he claims that bureaucracies in the United States tend to be of moderate size. In fact, most are extremely small. Bureaucracies do not invariably get bigger; bigger bureaucracies do not necessarily perform less well than smaller; and older bureaucracies are not necessarily more ossified than younger ones.

The commonly accepted view of political conservatives that government never performs as well as private business is shown to be a potent falsehood. Bureaucratic organization is not disappearing because it is outperformed by smaller market and network forms of organization. Bureaucratic organization may become more important in increasingly heterogeneous societies, as part of a public administration originated on the basis of several competing principles. Bureaucracy has a role as a tool for legislators and representative democracy and is positively related to substantive outcomes that are valued in contemporary societies.

Surprisingly to some, public bureaucracies have been found to mirror the demographic makeup and attitudes of the general population quite faithfully. Some scholars claim that the federal bureaucracy will make broadly representative decisions, on budgetary choices as well as on other issues, because it is a representative institution itself. Convincing evidence is offered that public administrators at all levels of government heed the preferences of a variety of social groups and produce outputs in accordance with their wishes. That there is a "bureaucratic mentality" is not supported by evidence.

One study found that senior executives and the general public largely reflect one another in their priorities for government spending. Public administrators are more frugal and less inclined to favor increased public spending than the general public. According to a work by Gregory Lewis, "government employers are no more likely than the average citizen to favor bigger government budgets" (cited in Dolan 2002). The assumption that bureaucrats prefer larger budgets is questioned; in fact, they are more likely to advocate decreased government spending. Further, there is little evidence that administrators inflate spending in their own programs while decreasing funds for competing programs (Dolan 2002).

Bureaucratic organization is not a panacea, and is not the necessarily preferred to organize public administration for various tasks nor under all circumstances. (For a negative look at a type of bureaucracy, see "A Closer Look" in the next chapter.) But the stereotype of a bureaucracy that is invariably inefficient and corrupt finds no empirical support. Bureaucratic organization is part of a repertoire of overlapping and supplementary forms coexisting in contemporary democracies.

Summary

Social interaction is the process by which people act and react in relation to others. People interpret and attach meaning to their everyday encounters.

Status is a social position an individual occupies. Usually one status implies another: husband-wife, employer-employee, teacher-student. An ascribed status is conferred at birth, while an achieved status requires effort on the part of the individual.

A role is behavior expected in a particular status. People often tend to become the roles they play. Role strain refers to an ambiguity or tension in fulfilling a single status; role conflict refers to ambiguity in fulfilling two or more roles.

The social construction of reality is the process by which people shape reality through social interaction. Through this process, people learn ways of interpreting their experiences in life.

Dramaturgy claims that social life is like a drama or a stage play. Many terms in sociology have been drawn from the theater: actor, audience, role, stage, script. Front stages are the public areas where people perform their roles; back stages are places out of the audience's sight.

A number of gender differences in interaction have been noted, particularly in nonverbal communication.

Social structure is the typical patterns of a group, heavily influenced by the statuses people hold. Lives always exist within groups, formal organizations, communities, and society. A primary group is one in which there is intimate, face-to-face interaction, such as a family. A secondary group is one to which people belong on a more formal basis. Social networks are clusters of people who associate together.

Organizations are coordinating mechanisms created to achieve stated goals. Organizations influence public decision making, which can be in a positive or negative direction.

Multinational corporations are enterprises that own or control production and service facilities in different countries. Such corporations spread goods and capital around the world and employ many workers, but have been criticized for exploiting people and resources.

Social institutions are social arrangements that channel behavior in prescribed ways, so society can meet its basic needs. Some claim that they perform vital functions, while others argue that they are controlled by those with privilege and power.

Bureaucracy is a government characterized by specialization of functions, adherence to fixed rules, and a hierarchy of authority. Weber thought that bureaucracy would increase efficiency but present certain problems. While many are critical of bureaucratic forms, evidence is presented that they can be effective.

References

Brodkin, Evelyn Z. 2007. "Bureaucracy Redux: Management Reformism and the Welfare State" (**Journal of Public Administration Research and Theory**, Vol. 17).

Burton, Paul E. 2007. **Dimensions of Social Networks as Predictors of Employee Performance** (Ann Arbor, Michigan: Proquest Information and Learning Company).

Charon, Joel M. 2007. **Ten Questions: A Sociological Perspective**, sixth edition (Belmont, California: Thomson Wadsworth).

Clark, Ruth Anne, Michael Dockum, Heidi Hazen, Meikuan Huang, Nan Luo, Jason Ramsey, Angel Spyrou. 2004. "Initial Encounters of Young Men and Women: Impressions and Disclosure Estimates" (**Sex Roles: A Journal of Research**, Vol. 50).

Dolan, Julie. 2002. "The budget-minimizing bureaucrat? Empirical evidence from the senior executive service (**Public Administrative Review**, Vol. 62).

Eitzen, D. Stanley, and Maxine Baca Zinn. 2007. **In Conflict and Order: Understanding Society**, eleventh edition (Boston: Allyn and Bacon).

Ferrante, Joan. 2006. **Sociology: A Global Perspective**, sixth edition (Belmont, California: Thomson/Wadsworth).

Goodsell, Charles T. 1994. **The Case for Bureaucracy: A Public Administration Polemic**, third edition (Chatham, New Jersey: Chatham House).

Harper, Charles L., and Kevin T. Leicht. 2007. **Exploring Social Change: America and the World**, fifth edition (Upper Saddle River, New Jersey: Pearson).

Henslin, James M. 2007. **Sociology: A Down-to-Earth Approach,** second edition (Boston: Allyn and Bacon).

Hinings, C. R., and Royston Greenwood. 2002. "Disconnects and consequences in organization theory" (**Administrative Science Quarterly**, Vol. 47).

Holzer, Marc, and Kathryn Kloby. 2006. "Bureaucracy and Democracy: A Happy Marriage?" (**Journal of Public Administration Research and Theory**, Vol. 16).

Macionis, John J. 2004. **Society: The Basics**, second edition (Upper Saddle River, New Jersey: Prentice-Hall.

McQuinty, Kristin, David Knox, Marty E. Zusman. 2003. "Nonverbal and verbal communication in 'involved' and 'casual' relationships among college students" (**College Student Journal**, Vol. 37).

Olsen, Johan. 2006. "Maybe it is Time to Rediscover Bureaucracy," (**Journal of Public Administration Research and Theory**, Vol. 16).

Patterson, Miles L. and Mark E. Tubbs. 2005. "Through a Glass Darkly: Effects of Smiling and Visibility on Recognition and Avoidance in Passing Encounters" (**Western Journal of Communication**, Vol. 69).

Schwebel, David C., and Milton Schwebel. 2002. "Teaching Nonverbal Communication" (**College Teaching**, Vol. 50).

Police station in Carrollton, Texas

Chapter 6: DEVIANCE AND SOCIAL CONTROL

The last two chapters have explored the ways people are socialized into their culture, the importance of social interaction in directing their behavior, and the social structures that mold their lives. The fact remains, however, that many people do not behave in ways considered appropriate for their social group. Most people witness or at least hear of such behavior every day. The name for behavior that does not conform to social expectations is *deviance* (Eitzen and Zinn 2007: 162).

Sociologists believe that it is not the act itself, but the reactions *to* the act that define deviant behavior. Because groups have different norms, what is deviant to one person or group would be *conformist* to another. Deviant behavior may vary in the same society in different time periods: cocaine was once legal in the United States. What is considered deviant may vary not only from one society to another, but between different groups in the same society (Macionis 2004: 135; Henslin 2007: 154).

A very large amount of deviance is lawful behavior. The previous chapter introduced the concept of *norms*, or rules for everyday behavior. Norms lay out the basic guidelines for how we should play our roles and interact with others. Whenever someone bumps into another person and fails to say, "Excuse me," whenever a married couple forgets to send thank-you notes to those who have given them wedding gifts, or whenever someone dresses casually on a formal occasion, deviant behavior has occurred.

It is possible to be considered a deviant without even *doing* anything. Erving Goffman used the term *stigma* to refer to characteristics that discredit people (Macionis 2004: 139). They might be violations of norms of ability (a badly scarred face, a mental handicap) or appearance (obesity, a noticeable birthmark). The famous reindeer Rudolph was labeled a deviant by the stigma of a very shiny nose.

Deviance must be viewed from within a group's own framework, for it is the meanings of a group that underlie their members' behavior. Establishing who is deviant doesn't answer questions of right and wrong

(Henslin 2007: 157). In the deep South in the 1950s, a white person who would associate with a black person publicly in a relationship of equality would be deviant under the norms of that time. Many ancient prophets, such as Isaiah, Amos, and Jeremiah, were considered deviant in their time.

A specific form of deviance is known as *crime*, the violation of rules that have been written into law (Henslin 2007: 154). Virtually all Americans at one time or another break the laws (Eitzen and Zinn 2007: 161). Cheating on one's income taxes, driving a few miles over the speed limit, copying computer software and music, cheating on examinations, using marijuana or another illegal substance, or embezzling from employers are all extremely widespread in American society.

Formal codes of crime vary from state to state and particularly from nation to nation. It is a crime in Iran for women to wear makeup. It is against the law in Florida to sell alcohol before 1:00 P. M. on a Sunday. It is illegal in Wells, Maine, to advertise on tombstones (Henslin 2007: 177).

In the 1980s a new crime appeared on the books: *hate crime.* This referred to crimes, especially physical assaults, motivated by bias or hatred toward the victim's race or ethnicity, religion, sexual orientation, disability, or national origin. Hate crimes carry sentences more severe than do the same acts not driven by hate (Macionis 2004: 145).

It is extremely difficult to establish accurate statistics for criminal acts (Macionis 2004: 147). In general, reported crime is crime known to the police, whether it is ever solved or not. The *Uniform Crime Reports* are compiled across the United States.

Obviously many crimes, such as shoplifting and attempted rape, are rarely reported. And police discretion, the decision of whether to arrest someone or to ignore an infraction, is a routine part of police work. There is, therefore, an inevitable bias in the statistics.

Types of Crime

Crimes may be divided into several different types, with slight overlapping.

(1) Common crime: includes both violent offenses, murder, rape, robbery, and aggravated assault, and property crimes, burglary,

larceny, automobile theft, and shoplifting. Young males are disproportionately involved in both. Discussion below will center on assault and murder in the U. S.

(2) White-collar crime: the violation of the law by middle and upper-class people in the course of their business and social lives (Macionis 2004: 143). Offenders may hold managerial, technical, or professional positions. Lies, misrepresentation, and deception are typically involved. Employees embezzle and pilfer an estimated $10 billion annually from their employers (Eitzen and Zinn 2007: 161).

(3) Corporate crime: this includes crimes committed *by* the corporation, such as false advertising, price fixing, and stock manipulation, and offenses committed *on behalf of* the corporation, such as negligence (health and safety violations), bribery, or polluting the environment.

(4) Organized crime: groups that provide and profit from illegal goods and services, such as drugs, prostitution, and gambling. Organized crime may also provide legal goods and services by illegal means, such as controlling garbage collection or tax service using intimidation to eliminate competition. Loosely known as the Mafia, organized crime is not Italian (it began in Ireland) but is found all over the world. These secret conspiracies generally evade law enforcement (Macionis 2004: 145).

(5) Crimes without victims: the willing exchange among adults of widely desired but illegal goods and services. These crimes offend public morals. Such crimes include prostitution, pornography, illegal drugs, and illegal gambling.

(6) Professional crime: refers to individuals (apart from organized crime) who make their livelihood from crime, such as jewel thieves, counterfeiters, and shoplifters. People involved in professional crime consider it a form of work, which is carefully planned. This type of crime is spreading through identity theft, electronic transfer of funds, and crimes using computers.

Assault and Murder

Under common crimes, the offenses that have elicited the most discussion, and the most fear, are assault (physical attack against a person or persons not resulting in death) and murder (homicide).

Experts who have studied these types of crime have found several patterns that usually prevail.

First, and true of all common crime, the perpetrators are overwhelmingly young and male. People ages 14 to 23 commit a disproportionate amount of all crime, although murder is likely to be committed by those slightly older, those in the late teens and twenties. Common reasons are that adolescents and young adults are going through an awkward transition between youth and adulthood; they may not have married or integrated into the occupational world; people of this age are more likely to become involved in delinquent gangs and other criminal subcultures.

Reasons males are more involved in violent assaults include the "macho" male culture that defines a man as more aggressive and "tough"; and that males are more likely to have access to weapons such as knives or guns.

Among other patterns of violent assault, most such behavior is *spontaneous* and the assailant is usually *known* to the victim. While planned murders are not unusual, most attacks occur in the heat of the moment, usually over an argument about money, drugs, girls, or territory. Attacks by strangers have been increasing slightly in recent years, but so is the tendency that the victim is known in some way to the assailant.

Alcohol (or alcohol abuse) is common in violent assaults, often by the victim as well as by the perpetrator. The role of illegal drugs in assaults is somewhat different: drugs are often involved as a source of contention, but seldom does the use of drugs (other than alcohol) embolden an individual to attack another. Most drugs actually have a lethargic effect.

When a weapon is used in a violent assault, it is likely to be a *handgun* (pistol or revolver). Although long guns (rifles and shotguns) are more numerous and more deadly, they are used for personal assault much less often than handguns. The main reason seems to be that the handgun is *concealable*: it can be brought into almost any public place without detection. There is evidence, however controversial, that the sheer *availability* of handguns contributes to their frequent use. "The presence of a firearm categorically changes the nature of the criminal intent" (Stanko et al. 2004: 10).

Further, handguns are much more lethal than a knife, the weapon next most often used. Estimates are that a handgun is at least four times more likely to result in death than is a knife. A study of youth crime in a British city found that although fighting and some violence were common, firearms incidents were *nowhere* near as common as they are in inner-city areas in major U. S. cities. No perpetrators used a gun, and most had never even seen one (Sanders 2005: 128-129). Most experts think that stricter gun control laws would reduce the level of deadly violence (Macionis 2004: 151).

Minorities are disproportionately involved in assault and murder, and they are also more likely to be victims (Sanders 2005: 18). Violent assault tends to be *intraracial*, meaning that the assailant and the victim are of the same race. An interesting observation is that when interracial violence has occurred, the black person is more likely to be the victim than the attacker. For further discussion about minority involvement in crime, see "Generalizations," below.

Somewhat surprising about violent crime, it comprises only about 10 percent of all crime. Further, violence is a relatively rare event among all groups, including blacks in America, and race is a poor predictor as to whether someone will be violent or not. In 2000, there were over 1.5 million arrests of young people in this country. Of these, 65,000 were for violent crimes and 800 for homicide (Lauritsen 2004).

Two more patterns of violent assault show that it generally occurs in *evenings* and *on weekends*. The emergency rooms of large hospitals consistently expect to receive a large number of victims of assaults from Friday night through Sunday morning.

White-collar Crime

White-collar crime refers to offenses committed by people of respectable and high social status in the course of their occupation (Henslin 2007: 168). Surveys by the Internal Revenue Service consistently find that three out of ten people cheat on their income taxes. An estimated 25 percent of the total labor force does not report all or part of its income from otherwise legal practices. Time theft by employees (such as faked illnesses, excessive breaks, and long lunches) costs U. S. business as much as $200 billion annually (Eitzen and Zinn 2007: 161). White-collar crime not only costs the country more money, but weakens public faith in a free economy and public morality generally.

Corporate Crime

Corporate crime has been big news in recent years. Michael Milken, the Wall Street wonder of the 80s, and associate Ivan Boesky, were dethroned in the "junk bond" scandal. The Archer Daniel Midland price-fixing scandal marked the 90s. E. F. Hutton was found guilty of 2,000 counts of defrauding American banks with a check manipulation scheme. The company paid a fine, but there were no prosecutions of the officials responsible. The Manville Corporation was convicted of asbestos exposure after thousands of people died of asbestos-related disease. The investigations prompted by the collapse of Houston's energy giant, Enron, were responsible for the indictments of at least 30 people (Jacobs 2006).

The Savings and Loan scandal of the late 1970s may have been the worst financial debacle in U. S. history: 450 institutions were declared insolvent and 11,000 cases were referred to the Justice Department for criminal prosecution. Over a ten-year period, some $250 billion was stolen or wasted. After the government cut back funds for regulation, many Savings and Loan officials took the opportunity to loot their firms. Estimates are that the scandal cost the American people upwards of one trillion dollars.

Generalizations about Crime

Criminologists have come up with a number of empirical generalizations about crime in the United States. That crime is committed disproportionately by males and by young people has already been discussed. Minorities are disproportionately involved in crime, but this generalization calls for explication. The disadvantaged social environment many minorities live in is believed to be primarily at fault. And there is evidence that the police and court systems may be biased against minority groups. Finally, the correlation is noticeable only with common crimes; whites are conversely overrepresented in white-collar and corporate crime.

Delinquent behavior by nonwhites is of special concern, underscored by mortality statistics and overrepresentation in juvenile detention centers and prisons. Blacks have higher rates of violent crime (homicide

112

and robbery), but for the vast majority of youth crime (assault, burglary, theft, vandalism, drug and alcohol violations), few differences exist (Lauritsen 2004). One study found that lack of parental control and supervision was strongly associated with delinquent behavior among young black males (Paschall et al. 2003).

Although males are much more likely to be involved in crime, the proportion of female offenders is growing. As more women work in factories, corporations, and the professions, their opportunities for crime increase. They are also enticed by illegitimate opportunities (Henslin 2007: 170). Women's crime tends to make less news.

More women are now being sent to prison for offenses that used to garner only a probationary sentence, but women still primarily commit non-violent crimes: larceny, theft, drunken driving, and fraud. In criminal enterprises, women function at the lower echelons as minor players. A majority of incarcerated women are women of color. Over 40 percent of women offenders reported a history of physical or sexual abuse prior to arrest (Jacobs 2006).

The crime rate in this country was relatively low in the 1950s, then had a dramatic upswing through the 1980s. But in the mid-1990s the rate began to decline significantly (Rosenfeld 2002; Stanko et al. 2004: 8). Despite a slight rise in some types of crime in the last few years, this decline has continued into 2008. Better employment opportunities in the late 1990s, fewer drugs on the streets, a smaller percentage of young people in the population, and firmer police practices are some of the reasons suggested for the decline.

The linkage between crime and drug abuse is well documented. In one study in 1993, about 60 percent of arrests in 22 large cities tested positive for drugs other than alcohol at the time of the arrests (Stanco et al. 2004: 79). As noted earlier, drugs seldom embolden a person to commit a violent act, but are involved in criminal activity in other ways.

Crime is highly underreported, that is, experts believe the true crime rate might be about twice what it is, due to unreliable statistics mentioned earlier and particularly the underreporting of many types of crime (Stanko et al. 2004: 7). Crime is repetitive, meaning that some of the same people tend to commit crimes over and over (see *recidivism* under social control, below). Finally, crime rates are higher in large urban areas than in smaller cities and rural areas.

The United States is one of the most violent nations in the world. More New Yorkers are hit with stray bullets than the number deliberately gunned down in most large cities elsewhere in the world (Macionis 2004: 150). Some reasons for this are a maldistribution of income, leading to economic stress, and social disintegration, reflected in high rates of divorce and social breakdown. Some experts believe the prevalence of gangs and the widespread availability of handguns are factors.

In a recent book on juvenile delinquency, Peter Greenwood says that research consistently links such factors as delinquent peer affiliations, neglectful parental supervision, low school achievement, and adolescent substance abuse to juvenile delinquency, and juvenile delinquency itself as a factor in adult criminality. Greenwood shuns the idea of tougher sentences and more prisons and recommends better, early preventive programming (Theriot 2007).

Theories of Deviance and Crime

Rather than look at biological or personality disorders, which seem to reveal little about why people deviate, sociology looks for factors *outside* the individual. It examines such influences as faulty socialization, membership in deviant subcultures, and social class (see chapter 8). Important considerations are people's relative standing in education, occupation, income, and wealth (Henslin 2007: 158).

Functional Theory

Functionalists contend that deviance is unavoidable and inevitable. The sociologist Durkheim recognized that deviance is actually functional: when it occurs, the rest of the community is bound together in opposition to the deviant act. It also helps prepare people for change. Violations that are increasingly tolerated become new, acceptable behaviors. They could force a group to rethink and redefine its moral boundaries (Ferrante 2006: 222). Though Durkheim did not stress this, deviance and crime also provide employment to a number of people: policemen, judges, prison guards, etc.

Structural Strain

An important theory of deviance is called *structural strain*, another functionalist view. "Strain" refers to a tension between the established goals of a society and the means for achieving them. In a conformist setting, people desire long-term cultural goals, usually of a material nature (money, success, valued possessions, etc.). The means desired to achieve these goals would be staying in school to get an education and working hard in a legitimate business until they are achieved. But when the valued goals are unclear, or if there is ambiguity about the means available to reach them, the goals may remain closed.

Americans tend to believe that anyone can achieve success. For many people, mainstream norms (working hard and going to school) don't seem to be getting them anywhere; people who experience strain find it difficult to identify with these norms. Particularly in depressed areas of the country, legitimate opportunities are too few to achieve the desired goals. People see too few peers from their area making it in the conformist sense.

Robert Merton, who proposed the theory of structural strain, set forth five theoretical responses to the situations available to people, four of which were deviant. They are diagramed as follows, with a plus sign (+) indicating acceptance and a minus sign (-) indicating rejection (Ferrante 2006: 238-239).

	Means for reaching goals	Long-term goals
conformist (non-deviant)	+	+
innovator	-	+
retreatist	-	-
ritualist	+	-
rebel	+/-	+/-

The conformist obviously accepts both the goals and the means for achieving them. The *innovator* accepts the goals—he or she would like very much to have the good things of life—but rejects the means for fulfilling them. Criminals want what most people want—material success—but they pursue illegitimate means to achieve it. Instead of staying in school and seeking a legitimate career, they typically turn to selling drugs, embezzling, robbery, or being a con artist.

Gangs are tempting to a disadvantaged young person from the inner city. Sanchez Jankowski did a participant observation study of 37 gangs in three large cities. The gangs earned money through gambling, arson, mugging, armed robbery, and selling moonshine, drugs, guns, stolen car parts, and protection. Jankowski, who lived with the gangs for a time, did not find that the motive for joining was to escape a broken home. Rather, the boys joined to access money, to find recreation (including girls and drugs), to maintain anonymity in criminal acts, and to help the community. (In some neighborhoods, gangs protect residents from outsiders.) Gangs will likely persist in city life (cited in Henslin 2007: 168).

A study of youth crime in a British city revealed that the phenomenon of gangs does not exist as it does in the United States. Territorial violence is far more prevalent in the U. S. There was no evidence of long-standing rivalries, gang rumbles, or territorial disputes (Sanders 2005: 128-130).

The *retreatist* has given up on *both* the long-term goals and the means for achieving them. He "retreats" into a shell, trying to avoid the pain of trying and failing. Examples of a retreatist: a Skid-Row alcoholic or drug addict who lives on the street, some forms of mental illness and some (probably not most) homeless people. A woman who enters a convent might be a retreatist, but for a different reason.

The *ritualist* is an interesting case: this person has become discouraged and has abandoned the long-term goals, realizing he will never achieve what most of society considers success. But rather than abandoning the means as well, he clings to conventional rules of conduct, slavishly conforming to the norms. An example could be a teacher who has experienced "burnout," but stays in the job without enthusiasm, or someone else who perseveres in a dead-end job.

The *rebel* is one who rejects both conventional means and goals, but who would like to replace them with new means or new goals, or perhaps both. Revolutionaries come from this category (Henslin 2007: 164-166).

Sanders (2005: 193), who studied youth crime in a British city, claimed that no theory of deviance or crime captured all behavior of the young people he studied, but he suggested that strain theory best explained the reasons why the young people committed the offenses they did.

Symbolic interactionists have proposed two theories to help account for deviant behavior, differential association and labeling theory.

Differential Association

This well-known theory of crime was developed by the prominent criminologist Edwin Sutherland. Basically, Sutherland claims that individuals *learn* techniques of committing crime from close association and interaction with those who engage in and approve of criminal behavior. They may become involved in delinquent subcultures (Macionis 2004: 137) such as gangs.

In the lives of some delinquents, deviant behavior is approved. They become disposed to commit criminal acts, especially in long-term interactions with those they admire and care about. Some areas, especially in inner-city slums, become filled with definitions and role models of deviance (Turner 2006: 149). One study found that affiliation with delinquent peers may be an important determinant of delinquent behavior among black male adolescents (Paschall et al. 2003). There is a sense, then, that some people become deviants by *conforming* to deviant companions.

The impact of families is crucial. Of all jail inmates in the U. S., almost *half* have a father, mother, brother, sister, or spouse who has served time. Children who have delinquent friends are likely to become delinquent, too (Henslin 2007: 159).

Labeling Theory

As noted earlier, sociologists believe that it is not the act itself, but the reactions to the act, that make it deviant. From the perspective of symbolic interactionism, labeling theory focuses on the significance of the labels (names, reputations) that people are given. These labels tend to become part of one's self-concept, and help set one on paths that are deviant. (A label might be "slob," "whore," "pervert," "troublemaker".) The labels people are given affect their own and others' perceptions of them, channeling their behavior towards either conformity or deviance (Henslin 2007: 161). Rudolph was labeled ("all of the other reindeer used to laugh and call him names").

Labeling theory emphasizes that the labels attached to people's behaviors are critical in the genesis and maintenance of deviance (Lemert, cited in Turner 2006: 148). When people are labeled, they often respond to the labels by fulfilling the expectations contained in the label. Some actually revel in a deviant identity: they make certain that their choices of clothing, music, and hairstyles reflect the rejection of adult norms (Henslin 2007: 162; Macionis 2004: 142).

Labeling theory is dramatically illustrated in the story of the "Saints" and the "Roughnecks," two groups in the same school in the same town. Boys in both groups skipped school, got drunk, and did a lot of fighting and vandalism. While the delinquent acts of the two groups were about the same, the community perceived the groups very differently. The Saints, eight middle-class boys, were perceived as "going somewhere." The Roughnecks, six lower-class boys, were viewed as headed down a dead-end road.

Seven of the eight "Saints" went on to graduate from college, and three studied for advanced degrees. Only four of the "Roughnecks" finished high school. Two did become coaches, but the remainder were undistinguished and two wound up in the penitentiary. It can be said that both groups lived up to the labels that the community gave them (summarized from Henslin 2007: 163).

Labels open and close the doors of opportunity. A judgment on people can lock them out of conforming groups and push them into contact with people who are similarly labeled (Henslin 2007: 164). Someone labeled could accumulate written transcripts of the label, such as a police file or a prison record. These could deny the person the chance to escape from deviance and force him into deviant roles (Turner 2006: 148).

Control Theory

This theory proposes that for deviants, there are no strong attachments to others who would disapprove of deviant behavior. For most people, the attachments they have to nondeviant others and groups who disapprove of deviants are strong. The more they have invested in education, years on the job, a house, family ties, a car, and other relationships and possessions, the more they risk by being deviant. Deviance is perceived as too costly.

From a control viewpoint, those who deviate have weak attachments to others, few investments in nondeviance, less time and energy committed to conformity, and fewer beliefs in conformity to mainstream norms. The costs of deviance are less to them (Turner 2006: 149-150; Macionis 2004: 141).

Conflict Theory

Unlike most approaches, conflict theory does not focus on the deviants themselves, claiming that that looks only at the symptoms, not the disease. The focus instead is on the failure of society to meet the needs of individuals. "The sources of crime, poverty, drug addiction, and racism are found in the laws, the customs, the quality of life, the distribution of wealth and power, and the accepted practices of schools, governmental units, and corporations" (Eitzen and Zinn 2007: 186-187). It is the established system, in this view, that is the primary source of social problems, and this is what must be restructured.

A conflict theorist would note vast discrepancies in punishment. The wealthy and privileged get light punishment for serious white-collar and corporate crimes, while common crimes are severely punished. Under federal law, causing the death of a worker by willfully violating safety rules is a misdemeanor punishable by up to six months in prison. Harassing a wild burro on federal lands is punishable by a year in prison (Henslin 2007: 169). The typical sanction for a corporate crime is a token fine. (See Social Control, below.)

Sociologist Jonathan Turner believes that these theories invite high rates of deviance in the United States. More punishment and enforcement will not work to reduce crime and other acts of deviance. Rather, policies must be directed at reducing the disjuncture between success goals and available means, at redressing the imbalance in how poor and rich criminals are treated, at mitigating the effects of labels, and at increasing the human costs of deviance by increasing attachments, investments, and involvements in the mainstream culture and structures of society (Turner 2006: 150).

The larger challenges are to find ways to protect people from deviant behaviors that are harmful, to tolerate those behaviors that are not harmful, and to develop systems of fairer treatment for deviants. Society needs a more humane system, one that would prevent the inequalities that tend to bring about deviance (Henslin 2007: 181).

Social Control

Social control refers to mechanisms that ensure conformity or punish deviance (Eitzen and Zinn 2007: 133). Social control is achieved through the application of *sanctions*, reactions of approval and disapproval to others' behavior. Positive sanctions are expressions of approval and reward: a smile, applause, an award. Negative sanctions are disapproval or punishment: ridicule, ostracism, imprisonment, even death. *Informal* sanctions are unofficial ones not backed by the force of law, such as ridicule. *Formal* sanctions are laws, regulations, and policies: medals, diplomas, fines, imprisonment (Henslin 2007: 156).

All social groups must deal with deviant behavior in some way. The socialization process itself, seeking as it does to ensure conformity, is a form of social control, as is gossip and ridicule. Such informal controls may work to a degree in some rural areas, but societies find that they are insufficient to ensure that people will behave in expected ways. Hence modern societies have increasingly moved to rely on the civil and the criminal justice system.

The police are charged with detection of crime, investigation, and arrest. They are the gatekeepers of the criminal justice system because they uncover criminal behavior. They gather as much evidence as possible to connect a person to a specific crime. At the same time, they are to abide by Constitutional safeguards (Stanco et al. 2004: 11). The police also exercise considerable discretion about which situations warrant their attention and how to handle them.

The procedure before the courts involved appearances, a preliminary hearing, formal charging, an arraignment, a trial, sentencing, and (in most cases) the setting of bail. A jury trial is rarely used; only about 5 percent of criminal cases go to trial, with about 90 percent resulting in plea bargaining. If a plea bargain is reached, offenders are 75 percent less likely to be sentenced to prison (Stanco et al. 2004: 13-14).

Traditionally, penalties for white-collar crimes such as fraud, embezzlement, and insider trading were significantly lower than penalties for violent, drug, or even physical property crimes. The crimes committed in the corporate world often do greater social harm because of a great number of victims suffer enormous economic loss. Pension funds and life savings are often lost (Podgor 2007). Yet perpetrators were more likely to receive probation, and (if given prison) short sentences.

Before Sentencing Guidelines became uniform in the 1980s, an average of 59 percent of fraud defendants received straight probation sentences, and the average prison time served was seven months (Bibas 2005).

Sentences for theft and fraud were raised on average in 1998 and again in 2001. The Sentencing Commission raised its penalties for fraud even further. But significant discretion is left in the hands of prosecutors: they have leeway to bargain over the facts. U. S. v. Booker (2005) made sentencing more flexible. Middle- and upper-class defendants receive better representation from their lawyers. Thus white-collar enforcement will never become as harsh as drug enforcement (Bibas 2005).

Institutional corrections include prisons, jails, and other regional detention facilities. Community corrections cover a wide range of alternatives such as probation, parole, home detention, electronic monitoring, community service, day reporting, and work or treatment programs (Stanco 2004: 17).

Prisons

Some 87 percent of prisoners are 18 to 44, and almost 90 percent are men. Close to half of all prisoners are black, even though they make up just 12.3 percent of the population. People who drop out of high school have a high chance of ending up in prison, while a college graduate is unlikely to be found there. While the popular view is that all prisoners are rapists and murderers, a majority of inmates are incarcerated for nonviolent offenses.

The United States has more prisoners than any other nation, and a larger percentage of its population in prison (Henslin 2007: 172, emphasis in original). Imprisonment rates have skyrocketed since the 1970s to levels not seen anywhere else in the world, except South Africa and Russia. The U. S. incarceration rate is higher than those in other developed nations for property and drug offenses. Over two million Americans now reside in prison or jail. More than twice that number is under some form of correctional supervision in the community, such as electronic monitoring (Rosenfeld 2002).

Prison costs are becoming some states' largest spending category. As the U. S. prison population grows, the costs associated with imprisonment grow as well. From 1980 to the late 1990s state corrections budgets tripled, and costs continue to rise. "Several large states now spend as much or more money to incarcerate young adults than to educate their college-age citizens" (J. Hagan and R. Dinovitzer, cited in Stanco et al. 2004: 21).

"Get tough" policies and three-strike laws have driven up the population. Though these laws were intended to keep violent offenders off the street, they had some unintended consequences. One 27-year old man was sentenced to 55 years for stealing a pizza. A man who went on a $17,000 shopping spree was given 200 years in prison. A young man who stole nine videotapes from K-Mart was given 50 years without parole.

Recidivism results when former prisoners are rearrested. For those sentenced for a violent crime and eventually released, 62 percent were rearrested within three years and 52 percent went back to prison. For those convicted of a property crime, the recidivism rate is even higher (Henslin 2007: 174).

Prisons are a reflection of society, a measure of civilization. They are warehouses of the unwanted. White-collar criminals usually get off with fines or short sentences, while street criminals are punished severely. There are more humane approaches than these (Henslin 2007: 181). The opinion that prisons are places where people get good meals, free medical care, and spend their time playing games and watching television is an erroneous stereotype (See "A Closer Look," below.)

Costly reliance on tougher laws and more prisons must hasten an informed debate over such policies. Many experts believe that the certainty of apprehension and conviction influence deterrence far more than severity of punishment (Bibas 2005). Greater knowledge of the social origins of public problems is surely needed.

We need more criminologists able and willing to say why so many families require 'intervention,' why so many students are alienated from their schools, why so few jobs are available to inner-city residents, why so many young adults are unfit for the available jobs, why Americans are so likely to sue guns to settle disputes, and why we incarcerate such a large fraction of our population, even controlling for our high rate of gun violence (Rosenfeld 2002).

A Closer Look: Life Inside Prisons

Prisons erect physical and social barriers to the outside world. The tendency is to disrupt the personalities of inmates and make their adjustment on the outside next to impossible. The process strips inmates of the supports of home and life on the outside, cutting them off from families, friends, jobs, and communities. All other social roles are subordinated to that of convict.

Inmate subculture maintains a subterranean, social order inside prison. Habits, customs, codes, opinions are all monitored. The inmate subculture has its own way of securing justice, revenge, discipline, the collection of debts, and the enforcement of contracts. What results is a distinctive social order that is often at odds with the outside world. This order rests primarily upon collective opposition to prison officials. "Never rat on a con," "be tough," and "have a connection" are powerful norms. Inmates display a predatory attitude towards money and property (Stanko et al. 2004: 66).

Thinly staffed and overcrowded prisons produce tension and violence. Many experts have observed that imprisonment actually increases criminality among inmates. They learn new or sophisticated methods of breaking the law. Some 90 percent of the men will eventually return to society, and they take with them the attitudes and actions they learned in prison. The concept of continual punishment as a means to deter crime is antiquated.

Prisons are reservoirs of drug abusers. A substantial portion of the inmate population continues to use drugs inside prison. Both visitors and correctional officers supply inmates with drugs, most often concealing them on their person. Marijuana, LSD, and ecstasy are among the most widespread drugs. Prison becomes simply another context in which the user must manage his or her habit (Stanko et al. 2004: 79-80).

Many prisoners are socialized into gangs. Some gangs dominate the prison social world. The gangs often differentiate themselves on the basis of race. They become involved in drug trafficking, strong-arming and extortion, often applied by violence.

In the 1990s, incarcerated individuals in the U. S. grew by 74 percent, while the number of beds in state and federal prisons grew only 41 percent. The more the overcrowding, the less the effectiveness of the incarceration. It is a source of strain that produces feelings of deprivation that can induce violence. Research indicates that prison crowding is associated with several pathologies: deaths, suicides, disciplinary infractions, and psychiatric commitments. Double cells result in negative housing ratings, poorer discipline, and complaints of illness. Crowding will likely intensify these problems if correctional trends continue (Stanko et al. 2004: 81-82).

Stephen Stanko provides a vivid account of several years in prison for a non-violent offense. He was stripped, shaved, showered, and deloused in less than one-half hour in full view of any passerby. He was stripped of all personal possessions, including clothes and jewelry. Pride was the first thing lost in the prison system, and the man who seeks privacy or any semblance of peace will never make it out.

Stanko believes that the majority of the public has no idea what goes on inside the typical prison. Freedom and privacy are quickly lost. Orders must be followed without hesitation. Any disobedience to officers is met with swift and immediate discipline. Force by officers is often excessive. Stanko claimed there are correctional workers who believe it is their purpose to create heavy and continual hardship on inmates. When an inmate's word conflicts with that of the correctional officer, the prisoner invariably loses. (For a more favorable view of prison guards, see Williams 2007.)

By consistently obeying the rules, guidelines, and procedures, inmates can move towards less restrictive custodies and receive added liberties. Most inmates are given a position of employment, assigned not on qualifications but on institutional need such as cafeteria work and yard detail. If an inmate is fired from his prison job, or violates any policy or procedure, he must earn anew his lost privileges. No matter how far an inmate advances, it sometimes takes only one disciplinary to send him all the way back to the most restrictive security.

Every inmate is assigned a new identity—a number. Names become secondary to the number. It is the only thing that signifies one's existence. Each is issued an ID card to be used like a credit card (most inmates are forbidden to have money in their possession at any time). The number, the ID card, and the rules eroded Stanko's individuality. He was ordered around by people in blue uniforms, many of whom had a third of his education and even less experience in life. This is a life where no emotions, save anger and control, can be shown unless you wish to become a target of predators.

At most institutions, cells are approximately six and one-half feet wide and eleven feet long. A set of steel bunk beds and an additional mattress are on the floor. Beds take up some 21 square feet of available space. There is a stainless steel toilet and sink, but no hot water. Most cells house three people, and all are present when business is done. Inmates are strictly forbidden to affix any items on cell walls. A lockdown prevails 23 hours a day Monday through Friday. The remaining hour men may walk in the open air if weather permits. On Saturday and Sunday the lockdown is 24 hours a day.

It is no surprise that anger and aggression can spark volatile confrontations in such tight and confined conditions. The small cells always gave Stanko a constant sense of confinement. Cell mates, already mentally stressed, begin to hate each other over an extended period of time. The only release from stress and punishment is communication with one's fellow inmates. The days became routine and mundane, making boredom a dominant factor of existence.

Showers are taken in community showers that have six to eight showerheads. Not only is this area usually unclean, but it often becomes a place where homosexual or violent activity occurs. In the case of violence, inmates usually do not identify the assailants for fear of being labeled a snitch; this is the code they must live by.

Eventually Stanko advanced to a medium and then a minimum-security prison. The experience was over 2,600 days of being told when to get up, when to eat, when to go to work, when to quit, when to shower, how to walk, where to go, what to do, and how to live. Surveillance included being told how fast to eat, what to watch on TV, and when to relax. He had to avoid contact with almost everyone around him.

Schedules in prison do not change from day to day. Each dorm is assigned one day per week for access to the mailroom, commissary, barbershop, library, canteen, and multipurpose building. These areas are only open at set times. The wrongful acts of a few inmates can cause the staff to deny an entire dorm its privileges for the day.

On each tier of a wing, there are recreation rooms where inmates can play cards and board games. When not in lockdown or at assigned jobs, they are free to play cards and other games. There are no computers or video games, but poker and other gambling games are plentiful. There is an upstairs dayroom for quiet study and reading, where no conversation or games are allowed. Most living areas have four TVs mounted in steel cages. There is no exterior volume on any TV; electronic transmitters are available to a limited number of inmates. The channel is determined by the warden. Comfort is not an option in prison.

Rehabilitation processes are few. Limited vocational courses are offered in such areas as plumbing, carpentry, brick masonry, and electrical work, but usually less than ten percent of the inmates are eligible for enrollment. Those who complete the course get only a certificate of completion, not a degree. In most states, college courses are not available.

It is common for 200 inmates to be guarded by only one or two officers. Thus opportunities abound for drug transactions, deal making, and sexual escapades.

Medical units are small. They are not equipped with frills and utilize equal if not more security supervision. A life-threatening problem or flowing blood are the only immediate opportunities to see a doctor in prison. All other requests must be submitted in written form. Little time is given to routine procedures and minor problems. Dental treatment is prioritized by pain and disease, and no cosmetic work is done. Teeth are routinely pulled, to hold down expense.

Food in the cafeteria barely meets the basic minimums for daily nutrition. Extreme security is kept in the cafeteria. Inmates are given no choice of selection or amount. The meals are neither varied nor select: taste is of little or no concern. Leftover food is often re-used. A dorm of 136 inmates per wing has 20 minutes to move single-file to the cafeteria, get trays, eat, and return to their wing. There is no opportunity for calm, quiet consumption, or neighborly chitchat.

Communication with the outside world requires proper paperwork and approval. Red tape surrounds a simple phone call. Officials automatically open mail as it arrives. Officials disallow envelopes, blank paper, or stamps in cells. Yet telephone and mail communications are the main links for many inmates in serving sentences. Contact with family and friends keep memories, hopes, and dreams intact. To withhold communication can cause stress and anger to skyrocket.

Life in prison rarely changes. Saturdays and Sundays are generally no different from weekdays. So many mundane routines have to be repeated every 24 hours in an inmate's life, it is not surprising that violent outbreaks and suicides are common. Fights occur on a daily basis for any and every reason. There is always the possibility of a riot. Over the years, Stanko saw men beaten, almost to death, over a piece of chicken or a pack of cigarettes. "I have seen what many would not see in a lifetime."

Isolation and confinement breed fear and uncertainty. A pad of over 200 men is an incubator growing fear and intimidation among men. Family and friends are seemingly out of reach. It became an absolute struggle to survive each day. For many convicts, anger, frustration, and rebellion grow stronger, leading to hatred and disrespect for any and all officials.

Emotionally, every day in prison is a series of challenges with great mental strains. Stanko spent each day wondering what he had lost on the outside while his life dragged along inside. Friends and family slowly became distant. "I fought insanity almost every breath."

(Most prisons have no VCRs, microwaves, movies, or weights, and few have recreational facilities. The cells contain no rugs, no comforters, or any such luxury. The floors are concrete; there are no pictures on the walls or lockers, no decoration. There are no choices of meals. Prison is no palace, no hotel, no vacation, and no life. Laughter is not a joy, but a mask over pain and depression (adapted from Stanco et al. 2004: 131-186).

(Stanko was released from prison in 2004, but unfortunately was arrested again and convicted on a murder charge. He is currently on death row.)

Summary

Deviance is behavior that does not conform to social expectations. Sociologists stress the reactions to the act rather than the act itself in explaining deviance. It varies greatly from place to place and from time to time.

Crime, a form of deviance, is a violation of rules that have been written into laws. Types of crime are: common crime, both violent and nonviolent; white-collar crime, those committed by middle- and upper-class people in the course of their business and social life; corporate crime, those done on behalf of a corporation; organized crime, activity that profits from illegal and goods and services; crimes without victims, a willing exchange of illegal goods and services; and professional crime, committed by those who make their living from the activity.

Several typical patterns of violent assault and murder have been identified. Males and young people are disproportionately involved. Minorities are disproportionately involved, but this fact should be assessed with care. Most assaults are spontaneous (emerging from an argument) and made by people known to the victim. A handgun is the most common weapon used in an assault, and alcohol is typically involved. Most assaults tend to occur on weekends and in the evenings.

White-collar crime costs more money than all other types of crimes combined. Corporate crime has been in the news in recent years, including the Savings and Loan scandal, costing the public upwards of a trillion dollars, and the Enron matter.

Several generalizations can be made about crime in this country. Two, that it tends to be committed by males and young people, have been mentioned. Crime increased dramatically from the 1950s through the 1980s, but has leveled off and declined somewhat in recent years. Crime is underreported, meaning there is much more actual crime than we have figures for. It is repetitive, meaning the same people tend to commit crime, and the rate is higher in urban areas.

Functionalists believe crime is inevitable and unavoidable. One functionalist theory, structural strain, holds that there is a tension between desired goals and the means available to achieve them. Three of the deviant styles according to this theory are the innovator, who accepts the goals but uses deviant means to achieve them; the retreatist, who rejects both the goals and the means; and the ritualist, who rejects any long-term goals but continues with the means.

Two theories based on symbolic interaction are differential association and labeling theory. Differential association maintains that crime is learned by association with peers who favor criminal behavior. Labeling theory holds that the important fact about deviance is the way other people attach labels to the behavior, which affects people's self-concept so that they tend to live up to the expectation.

Control theory believes that deviants lack strong attachments to groups and others who disapprove of deviance. Some people with strong control mechanisms find deviance too costly, but these attachments are weak for others. Conflict theory concentrates on the failures of society to meet the needs of individuals, and notes how the justice system is lenient on upper-class and white-collar criminals.

Social control refers to mechanisms to reward conformity and punish deviance. These range from informal controls like ridicule to formal systems such as police, courts, and prisons. America currently has about two million people in prisons, but the idea that this will reduce crime is doubtful. A first-hand account of life in prisons reveals the overcrowding, violence, and little rehabilitation found in these institutions.

References

Bibas, Stephanos. 2005. "White-Collar Plea Bargaining and Sentencing After Booker" (**William and Mary Law Review,** Vol. 47).

Eitzen, D. Stanley, and Maxine Baca Zinn. 2007. **In Conflict and Order: Understanding Society,** eleventh edition (Boston: Allyn and Bacon).

Ferrall, Bard R. 2004. "Criminal Law and Criminology: A Survey of Recent Books" (**Journal of Criminal Law and Criminology,** Vol. 94).

Ferrante, Joan. 2006. **Sociology: A Global Perspective,** sixth edition (Belmont, California: Thomson/Wadsworth).

Henslin, James M. 2007. **Sociology, A Down-to-Earth Approach: Core Concepts**, second edition (Boston: Allyn and Bacon).

Jacobs, Michelle. 2006. "Loyalty's Reward—a Felony Conviction: Recent Prosecutions of High-Status Female Offenders" (**Fordham University Law Journal**, Vol. 33).

Lauritsen, Janet L. 2004. "Searching for a Better Understanding of Race and Ethnic Differences in Violent Crime" (**Criminal Justice Ethics,** Vol. 23).

Macionis, John J. 2004. **Society: The Basics**, seventh edition (Upper Saddle River, New Jersey: Prentice-Hall).

Podgor, Ellen S. 2007. "The Challenge of White Collar Sentencing," **Journal of Criminal Law and Criminology**, Vol. 97.

Sanders, Bill. 2005. **Youth Crime and Youth Culture in the Inner City** (London: Routledge).

Stanko, Stephen, Wayne Gillespie, and Gordon A. Crews. 2004. **Living in Prison: A History of the Correctional System with an Insider's View** (Westport, Connecticut: Greenwood Press).

Theriot, Matthew T. 2007. "Peter W. Greenwood, Changing Lives: Delinquency Prevention as Crime Control Policy" (**Journal of Social Policy and Social Welfare,** Vol. 34).

Turner, Jonathan H. 2006. **Sociology** (Upper Saddle River, New Jersey: Prentice-Hall).

Williams, Jeffrey J. 2007. "The Professor Was a Prison Guard," **The Chronicle of Higher Education** (April 6).

Skyline of Dallas, Texas

Chapter 7: COMMUNITIES

Anyone who has lived in both a small town and a large city knows that the locale where one lives influences the lifestyle of the residents. There is something fundamentally different between living in a rural area and in a large city. It is not that one is good and the other bad; each area has its own features that may attract or repel. So the differences between communities are real indeed. It is not surprising that sociologists have made community, whether that be rural or urban, a subject of special study.

Let's visualize Main Street in the county village, several stores and a post office, streets, houses, and lawns that surround it in the setting of a prairie, dairy-farm country, or forest. Or think of a small city with a larger population, greater variety of shops and services, a daily newspaper, wholesale establishments, perhaps a college or university, a hospital, and a number of industries (Warren 1978: 1).

A *community* is a physical place where people settle and where basic institutional activities are conducted (Turner 2006: 194). A community describes something both psychological and geographical. Psychologically, it implies shared interests, characteristics, or association. Geographically, it denotes a specific area where people are clustered. Sociologically, the term combines these two things. It suggests the shared interests and behavior patterns people share by virtue of their common locality (Warren 1978: 5-6).

At one time in the past, observers thought of communities as relatively autonomous places where people carried on their activities. The community was viewed as a limited geographic area with definite boundaries. This way of thinking of communities has become problematic for several reasons. For example, many people live in one locality but earn their living in another. Another is that large metropolitan areas make a clear division of communities difficult. A metropolitan area consists of one or more cities and the relatively densely populated territory surrounding it. A Standard Metropolitan Statistical Area (SMSA) contains at least one city or twin cities of 50,000 or more inhabitants. Generally they include the city's surrounding county and adjacent counties that have a metropolitan character (Warren 1978: 3). It is estimated that approximately every second human being lives in urban settlements today, and by the year 2030 over 60 percent of the world's population will be urbanized (Parker 2004).

Another reason the concept of autonomous communities is problematic is that local community units have become more closely tied with state and national systems, leaving a narrower scope of functions for local units. A small town may have a post office, local bank, welfare department, national manufacturing company, and a branch of a supermarket chain, but the formulation of the policies of these agencies is less subject to local control than it was in an earlier period (Warren 1978: 5).

Because a community is considered a social unity, that is, its members share certain behaviors and attitudes, there is disagreement as to what constitutes a true community. A city the size of New York or Los Angeles could hardly be considered a community because of its size and diversity. There are communities within communities. Some studies have been made of a whole city as a community while others have taken only one small part of the city for the basis of a study.

Historically, people existed for thousands of years without developing communities of any real size. Cities could only develop with the capacity to produce enough food to feed all those who do not harvest the land. This required using nonhuman sources of energy from animals, wind, and water. Settling in communities led to a dramatic increase in the amount of work that people had to perform to sustain themselves. The larger communities became, the more specialized were the activities of individuals, not only in food production but trades, services, and crafts (Turner 2006: 194).

Even as the workforce needed to produce an adequate food supply has declined, a rural way of life is still important in the United States and in other countries. When the economy required most of the people to be farmers or to work in agricultural related fields, few large cities could develop. When it became possible for a relatively few people to farm, towns and cities could grow, aided by rails and roads. The rural population, consisting of those who live on farms or in towns of fewer than 5,000 people, declined throughout most of the twentieth century, but experienced a modest gain late in the century, partly because some people wished to escape some of the highly-publicized urban problems.

The significant growth in recent decades has been *urbanization,* the process whereby an increasing proportion of the population lives in cities. Today, a majority of the population in the developed world resides in urban areas, composed of a core city and its surrounding suburbs (Spates and Macionis 1987: 18). For the first time in history, half the world's population is now classified as living in urban areas (Simon 2007).

Despite occupying just 12 percent of United States land mass, the nation's 100 largest metropolitan areas account for 65 percent of its people and 75 percent of its economic output. They hold the keys to America's prosperity, generating 78 percent of the nation's new patents, 81 percent of jobs devoted to research and development, and 94 percent of venture capital funding (Katz and Williams 2008).

The Folk-Urban Distinction

A number of theorists have distinguished between certain attributes of social life that find a fundamental distinction between urban and the rural. While legitimate criticisms have been made of these distinctions, it is worth considering the most important of these to understand how social scientists have compared a rural way of life with an urban one.

The German sociologist Ferdinand Tonnies conceived of a type of social structure he termed *Gemeinschaft,* which roughly corresponds to a "folk" society, or one of an earlier era characterized by a social order handed down from the past. The more modern or urban society Tonnies called *Gesellschaft,* a deliberately instituted social order (Spates and Macionis 1987: 102-104).

Emile Durkheim, discussed in Chapter 1, compared actions that conform to a homogeneous, coercive value system (cf. a "folk" society) to behavior that reflects the individualized interests of persons related to each other as rational and functionally interdependent specialists (the urban society). The older society was held together by its sameness; the modern society by its specialization and interdependence (Spates and Macionis 1987: 104-105; Cousins and Nagpaul 1979: 94)

Georg Simmel, the German philosopher and sociologist, wrote a famous article, "The Metropolis and Mental Life," in which he spoke of a great historical transformation from the rural society to an urban one. Urban life, he said, is stimulating and sophisticated. People tend to be more anonymous and regarded with impersonal objectivity. "Occupational specialization, style-of-life preference, and mobility all contribute to greater subjective and behavioral liberty in the city than in the country" (cited in Cousins and Nagpaul 1979: 96; Spates and Macionis 1987: 106-107).

The typology emphasized here is that made by Robert Redfield, a University of Chicago anthropologist, who devised the idea of the folk society as the direct opposite of urban society. In doing so, he used many of the constructs made by several other scholars. The "folk" society may be thought of as a set of attitudes typical of small rural communities in the past, while the "urban" is the more complex, modern way of life that has come about in almost every country in the world. This does not mean that all these traits are always found in any large city; some "folk" characteristics persist in many urban locales.

A folk society, for Redfield, is small, isolated, and its members not highly educated. Its members exhibit the homogeneity of a local, inbred population. Very intimate with one another, they possess a sense of belonging together. Their technology is relatively simple, and the division of labor is rudimentary. By inference, an urban society is large, with a high degree of specialization, and less sense of community.

The major distinctions are listed below. (The "folk" characteristics roughly correspond to Tonnies' *Gemeinschaft;* the "urban" characteristics to *Gesellschaft.)* We also add some insights from other thinkers who have contributed to this subject. (Movement from traits on the left to those on the right helps us understand social change, discussed in chapter 13.)

FOLK	URBAN
sparsely settled	densely settled
homogeneous	heterogeneous
generalized labor	specialized labor
traditional	rational, progressive
oriented to the past	present and future-oriented

fatalistic	self-guided
communal	associational
primary relations	secondary relations
informal	formal, bureaucratic
religion dominant	secular
absolute ethics	situational ethics
extended family	nuclear family
patriarchal	egalitarian (or matriarchal)
restricted roles for women	opportunities for women
sex segregation	shared activities
ascribed status	achieved status
little mobility	high potential mobility
education for the few	mass education
parochial	cosmopolitan
simple entertainment	sophisticated entertainment

Dense settlements, along with size, are an obvious trait of urban areas. There are areas of Montana and Idaho where one cannot see a human being, or even a house, for many miles, whereas almost all urban areas are characterized by high density.

A *homogeneous* society is one marked by the overall similarity of the population. There have been agrarian societies where everyone was a farmer or a member of a farm family. Everyone might be of the same ethnic group, the same religion, and of the same social class.

By contrast, h*eterogeneity,* indicating a mixture of many different types of people, typifies urban areas. Specialization (see the next trait) creates a wide variety of occupations in the city. Migration brings people of various nationalities, racial and ethnic composition together. A number of different religions will be represented, as well as a sizeable number with no religion at all. And social classes will be found all the way from the upper class to the lower class.

It is worthy of note that the Chicago sociologist Louis Wirth defined a city in terms of size, density, and heterogeneity (Spates and Macionis 1987: 114).

A subsistence economy marked the folk society and farming or fishing likely the dominant occupation. Durkheim called the solidarity (unity) in this type of community *mechanical.* In contrast, the growth of cities encourages new kinds of economic activity not directly related to food production. "Someone has to construct boats, houses, streets, ports, canals, and buildings; trade creates new kinds of economic positions, from merchants to bankers and accountants and insurers" (Turner 2006: 196). Crafts trades come into existence to produce many different kinds of goods that meet the needs of the urban population. Durkheim referred to the modern society with high specialization as *organic* solidarity.

The folk society is based on tradition, an orientation towards the past. In this mindset, an adequate reason for doing something is "that's the way we've always done it." In an urban society, the emphasis is on rational analysis, which often results in a progressive attitude oriented towards the present and the future. The sociologist Max Weber has a lengthy discussion of this shift from a tradition-based society to one based on rationalization.

A "communal" mentality marked the folk society: everyone was considered to be a member of the community and associations were based largely on proximity. (Your neighbor was almost unavoidably your friend.) In an urban society, one may well know one's neighbor, but contacts tend to be *associational,* meaning that people who may not live near each other come together on the basis of common interests.

Primary groups and *primary relations* characterize the folk society. A "primary" group is one in which personal, face-to-face interactions dominate. One tends to know the people with whom he or she interacts personally. While primary relations are by no means absent in the urban society, a higher percentage of people's relationships are *secondary,* meaning they relate to many people on a regular basis whom they may not know personally. The interaction tends to be *instrumental,* designed to accomplish a particular goal.

Religion tends to be dominant in the folk society. This means that religion is woven into practically all relationships and activities. More modern societies tend to be secular, meaning that tangible and practical realities are perceived as more important than religion in day-to-day activities. Religion is still important for many in urban areas, but it tends to be perceived in a more optional framework (see chapter 12).

Ethical behavior, usually rooted in religious beliefs, was a major aspect of the folk society. The rules governing ethical behavior tended to be *absolute,* meaning there were rarely if ever exceptions to the rule. Ethical rules are still found in the urban society, but they are more likely to be *situational,* meaning the rules are applied more flexibly to specific circumstances. An example could be divorce: a folk society might consider divorce to be unquestionably wrong, while the modern society, though discouraging divorce, would deem it justified in certain circumstances.

The family, particularly the *extended* family, was the dominant institution in the folk society. One might even say that the folk society consisted of families rather than individuals. An "extended" family is one that includes grandparents, aunts, uncles, cousins, and others who may be related by marriage. The extended family often lived under the same roof or at least fairly close to each other. In the urban society, the *nuclear* family, consisting of husband, wife, and their immediate children, has been the norm. (See chapter 11.)

Most folk societies were *patriarchal* or male-dominated. The father was considered the head of the household; the village elder was almost always male. In the modern society, this tends toward an *egalitarian* system in which the husband and wife are on equal footing, or in many cases into a *matriarchal* society, especially in cases in which the mother is the only parent in the home. However, patriarchal attitudes may still be found in many urban locations.

Women held highly restricted roles in the folk society. In most cases, their roles were limited to mother, parent, cook, and housekeeper (although in some rural areas, women did considerable work in the fields). In the urban society, at least in the Western world, a much larger array of opportunities have been open to women.

Sex segregation marked many folk societies, in which the men of the community would gather for various activities and the women would gather for theirs. The men might hunt together while the women came together to knit and sew. In an urban society, shared activities by couples are more common, although some sex segregation is not unknown.

Social status tended to be *ascribed* in the folk society; one's station in life was largely determined by conditions over which one had no control, such as who one's parents were. While ascribed status is still a factor in the urban society, social status is much more likely to be *achieved,* that is, determined by one's particular accomplishments. Further, *mobility,* the ability to move to a higher social class, was extremely limited in the folk society but more common in an urban area (see chapter 8).

Education was much less important in the folk society. In the past in many rural communities, it was not unusual for only a handful of the population to be literate. Even as education became more widespread, it tended to be limited to a relative few who saw the need for it. But in the urban society, education came to be seen as essential in life and the philosophy of mass education developed.

Entertainment in the folk society was likely to be rather simple, such as some simple games and what is now known as bluegrass music. In an urban society, a wide array of sports, both for participants and spectators, as well as more sophisticated arts such as the symphony, opera, and ballet, are available.

The folk society tended to take a *parochial* attitude toward the world, confining their interests to the local scene. The larger world tended not to affect them that much and went largely ignored (except for trade and essential transactions). But in the urban society, a more *cosmopolitan* approach was more common. Largely through the mass media, people became aware of the larger world and often took an active interest. Many would travel to different countries and subscribe to national and even international periodicals. Cosmopolitans are more rootless and think in terms of wider possibilities (Merton 1968).

It is important to realize that these traits are descriptive terms that show general tendencies as communities move from a more simple society to a more complex one. They do not necessarily apply to all rural or urban areas. Research has discovered rural villages that were not stagnant or uninterested in going into modern commercial farming. Some small towns have highly specialized occupations and possibly a cosmopolitan attitude. Some communities which are part of large cities have developed close primary relations, and the extended family is important to many urban dwellers.

The Study of Cities

Studies of cities have become complex and interdisciplinary. A student of urban areas would need to examine not only sociology but history, government, education, architecture, geography, urban economics, urban planning, urban ecology, urban housing, and comparative studies.

An important locale for study on the American city developed at the University of Chicago, in what came to be called "The Chicago School." Robert Park, Ernest Burgess, Louis Wirth, and others made extensive empirical studies of Chicago and other cities. These early studies were extremely important in stressing the need to study the city first-hand, and producing some early ecological models of a typical city. Some of their accounts of aspects of city living makes fascinating reading to this day.

Many of the observations of this school supported a view of the city as encouraging impersonal relations; the residents tended to be isolated, alone, and alienated (powerless). Louis Wirth, after describing urban life, wrote that "personal disorganization, mental breakdown, suicide, delinquency, crime, corruption, and disorder might be expected under these circumstances" (quoted in Cousins and Nagpaul 1979: 99; Spates and Macionis 1987: 118-119).

More careful and recent research, however, has revealed that city dwellers show strong family and friendship ties, have a sense of neighborhood and community, and have strong ties to fellow ethnics and to religious organizations. Other observers found a proliferation of voluntary associations in cities, such as physical fitness groups, meditation and yoga, singles bars, and the like. People seem to find a way to form strong social ties and a sense of community (Spates and Macionis 1987: 119; Turner 2006: 200).

Herbert Gans (1968) felt that the Chicago School stressed poverty and the seamy side of city life, where actually, it is a kaleidoscope of *many* lifestyles, which are the result of more general social characteristics, such as age, sex, income, and educational level. Among the city dwellers noted by Gans were the ethnic villagers, who showed almost *none* of the alleged urban characteristics identified by Wirth. He does grant that there is an element of the deprived and trapped in the city.

The Suburb

Suburbanization refers to a large city surrounded by smaller cities composed of extensive housing tracts, small central business and retail districts, and regional malls. People have moved to suburbs to escape high taxes, high crime rates, decaying neighborhoods, a declining business district, noise and crowding, declining city services, and environmental pollution (Turner 2006: 200).

People also move, of course, for the attraction of the suburb itself: larger houses with yards, the ability to commute to work, the movement of jobs to the suburbs, lower crime rates, lower taxes (at least initially), better recreational facilities, less crowding and pollution (Turner 2006: 201). Some corporate headquarters or regional centers have moved to suburban areas, creating white-collar jobs outside of the city.

The suburb can be viewed as an attempt to recapture the characteristics of small-town community living, but it is different from the traditional small-town community in several ways. It is dominated to a much greater degree by the neighboring large city than is the small town. Another important characteristic of the suburb is the transience of its population, which militates against the development of strong community ties among its residents (Warren 1978: 4). (That there are weak community ties in suburbs has been disputed.)

Some of the early sociological studies examined life in these new (at that time) suburbs and were decidedly critical. They reported superficial conformity, an emphasis on personal appearance, gossip, and life centered around maintaining status. Family life was disjointed and extramarital affairs a preoccupation. (This shallow lifestyle is depicted in the television show, "Desperate Housewives.")

Later studies, however, found that these studies were biased. Several careful investigations showed little difference in behavior of city and suburban dwellers. In the suburbs they studied, commitment to community was strong, there was involvement in civic and school life, and most people seemed to live pleasant and happy lives in the suburbs (Spates and Macionis 1987: 312). It is true, however, that many of the urban problems they sought to escape have been recreated.

That poor people live in cities and the wealthy in suburbs is a stereotype. For the first time in history, more of America's poor are living in the suburbs than the cities, according to a 2005 survey. "The suburbs have reached a tipping point," says Brookings Institution analyst Alan Berube, who compiled the data. "For example, five years ago, a Hunger Network food pantry in Bedford Heights, a struggling suburb of Cleveland, served 50 families a month. Now more than 700 families depend on it for food" (Tyre and Philips 2007).

Exurbia

Exurbia refers to communities located some distance from suburbs. The area is tied together by freeways, jetways, and jogging paths. They contain corporate headquarters, fitness centers, and shopping plazas. Many jobs have moved out here from the city, and most residents do not make a daily commute to a core city. "We (Americans) created vast new urban job centers in places that only 30 years before had been residential suburbs or even corn stubble" (Garreau 1991: 4).

Fairfax County, Virginia, is more populous than Washington, D. C. or San Francisco. The Edge City called the Galleria area west of downtown Houston—crowned by the sixty-four story Transco Tower—is bigger than downtown Minneapolis (Garreau 1991: 6). It is possible, however, such places could grow and become more like larger cities. These developments are changing our lives in countless ways.

The Megalopolis

The megalopolis or conurban region refers to metropolitan areas now blending into each other. A whole countryside from Portland, Maine, to Virginia constitutes one solid metropolitan complex of overlapping and intermingling metropolitan areas. Similar complexes are developing in the Middle and Far West. At the start of the 21st century there were 22 megalopolis with eight-figure populations (Parker 2004: 1).

The five largest megalopolis areas in the United States are:

The New York area, with Long Island, northern New Jersey and Connecticut—about 21.2 million;

The Los Angeles area, with Riverside, Long Beach, and Orange County—16.1 million;

Chicago, with parts of northern Indiana and southern Wisconsin—9.1 million;

Washington-Baltimore, with parts of Maryland, Virginia, and West Virginia—7.6 million;

The San Francisco Bay areas, with Oakland, San Jose, and other cities extending from the bay—7.1 million (Turner 2006: 203).

Clearly, government regulation becomes very difficult across the entire region, funding for necessary infrastructures is difficult; police, fire, education, and other public service issues become difficult to manage. Residential segregation among ethnic groups means that the poorest people are trapped in the neighborhoods of core cities (Turner 2006: 203).

World Cities

To discuss world cities in any depth lies beyond the scope of this chapter. In general, cities in Latin America, Africa, the Middle East, and Asia "vary enormously from the Western cities with which we are most familiar. The diversity of history, cultural traditions, religion, and politics accounts for these differences" (Spates and Macionis 1987: 275). Cities of the non-industrial world vary tremendously among themselves.

Such world cities as New York, London, Mexico City, and Rio De Janeiro, are oriented toward the global economy, and the production of wealth depends heavily on international banking and trade (Harper and Leicht 2007: 30; see chapter 13).

The number of "megacities," with populations of over 10 million, has increased to 19, while another 22 cities worldwide are home to between 5 and 10 million people each. Another 370 cities house between one and five million people. The most rapid growth within cities is occurring in poor and middle-income countries (Simon 2007). In 1978, there were only 172 million urban residents of China; now there are 577 million, over 40 percent of the population. Each year roughly 10 million rural Chinese move to the cities (Hessler 2008: 176).

Any city "is linked intricately to the broader society of which it is a part. Any city's physical and social forms are shaped by the cultural values of that society and its historical epoch" (Spates and Macionis 1987: 210). Recent research has shown that cities and their hinterlands are bound together in a complex interdependence that allows each significant influence over the other.

Many of these cities were colonized, which has left an underdeveloped economy. Their difficulties are well summarized by Spates and Macionis (1987: 277): "Most cities in the non-industrial world are being inundated with so many people that they cannot hope to provide adequately for their populations without major advances in economic vitality and technical efficiency." Exceptions include Singapore, Hong Kong, and Japan.

Urban growth in the developing world is increasingly associated with the growth in slums around the fringes of established cities. In America, usually the slums are in the inner city. The United Nations estimates that 837 million people lived in urban slums in 2001 (Parker 2004: 168).

Urban Problems

Social problems in the United States are more visible in urban areas. Small towns certainly experience crime, poverty, and other problems, but they tend not to get the national attention the same problems do in large cities. The problems that seem particularly acute in urban areas are crime and delinquency, including gang activities and illegal drugs, poverty, especially slums and inadequate housing, inadequate schools, racial conflict, family problems such as abuse, and pollution. We lack space to examine these in any detail, but will touch on a few and refer the reader to related chapters.

Higher Crime Rates

Most forms of crime and delinquency occur more frequently in urban areas. Researchers have found a positive correlation between unlawful behavior and city size; that is, not only is there more crime in a large city but the *rate* will be higher than in a rural area or small city (Spates and Macionis 1987: 384) The difference is especially marked when we consider crimes against property. However, there has been a slight decrease in crime rates since 1995.

Sociologists have given a number of reasons why crime is more common in large urban areas. Individualism is more intense in the city, and wider latitude is allowed for personal choice, which sets up a tendency towards violations of the law. With more heterogeneity and conflict in the city, there is more need and opportunity for deviance. More mobility and social change in urban areas may lead to moral ambiguity. The greater wealth in the city also furnishes added opportunity for illicit behavior. The availability of property motivates criminal conduct. Finally, the larger the police force and the more efficiently it is organized, the greater the volume of crime it will be able to detect. (Cousins and Nagpaul 1979: 397-98)

Much of a high crime rate can be explained by high unemployment and the loss of jobs. As many studies have revealed, the decline in legitimate employment opportunities among inner-city residents has increased incentives to sell drugs. The distribution of crack in a neighborhood attracts individuals involved in violence and lawlessness. The high rate of violent crime among younger males has accompanied the widespread outbreak of addiction to crack-cocaine. This is especially common in inner-city ghetto neighborhoods plagued by joblessness and weak social organization (Wilson 1996: 21).

The emphasis on unemployment rates and the social disorganization of the streets suggests that the best way to reduce crime rates would be to promote policies that renew economic opportunities in the inner cities. Several observers see urban crime as an inevitable consequence of a society that produces great disparities in income, which produces great frustration. Reducing these disparities should reduce the violence in American cities (Spates and Macionis 1987: 391). Cooperation between government and the private sector might be the most feasible way to accomplish this end.

For a longer discussion on crime in general, see chapter 6.

Poverty

It comes a surprise to many to learn that the rates of poverty are actually higher in rural areas than in urban ones. Rural areas have been hurt by the farm crisis, especially that of the 1980's, the growth of agribusiness which hurts the small farmer, a tendency for most jobs to pay lower wages, and (in most cases) a more stagnant economic base. "Hidden in the hollows of Appalachia (the area in eastern United States from southern Pennsylvania to eastern Tennessee), in makeshift villages along the Rio Grande, in shriveled industrial towns in Pennsylvania, on the back roads of Maine, and at the edge of cotton fields in Mississippi, the world of rural poverty endures" (Burton, 1992: 14).

In large cities, there are growing numbers of the so-called "underclass," the static poor who are trapped in their situation by restricted opportunities and a variety of other forces. These are people who have been excluded from the regular labor market and who find, at most, sporadic employment. There are many female-headed households, long-term recipients of welfare, and the source of much violent crime and drug addiction.

The major factor creating an underclass in our cities has been economic deprivation, and this has been abundantly documented. According to William Julius Wilson, an underclass has been produced by changes in American economic organization, demographic changes, and changes in the laws and practices of the government as well. Wilson emphasizes the relationship between joblessness and family structure and such things as crime, teenage pregnancy, and welfare dependency (Wilson 1987: 18; Wilson 1996: xiii-xix). Younger men, particularly those of minority status and low education, have seen their economic position worsen since the 1960s.

In the older inner city, the job opportunities that exist are likely to pay minimum wage or only slightly above. Public programs and institutions are weak. Temptations of the street, including deviant gangs and drugs, are highly visible. Dwellers in the inner city will pay higher prices for apartments, food, and other essentials. With the combination of these problems, an underclass-like trap can envelop poor households.

Residents lack many concrete examples of hope that help instill a value system in the young. In today's ghetto, it is rare to find neighbors whose lives demonstrate that education is meaningful, that steady employment and a stable family are aspects of normalcy (Schorr 1988: 20).

There are some who view the behavior of these inner-city poor people a primary source of their problems. Their claim is that they have violated rules most Americans regard as reasonable. In light of the structural arguments, especially the record of massive job losses in these areas, this judgment seems simplistic. Most analysts view the members of the underclass as those victimized by conditions over which they have little or no control. One sociologist thinks we should avoid the term "underclass" altogether, since it has a pejorative meaning (Gans 1995).

(For more on poverty in general, see chapter 8.)

Urban Schools

There is, of course, a wide variety of school systems across the United States. Many public schools, particularly in affluent suburbs, are well-funded and offer a variety of challenging programs for students.

Effective schools may also be found in other urban areas and in many rural areas.

But there are severe problems in many inner-city schools, including inadequate funding to overcrowded classrooms to indifferent teachers. Wilson shows that consignment to inner-city schools helps guarantee the future economic subordinancy of minority students. Inner-city schools train minority youth to feel and appear capable of performing only jobs in the low-wage sector. In many schools the repressive, arbitrary, chaotic, and authoritarian structure mirrors the characteristics of inferior job situations (Wilson 1987: 103)

Even if poor students go to a reasonably good school, they face a number of problems. They may face teasing by middle-class students for their dress or other signs of a lower-class background. An inadequate diet, such as coming to school without breakfast, will be a handicap. Their home life may not encourage academic success; for example, home is less likely to have a computer, books, or even a quiet place to study. Parent-teacher interaction is less common. And many poor students may face pressure to leave school early to help support the family.

Trouble in school virtually guarantees bleak prospects for the future. Many poor students will lack a personal sense of mastery and self-esteem. They are less likely to believe in their own power, command a rich language, and be confidant of success. Higher education and a white-collar job will appear beyond their grasp.

The development of skills necessary for the field of work in the mainstream economy is adversely affected. Teachers become frustrated and do not teach and children do not learn. A vicious cycle is perpetuated through family, community, and schools. (Wilson, 1987: 57; Wilson 1996: 8) The social disorganization of the community inevitably affects the climate of the public schools. (For more on schools, especially colleges, see "Society and Government" at the end of chapter 10.)

Racial Conflict

Blacks and other minorities are heavily concentrated in urban areas in this country. Given the decline of industrial jobs in the inner city, the deterioration of much of the housing, and the problems of the public school, problems for minorities have been exacerbated in these settings. Almost all the growth in entry-level and other low education requisite jobs has occurred in the suburbs and other areas far removed from urban blacks (Wilson 1987: 45).

Wilson stresses the geographic and social isolation of the ghetto underclass. In urban areas, there tends to be a disproportionate concentration of the most disadvantaged segments of the urban black population. Poverty within the inner city is debilitating when it is intensely concentrated (Wilson 1987: 47). A related problem is social isolation, aided by the movement of the middle-class to suburbs.

Both middle-class and working-class blacks—who have historically reinforced the traditional patterns of work, family, and education—have departed many ghetto neighborhoods in significant numbers. Hence there is a paucity of such families not only because the higher-income families leave, but because of declining employment opportunities associated with the economic restructuring that afflict Americans in all racial and ethnic groups (Wilson 1996: xvii). (For more on race, see chapter 9.)

The Challenge of Cities

Despite a myriad of problems, many cities have remained viable in many respects. While cities such as Detroit and Cleveland have severe economic problems, others, such as New York, San Francisco, Boston, Atlanta, San Diego, Houston, and Dallas, have remained strong core cities. The appeal of cultural and recreational facilities, urban renewal of older housing, improvements in infrastructures, and efforts to reduce crime and pollution, have lured a number of people back to the city (Turner 2006: 204).

Spates and Macionis sum up the challenge of cities when they write:

> Cities seem to do better when they have vital economies; responsive governments; nonexploitative relationships with their physical environments; superlative health, transportation, housing, artistic, and educational facilities; open, tolerant, and relatively egalitarian social structures....and relatively small in population (Spates and Macionis (1987: 476).

Some observers have complained about the loss of community in the United States over the last generation or so. Membership in grassroots community organizations has declined. Others, however, have found a growing number of Americans who regularly participate in small groups where they find friends, emotional support, overcome addictions, and grow in spirituality (Harper and Leicht 2007: 78). It is a commonplace in sociology to point out that we find ourselves not independently of other people and institutions but through them. All of our activity goes on in relationships, groups, associations, and communities ordered by institutional structures and interpreted by cultural patterns of meaning. We are part of a larger whole. Our connectedness to others in work, love, and community is essential to happiness, self-esteem, and moral worth (Bellah et al. 1985: 84)

Summary

Most people are conscious of the differences between living in a large city and a small town or rural area. A *community* was defined as a place where people settle and institutional activities conducted. Among several attempts to distinguish between rural and urban, we discussed Redfield's "folk society" in some detail. *Urbanization* is the process where an increasing proportion of the population lives in cities.

The importance of the Chicago School, with its strong empirical research, as discussed earlier, noted that the claim by some that urban life leads to impersonality was challenged. The suburb, smaller urban settlements around large cities, "exurbia" or edge cities away from suburbs, and the megalopolis, metropolitan areas blending into each other, were described.

After a discussion of problems affecting cities, including crime, poverty, schools, and race conflict, it was noted that many cities remain viable. There has been a concern over the loss of community in the United States in the last generation or so. It is a commonplace in sociology that we find ourselves not independently of others but through them.

References

Bellah, Robert N., Richard Madsen, William M. Sullivan, Ann Swidler, Steven M. Tipton. 1983. *Habits of the Heart:* Individualism and Commitment in American Life (New York: Harper and Row).

Burton, C. Emory. 1992. *The Poverty Debate* (Westport, Conn., Greenwood Press).

Cousins, Albert N., and Hans Nagpaul. 1979. *Urban Life* (New York, John Wiley & Sons).

Gans, Herbert J. 1968. "Urbanism: Suburbanism as Ways of Life: A Re-evaluation or Definitions. Pp. 34-52 in *People and Plans* (New York: Basic Books).

Gans, Herbert J. 1995. *The War Against the Poor* (New York: Basic Books).

Garreau, Joel. 1991. *Edge City: Life on the New Frontier* (New York: Doubleday).

Harper, Charles L., and Kevin T. Leicht. 2007. **Exploring Social Change: America and the World**, fifth edition (Upper Saddle River, New Jersey: Pearson Education).

Hessler, Peter. 2008. "The Road Ahead." **National Geographic** (May).

Katz, Bruce, and Don Williams. 2008. "We Need Washington." Dallas Morning News, 5P (February 24).

Merton, Robert. 1968. *Social Theory and Social Structure* (New York: The Free Press.)

Parker, Simon. 2004. *Urban Theory and the Urban Experience: Encountering the City* (Boca Raton: Routledge).

Simon, David. 2007. "Cities and Global Environmental Change: Exploring the Links" (**The Geographical Journal**, Vol. 173).

Spates, James L., and John J. Macionis. 1987. *The Sociology of Cities,* second edition (Belmont, California: Wadsworth).

Turner, Jonathan H. 2006. *Sociology* (Upper Saddle River, New Jersey, Prentice Hall).

Tyre, Peg, and Matthew Philips. 2007. "Poor Among Plenty: For the first time, poverty shifts to the U. S. suburbs." *Newsweek,* CXLIX, No. 7 (February 12).

Warren, Roland L. 1978. *The Community in America*, third edition (Chicago, Rand McNally).

Wilson, William Julius. 1987. *The Truly Disadvantaged: The Inner City, the Underclass, and Public Policy* (Chicago: University of Chicago Press).

Wilson, William Julius. 1996. *When Work Disappears: The World of the New Urban Poor* (New York: Vintage Books).

A Home on Prominence Drive

Chapter 8: SOCIAL STRATIFICATION

Every society distinguishes among clusters of people in its population. Some have more money, schooling, health, and power than others. Social stratification is a system by which a society ranks categories of people in a hierarchy (Macionis 2004: 188). These categories are called *classes*. Few subjects are more important for the individual seeking to better his or her lot in life, or for gaining a better understanding of American society.

One important feature of social stratification is that it is a trait of society, not simply a reflection of individual differences. Of course personal talent and effort are involved, but most people exaggerate the extent to which they control their own destinies. The privileged (or underprivileged) position of people exerts a strong influence on the type of life they will enjoy. Further, social stratification tends to persist over generations.

Sociologists distinguish between closed systems, which allow little change in social positions, and open systems, which permit some social mobility. If a system is completely closed, it is called a *caste* system; if it is relatively open, the term *class* is used.

A caste system bases social stratification on birth or some form of *ascribed* characteristics. Ascribed traits are those the individual has no control over, such as race, parental background, gender, and age. The standard example is traditional India, where, historically, caste position determined the direction of people's lives. A type of caste system existed when slavery was practiced in the United States.

A class system is based on *achieved* status characteristics, those the individual has some control over, such as education and accomplishments of various kinds. While it is not always possible to distinguish between the two (for example, having wealthy parents makes it easier for the offspring to achieve an education), the emphasis on achieved status implies a *class* society.

Karl Marx, introduced in chapter 1, believed that increasing industrialization and capitalism led to increasing inequality; the stratification became more rigid. The people at the top, the owners of property, exploited the larger group of workers below them. Alienation, a sense of powerlessness, was widespread. Classes have different and often opposing interests: a simple example is the working class pressing for higher wages and benefits, often opposed by their middle-class employers. Marx showed how the historical context in which people act affects their behavior (Beeghley 2005: 3-6).

Actually, there has been much more mobility (movement to a higher class) in capitalist societies than Marx anticipated. As applied to an industrialized country like the United States, his theory seems somewhat simplistic, giving little discussion to a relatively affluent middle class. However, Marx's analysis of stratification has been very influential because it points to the importance of privileged position and power.

Some scholars argue that labor market statistics indicate that Marx was at least partly right. Most of the increases in total income in recent years have gone to the owners of capital; very little has found its way into the hands of workers. Wages are once again falling behind the rise in prices. Real wages have declined even when the economy was supposedly heating up. Counting only salary and cash bonuses, CEO pay more than doubled between 1989 and 2004. The share of the pie (total resources) to those at the bottom has shrunk (cited by Yates 2005). Fully 70 percent of the wealth in this country is owned by only 10 percent of the nation's families (Henslin 2007: 204). The top 1 percent of families had 20.3 percent of all income in 2006 (Gudrais 2008).

Max Weber, discussed in chapter 2, claimed that there were three major dimensions of social class: wealth (he used another term), power, and prestige. *Wealth* refers not only to income but to all of one's assets, such as land, stocks, and other holdings. *Power* refers to the ability to achieve one's ends or goals, even against opposition. *Prestige* (Weber would say *status*) refers to social honor or esteem (Spates and Macionis 1989: 314-315).

Weber thought these terms were analytically different. A clergyman might gain high prestige but little wealth or power. A gangster might have wealth and power but little prestige. In practical terms, these measures are considered by looking at such things as family background, income, education, occupation (some think the most important of all), memberships, leisure activities, and influence in the community and nation.

Weber noted that the culture of capitalism became the dominant value orientation in modern societies. Individualism, stressing the need to make it on one's own, came to be a dominant value. Yet ascribed characteristics, such as family background, were still important. Prestige means the evaluations people make of others' lifestyle, their choices and values. Families in the same class share a style of life and tend to associate with those of the same class (Beeghley 2005: 8-10).

By applying the relevant criteria, sociologists have found several rather distinct classes in America, including both ascribed and achieved characteristics. Most would list five or six such classes: a description of each follows.

The Social Classes

The Upper Class consists of people who have top-level positions in big business, industry, entertainment, the government, and the military. Upper-class status suggests more than simply being well-off financially: most of the members have shared this status over a number of generations, and their prestige is well recognized among their peers. Most have a degree from a prestigious college or university, and many have graduate degrees. This is sometimes called the "capitalist class," but most scholars restrict that term to the extremely rich.

Upper-class people seek to maintain an elegant lifestyle, tending to live in large but not necessarily new homes. Many have paid help in the homes such as a maid, butler, cook, and/or gardener. Even the neighborhood may carry a certain prestige, such as Beacon Hill in Boston or the Gold Coast of Chicago. For many in this class category, the extended family is important: for example, a first cousin may be considered almost as important as a brother or sister.

Most in these social strata tend to be exclusive: they belong to prestigious private clubs and encourage their children to associate with those of the same social class. They have influence in what is going on in the community and the nation, but frequently their power works behind the scenes. They are able to use their power to influence decisions that are made in the business and governmental arenas. The upper class has more class consciousness (awareness) than other classes.

There is a difference of opinion on the numbers in the upper class. Some sociologists consider those making more than about $200,000 to be upper class, which would amount to about two or three percent of the population. Others believe a true upper, or capitalist, class would be those making over about $500,000, or about 0.5 percent of the population. Remember, though, income alone is not a complete measure of class position.

The middle class is usually divided into two groups, *upper* middle and *lower* middle, though they share some things in common. With very few exceptions, all middle class people are college graduates, are employed in professions or other white-collar occupations, and are active in their communities. The middle class as a whole is about 35 percent of the population.

The essence of middle-class life is to do nonmanual labor. Persons in white-collar jobs usually sit behind desks, nearly always stay physically clean while they work, often supervise others, sometimes engage in entrepreneurial activity, and frequently have high incomes (Beeghley 2005: 183). These people generally like their jobs and feel superior to the working class.

For just about all of the middle class, *work* is a central interest in life. It tends to be a challenging and fulfilling occupation in which one works without close supervision. The work is likely to be with ideas and with other people, rather than manual labor. The people work for a salary with good benefits such as health care and pensions.

Further, many companies provide higher-level employees with such benefits as expense accounts, use of company-owned cars, membership in private clubs, entertainment, and stock options. Beeghley (2005: 186) considers these benefits fundamental aspects of remuneration and constitute a significant element in the structure of stratification in the United States.

About half of professional and technical workers can stay at home and still get paid if they get the flu. Further, about half of professionals and administrators have long-term disability benefits as part of their employment package, compared to 27 percent of clerical and sales staff and only 14 percent of blue-collar employees (Beeghley 2005: 190). In short, middle-class people have a greater ability to protect their economic situation and lifestyle than do working-class people.

Middle-class people tend to marry later than lower classes, and to have fewer children. The nuclear family (husband, wife, and immediate children) is the norm in these families. Discipline for children is likely to be withdrawal of privileges rather than corporal punishment. There is less sex segregation in the middle class: men may occasionally get together with other men for an activity such as golf, and women could get together too, but couples tend to do most things as couples. A dead giveaway for middle class status would be the assumption that the high school junior or senior in the family is going to college. There's no debate: attending college is simply what successful people do.

The upper middle class—perhaps 10 percent of the population-- may be graduates of colleges somewhat more prestigious than the lower middle class. More importantly, they are employed in recognized professions such as medicine, law (usually a large firm), or as architects, deans and tenured professors in prestigious colleges, officers in the military, or a high position in a corporation. (A CEO in a major corporation, of course, would be upper class.)

The lower middle class, about 25 percent of the population, is composed of professionals at lower pay scales, such as nurses, school teachers, social workers, small business owners, insurance agents, policemen, and successful salespersons. Even at this level, the type of work is of a higher status than what we will find in the working class.

Middle-class people tend to be active in their communities, belonging to a number of organizations such as churches, neighborhood associations, garden clubs, and the like. They read more books and watch less television than the classes below them. Many take interest in hobbies and travel is common, often to distant destinations such as Europe or Asia.

Middle-class people take an active interest in elections and turn out in large numbers. Along with the rich, middle class people dominate the political process. Contrary to widespread belief, the upper and middle classes benefit much more from government transfers than do poor people (Beeghley 2005: 195-207).

While this description of the middle class might make it sound idyllic, a number of writers have expressed concern about problems affecting this group, including dissatisfaction with work and lifestyle, and the possibility of falling into a lower class because of job loss

(Newman 1988; Ehrenreich 2005). Some claim that the middle class is shrinking for these and other reasons.

With the economic downturn of 2001, unemployment was running at about 5.9 percent, but in contrast to earlier economic downturns, a sizable portion—almost 20 percent, or about 1.6 million—of the unemployed were white-collar professionals. In the next few years, stories surfaced of people ejected from their office suites, and later finding work behind the counter at Starbucks (Ehrenreich 2005: 4). The housing crisis of 2007-2008 has also affected many.

A 2004 survey of executives found 95 percent expecting to move on, voluntarily or otherwise, from their current jobs, and 68 percent were concerned about unexpected firings and layoffs. One doesn't have to actually lose a job to feel the anxiety and despair of the unemployed (Ehrenreich 2005: 5).

Wages have been growing slowly of late, and middle-class and even upper-middle class Americans are reminded every day that their families are just a bad break or two away from a financial crisis. In the last several years, real wages have stalled, even though workers' output and corporate profits kept rising (Regnier 2007). Recent statistics reveal that credit card debt is $800 billion, a figure which has almost tripled since 1989, and personal savings are the lowest since the Depression (20/20: 2007).

In 1970 Americans averaged a 7 percent chance of experiencing a 50 percent drop in family income; by 2002 it was a 17 percent chance. Among the causes are offshoring, jobs being supplanted by technology, the rise of two-income families and divorce, and the decline of unions. A study by economist Henry Farber found that the average college-educated person who loses a job earns 14 percent less on the next job (cited by Regnier 2007).

Ehrenreich (2005: 5) cites a business journalist who describes stressed-out white-collar employees who put in ten-to twelve-hour-long days at the office, continue to work on their laptops at home, and remain tethered to the office by cell phones even on vacations and holidays. Ehrenreich probably exaggerates the problem, but she has touched on a legitimate concern that affects many white-collar workers.

The *working class* comprises about 40 percent of the population. Most members of this class have only a high-school education, though some may have some college experience. They tend to work in manual-labor type jobs such as truck drivers, factory workers, firemen, lawmen, mechanics, waitresses, or small farmers. They often work with their hands, get physically dirty while doing their jobs, and obtain wages by the hour rather than by salaries. Further, blue-collar employees are nearly always subordinate to white-collar people.

Working-class people are not poor, that is, almost all of them are above the poverty line, but most struggle. They generally have the basic necessities of life and a few of the comforts, but most have little savings, and a catastrophe such as a layoff, a serious accident or illness might drop them into a lower class. Many, in fact, have little or no health insurance. Working-class people are easily hurt by layoffs, which have increased as U. S. manufacturing has shrunk.

The skilled working class, such as plumbers or electricians, often make more money than neighbors in the lower-middle class, such as school teachers. Nevertheless, school teachers are considered to be in a higher class because of the nature of their work, the flexibility of their schedules (summers off, for example), and their general regard in the community.

In general, working-class people belong to relatively fewer organizations than the middle class. They might belong to a union if their occupation is unionized, and many belong to churches (though they are not as likely to be active), but usually they are not involved in many other groups.

Their outlook is more parochial than the higher classes, as they tend to be oriented towards family (often extended family) and neighborhood. They watch more television and read fewer books and magazines than the middle class, and travel less. When they do travel, it is more likely in the same state or an adjoining one, except for an occasional flight to visit relatives.

Working-class people are often stereotyped with "redneck" stories and jokes, but the truth is that most are hardworking people who pride themselves on their honesty and basic values. While dissatisfaction with the job is common, many at this class level take pride in doing their work well.

A good case can be made that the distinction between middle class and working class is the most important in the stratification system. Some claim that these two classes are merging, so that the characteristics of working-class people now resemble those of the middle class. However, Beeghley (2005: 211-229) convincingly shows that this is basically incorrect, that the working class differs from the middle class in fundamental ways.

First of all, the working class labors in work settings that are ill-suited to the view that the two classes are merging. Blue-collar work is often conducted under conditions that are unpleasant, even dangerous. Those who work inside frequently operate machines that are hazardous if unreliable or handled incorrectly. They often must face high noise levels, toxic dust and dirt, noxious odors, and other conditions that can lead to long-term health problems. Those who work outside often work in the rain and the snow and the heat and the cold.

None of these situations characterizes white-collar jobs. It is common for office workers to have windows and to surround themselves with flowers and pictures. Health hazards and injuries occur far less often among those who think, administer, or process for a living. Beeghley correctly concludes that blue-collar jobs are much more dangerous than white-collar jobs.

Further, many blue-collar work settings are distinguished by close supervision and petty work rules. The pervasive time clock suggests how closely supervised blue-collar workers are. Many blue-collar jobs are characterized by work rules that resemble those in elementary school, so that many workers themselves claim to be treated like a machine instead of a human being. This is fundamentally different from middle-class work, where people deal with ideas, sales, blueprints, computer programs, and other things that cannot be standardized.

Job security, as indicated by the unemployment rate, is far less for those engaged in working-class occupations. Unemployment rates are much higher in all working-class occupations. For example, precision production workers, who have median incomes above that of administrative support workers, have an unemployment rate higher than those in administrative support occupations. Long-term unemployment is devastating to working-class families, not only financially but in terms of personal ills like stress and family disruption.

Labor market statistics bear out these contentions. They point out that workers in America have been taking a beating for the last thirty years (the only exception was in the late 1990s). Gains made by minorities and those at the bottom of the income distribution have eroded. Most of the increases in total income have gone to the owners of capital; very little has found its way into the hands of workers. Wages are once again falling behind the rise in prices. In the 2001-2005 period, manufacturing shed jobs for 41 consecutive months, indicating a loss of 1.1 million jobs (summarized by Yates 2005). Of course, job losses were enormous in 2008-09.

This analysis does not imply that there are no working-class people who lead satisfying and productive lives. It does indicate, however, that working-class people labor in less safe and comfortable occupational settings, which carry with them lower incomes, less job security, and make possible a less affluent and prestigious lifestyle.

While some would consider all below the working class to be simply one lower class, it seems reasonable to divide the remaining population into two groups, the *working poor,* which could be called the *upper lower class,* and the (true) *lower class.*

The working poor are those whose jobs do not pay enough to keep them above the poverty line. (Some who live precarious lives barely above the poverty line could also be considered in this class.) In some cases the work is seasonal, part-time, or temporary. In some cases the pay would normally be adequate but family conditions, such as a handicap or a recurrent illness, keep the family at a near-poverty level. Perhaps ten to fifteen percent of the population would be considered working poor.

This group includes the unskilled laborers, most of these in service jobs, and some of the lower-paid operatives (especially in marginal firms). Many employed single mothers find themselves in this class. Their incomes depend on the number of weeks a year they are employed and on the number of workers in the family. Unable to save money to cover contingencies, insecurity is a normal part of their lives (Gilbert and Kahl 1987: 336).

What keeps this class from being a truly lower class is that at least one family member is tied in to the job market on a more or less consistent basis. These are families who regularly go to work, have a bank account, and in most cases try hard to keep the family going. A very real illustration would be a family of three holding five jobs among them but still living below or barely above the poverty line.

Some people are surprised to learn that hard-working people can be poor. Their plight has been well documented by many observers (Schwarz 1992; Ehrenreich 2003; Shipler 2005). The minimum wage was raised July 24, 2007 from $5.15 an hour to $5.85 an hour, then increased to $6.55 an hour in July of 2008, and is scheduled to go to $7.25 an hour in 2009 (Armour 2007). Even if we assume a salary of $6.55 an hour, that translates into an annual salary of about $14,000 a year, which is below the poverty line for a family of three and well below the line for a family of four.

As might be expected, those in this social class have a poor education (perhaps high school but often less than that), have few if any of the comforts of life, and do not participate actively in community organizations. They are much more likely to rent rather than own their own homes.

The *lower* class, roughly 12 to 15 percent of the population, represents school dropouts, and those without a strong attachment to the job market. Even at this level, however, many in the lower class have work experience, but usually in the lowest-paying and least secure jobs. The members tend to have few marketable skills. While some could be trained to perform certain types of work, others have serious mental or physical handicaps that render them all but unemployable. Welfare is the main source of support for many in this class. A significant minority are homeless. (This class is sometimes referred to as the *underclass*, a somewhat controversial term.)

Lower-class members tend to be resigned to their fate and distrustful of others. They have few resources to enable them to escape their plight. They vote less and are not able to participate in community organizations. Apathy is a common condition (rather than apathy causing their lower-class status, it is more likely that their lower-class status had produced apathy). *Alienation* is a word often applied to the working and lower classes: the term refers to people who feel powerless, so much so that dominant norms and values seem remote (Beeghley 2005: 7). Further, the lower class is the one most discriminated against. (For more on poverty, see "A Closer Look," below.)

These class descriptions are drawn from a number of sources. For a description of the major classes similar to that shown above, see Gilbert and Kahl 1987: 329-337.

Caveats

Determining people's social class position is not as clear-cut as this analysis might suggest. It is not uncommon to find a well-educated person among the working poor, for example. (This situation is what is called *status inconsistency*. A government official may administer a multimillion dollar budget yet earn a modest personal income. Another example would be a high school dropout who holds a job with high pay.) Also, social position may change during a person's lifetime.

Mobility

A question that sociologists have given considerable attention to is *mobility*, movement from one social class to another. This is known as *vertical* mobility. *Horizontal* mobility refers to moving to another area or to another position with no significant change in social status. Stories of someone such as Oprah Winfrey, who rose from abject poverty to great fame and riches, fascinate people. (For an interesting and sophisticated account of cases of upward mobility, see Harrington and Boardman 1997).

Obviously, some mobility is possible. Stories abound of people born of poor parents in a depressed area, who, either by great determination or luck or a combination of the two, eventually move into a higher status, perhaps upper middle class. Conversely, *downward* mobility may also occur. It is not difficult to conceive of a person, born of wealthy parents, through circumstances such as alcoholism, mental illness, or bad luck, who winds up in a lower-class position or even homeless.

An important study of mobility was carried out by Peter Blau and Otis Dudley Duncan in 1967. They were particularly concerned about changes in occupation, which is ordinarily the most significant measure of social status (cited in Gilbert and Kahl 1987: 156).

Blau and Duncan found frequent occupational inheritance in this country: a pattern in which fathers in white-collar occupations have sons who work in white-collar occupations, and fathers in blue-collar occupations have sons who work in blue-collar occupations. Thus, the sons tended to duplicate the social class of their fathers. The social structure sets the range of opportunities available to individuals: the class structure is reproduced as a child grows up with certain experiences and learning specific skills.

To be sure, opportunity is widespread in the United States. Short-distance movements, however, exceed long-distance ones. This means that when someone moves up from a working-class position, he or she will probably settle no higher than a lower-middle-class status. People who move from entry-level work all the way to the top probably make it less than 1 percent of the time.

The work experience of women tends to parallel that of men, but women still face some discrimination. When women work for pay they are often guided into "support jobs" such as a clerk, assisting men. Like the men, their upward mobility is limited. Only 1 percent of daughters of farmers become professional workers. Many women get locked into jobs without a promotion ladder. Ehrenreich (2005: 171) speaks of the "invisibility" of middle-aged women in our society.

Of course ability and effort are important, and become more so as one reaches college and early work experience. But people's class of origin indicates the opportunities with which they begin seeking a place in society. To be sure, a significant minority of working-class children is able to get into and complete college, and this translates into white-collar prestige and income.

The rewards of hard work go mostly to those who start life with some advantages. Ascribed factors (family background, race, gender, etc.) influence status attainment at every stage. People's family background is significant because it allows them to obtain educational credentials and provides them with knowledge, interpersonal skills, social contacts, values, psychological traits, and other characteristics that enable them to obtain and keep better jobs.

Women, blacks, and Hispanics have lower rates of mobility. Among the reasons for this are that they were born to the wrong parents, worked in the wrong industry, or lived in the wrong region of the country. Studying poverty many years ago, Michael Harrington noted that poor people can be paragons of hard work and morality and still remain poor or live on the edge of poverty.

The extent of equality of opportunity and mobility varies greatly from one society to another. Yet the rates of mobility in the United States are neither much higher nor lower than those in other industrialized nations. One study found that the United States had slightly less mobility than Sweden, but somewhat more than England or France.

(This discussion of mobility is adapted from Beeghley 2005: 103-129). A recent report claims that mobility is higher in Norway, Finland, and Denmark than in the U. S. (Gudrais 2008).

Ehrenreich chronicles the difficulty of getting a high-paying middle-class job. She claims that a gap in one's work history for any purpose—child rearing, caring for an elderly parent, recovering from an illness—is unforgivable. With only slight exaggeration, she writes, "If you haven't spent every moment of your life making money for somebody else, you can forget about getting a job" (Ehrenreich 2005: 169).

Despite the obstacles, some do move up. One study of upward mobility found that individuals who moved to a higher status had psychological resources to help them; they tended to have an internal locus of control. This meant they were capable of comforting themselves during times of emotional stress. For those with an internal focus of control, external rewards may be less salient.

However, the same study stressed that "resilient" children and adolescents made use of an extended network of support: teachers, ministers, peers, friends' parents, extended family members, and the like. Having had at least one teacher who shares the student's background was found to be critical (Harrington and Boardman 1997: 172-184).

Consequences of Stratification

Position in the social stratification system has enormous consequences in almost every area of life, sometimes called "life chances," the opportunity to live a full, healthy, and meaningful life. Social class influences one's family, friends, work, income, wealth, leisure activities, travel, and just anything else one can think of. In general, social class position is positively related to overall happiness and success, just as it is negatively related to the disagreeable or unsatisfying things of life. Without question, social stratification is one of the crucial factors of social life in our time

A Closer Look: Poverty

Because poverty is the salient condition of the bottom two classes (and may threaten even working-class people), it prompts further discussion.

Currently, 38 million people live below the poverty line in the United States, some 12.6 percent of the population. The federal government defines the poverty line as an annual income of $20,000 or less for a family of four. (The reader might try to devise a budget for such a family with this level of income.) The poverty rate increased every year from 2001 to 2004, and is roughly unchanged since. This translates into 7.7 million families in this country who are poor. About 17.6 percent of all children in the country are poor, and that is the age group with the highest rate of poverty (U. S. Census 2006).

The United States has symbolized a land of opportunity as the breadbasket of the world. Yet poverty touches every corner of this affluent nation, in every state, city, and village across America. Not only have several studies supported this contention, but social service agencies and homeless shelters report continuing and increasing use. The conclusion that poverty in America is extensive and debilitating seems overwhelming (Rank 2004: 3-4; Burton 1992: 10-20).

From the early 1970s to the present, wages and income have stagnated, he gap between rich and poor has widened, increasing numbers of working families fall below the poverty line, inner cities and rural areas have become ever more economically isolated, and so on down the list. Roughly one-fifth of our population is either in poverty or precariously close to falling into poverty at any point in time. In fact, the United States has far and away the highest rates of poverty and income inequality among Western industrialized countries (Rank 2004: 5).

A recent survey of child welfare in 21 wealthy nations that assessed everything from infant mortality to whether children ate dinner with their parents concluded that the United States and Britain ranked at the bottom (UNICEF 2007). Children fared worse in the U. S. because of greater economic inequality and poor levels of public support for families. The lack of day-care services and poorer health coverage in the U. S. were important factors.

In the recession of 2008, more and more people are turning to food banks, soup kitchens, and other emergency food assistance programs. Food prices were up 6.1 percent from June of 2007 to June of 2008. Working Americans comprise an increasing percentage of recipients of these programs. In Atlanta, half of the people have full-time jobs but don't earn enough to keep up with rising prices (Jaret 2008).

As of late 2008, food pantries cannot keep up with the demand. Some six million Americans are turning to pantries for the first time. The numbers of food pantry visits are up 25 percent in Dallas, 33 percent in Chicago, and 41 percent in Los Angeles. Further, donations to these agencies are down when they are most needed (CBS News 2008).

There is considerable movement in and out of poverty. While a few people (about 2 percent of the poverty population) never get out of poverty during their whole lives, most do—at least for a time, though some slip back into poverty (Spates and Macionis 1989:365). In one study, only 1 percent of the poor remained poor during a nine-year time span (Rank 2004: 29). The popular image that most poor people remain poor forever is incorrect.

Many people blame the behavior of the poor as the main cause of their problems. The contention is that if only the poor would stay in school, delay marriage and childbearing, look hard for work, and be frugal with their resources, they would find a way out of poverty. It is tempting to believe this because it provides a simplistic answer to a problem and fits in well with an individualistic philosophy so strong in America. But like most stereotypes, it has an element of truth but represents a serious misunderstanding of poverty in this country.

To blame the behavior of the poor as the cause of their problems is to overlook the powerful social and economic circumstances which constrain their lives. The poor are characterized by their vulnerability and limited choices: most choose among severely restricted options. They tend to learn that their chances of solving their problems are not very great. Restricted opportunities and unpleasant experiences most frequently shape the behavior of the poor.

After summarizing some of the alleged behavioral deficiencies of the poor, Gans (1995: 2-3) argues that the causes of their behaviors are in fact usually *poverty-related* effects; that sometimes poor people are driven by these to actions that violate their own morals and values. These pressures develop because poor people lack the funds, the economic security, and often the social supports and emotional strength, to behave in mainstream ways.

Many of the welfare poor have a sense of hopelessness and feeling trapped; they find few attractive alternatives to receiving public assistance. In a careful study of families on welfare, Mark Robert Rank found families that sounded remarkably like the families one might encounter in the grocery store or down the street. They wanted to get ahead in their lives, wished the best for their children, and were willing to put in the effort to achieve it (Rank 2004: 6).

Poverty is a result, not of incompetence on the part of the poor, but of the characteristics of the labor market. Poverty results primarily from an imbalance between the jobs the poor seek or hold and the jobs made available by the U. S. economy. In inner cities, changes in the urban economy have resulted in isolation that exacerbates their plight. Many of the poor are individuals whose strong endorsement of mainstream values has not relieved their poverty.

Changes in the economic and social situations of the ghetto underclass will lead to changes in culture norms and behavior patterns. The poor have a marked ability to move out of poverty when economic opportunities have improved.

Numerous studies have found considerable work effort on the part of the poor. (Recall our discussion of the working poor). In general, impoverished people work whenever there is opportunity to do so. Millions of people in the United States work long and hard at the best jobs they can find, and end up poor. One problem is the poor worker has no reasonable expectation that his job will lead to better things.

Most of the unemployed working-age poor are not employable because of personal handicaps, child care responsibilities, or lack of suitable job opportunities. (Only about 10-15 percent of jobs listed in newspapers are jobs poor persons might have a chance to get, and nearly all were filled in a day or two.) (For a summary of many of these arguments, see Burton 1992: 25-33.)

In explaining poverty, most sociologists give more importance to structural characteristics of a society than to lack of individual effort, though the latter is clearly a factor. (Structural characteristics, discussed in chapter 1, refer to systemic features of a society over which the individual has little or no control.) A good example is the Great Depression of the 1930s: people were not poor because they lacked initiative, but because the economy had collapsed and jobs were all but unavailable.

Today, of course, the economy has not collapsed (although the nation went into a recession in 2008) and some jobs are available, but important structural characteristics still prevail. There has been a serious decline in manufacturing jobs in this country since the 1970s Some have just disappeared while others have moved to other areas of the country or to third-world countries where labor costs are much lower. In February of 2008 the nation lost 63,000 jobs (CBS News 2008). The disadvantages of some poor students make it less likely they can complete their education (see chapter 4). There is a marked lack of low-cost housing in most areas of the country. Discrimination affects not only minorities but poor people in general and often residents of certain low-status areas.

There are several categories of persons who are more vulnerable to poverty than others. The most important of these are the uneducated; single parents (particularly when the parent is a woman, which is usually the case); a handicapped head of household; minorities, particularly African Americans, Hispanics, and Native Americans; residents of a deteriorating inner city; residents of an isolated rural area; and very old (over 85) females, particularly black.

I should stress that one, or even two, of these characteristics does not necessarily mean one is poor. I was raised in a single-parent family, for example, but we were not poor. Many African Americans and many elderly females are not poor, and so forth. However, in every case the *percentages* of these people who are poor will be higher than the average. And if several of these characteristics prevail, poverty is very likely.

A word should be added about the plight of single-parent families. Many women with children find themselves without a husband (never married, divorced or abandoned) and in dire straits. Child support is usually either nonexistent or very small. Getting a job, particularly for a woman with low education in a declining area, can be a daunting task. Child care is a critical issue. Women earn less than men in this country, particularly when less-educated women are steered into "pink collar" occupations such as clerks, child care workers, and waitresses, and most such jobs lack health care coverage.

(For a sympathetic treatment of single-parent females, see Berrick 1995.)

The Role of Welfare

Students may ask, "But does not welfare take care of the poverty-stricken in our country?" Obviously public assistance programs help relieve some of the worst symptoms of poverty, but many poor receive none of this aid. Further, welfare payments do not eliminate the condition itself: in order to receive welfare, recipients must remain poor in order to continue receiving benefits. Although it is not generally recognized, most of the cash benefits go to middle-class people. Money from food stamps goes to grocery stores, money from Medicaid goes to the health care industry, money from housing vouchers goes to landlords, and so on.

It is true that at least one program, Temporary Assistance to Needy Families, provides cash to single heads of families. But since the changes instituted in 1996, severe restrictions apply to this aid. Most women must be actively looking for work, the benefits are extremely small, there are time limits on almost all grants, and there is great variation by states. The claim that women have children in order to receive these benefits has been dismissed by almost all who have examined it (summarized in Burton 1992: 81-83, 96-97).

After an extensive analysis of welfare grants, Beeghley (2005: 252) suggests that "grandiose notions about America's generosity toward the poor are misbegotten." (For an excellent discussion of welfare, see Rank 1994.)

Being poor is highly correlated with poor health care, inferior education, inadequate housing, higher crime rates and poorer access to justice, and a dysfunctional family life. The poor get sick more than anyone else. Poor children are less likely to receive adequate nutrition, decent medical care, and access to early childhood programs. Poor children are more than three times as likely to die in childhood (Burton 1992: 12).

Poverty is extremely costly to the rest of the society. There is significant waste of a relatively unproductive mass of people. The cost to other taxpayers is large not only because of welfare but also because of urban renewal and crime prevention. The entire society would prosper with the elimination (or at least significant reduction) of poverty because of the purchasing power and larger tax base that would result (Burton 1992: 152).

There is evidence that living in a society with wide disparities—in health, in wealth, in education—is worse for *all* the society's members, even the well off. High inequality reverberates through societies on multiple levels, correlating with, if not causing, more crime, less happiness, poorer mental and physical health, less racial harmony, less civil and political participation (Gudrais 2008). And as Rank (2004: 9) says, poverty drains us individually and as a society. Each of us directly and individually pays a high price for allowing poverty to walk in our midst.

For too long, poverty has been neglected as a major problem in American life. As Jargowski (1997: 213) says, "(W)e must find the political will and the means to ensure that millions of our fellow citizens need not live in economically devastated and socially isolated neighborhoods."

Summary

Social stratification is a system by which a society ranks groups of people in a hierarchy called classes. A closed system based on ascribed status characteristics (things no one can control) is called a caste system. An open system based on achieved (earned) characteristics is called a class system.

The upper class consists of people in top positions in business, government, and other areas, particularly those with recognized prestige who live an exclusive life style. The upper middle class consists of college graduates who are in professions or other white-collar jobs, receive good salaries and benefits, and are active in their communities. The lower middle class belongs to lower-level white collar jobs but share most of the characteristics of the upper middle class.

The large working class generally has only a high school education, and labors at manual labor jobs for an hourly wage. They have the necessities of life and a few comforts, but tend to have little savings and are vulnerable to changes in the economy. They are not very active in their local communities.

The working poor have little education and a precarious position in life, but do have some regular ties to the job market. The true lower class, consisting of school dropouts, is the most precarious of all, holding few marketable skills.

Mobility, or movement from one class to another, is possible but limited in scope. Those who do move to a higher class generally move only one level. Scholars have found that social class position tends to duplicate itself in the lives of children.

Poverty is a major problem in the United States. Its members are marked by vulnerability and limited choices. Most poor people are poor not from individual failures but from the characteristics of the labor market. Those most vulnerable to poverty include the uneducated, single parents, handicapped head of family, minorities, residents of the older inner city or an isolated rural area, and the very old. Welfare helps poor people less than is commonly thought.

References

Armour, Stephanie. 2007. "Minimum wage increase kicks in today." **USA TODAY** (July 24): 1.

Beeghley, Leonard. 2005. *The Structure of Social Stratification in the United States,* fourth edition (Boston: Allyn and Bacon).

Berrick, Jill Duerr. 1995. *Faces of Poverty: Portraits of Women and Children on Welfare* (Oxford: Oxford University Press).

Bureau of the Census. 2006. Washington, D. C.: U. S. Government Printing Office.

Burton, C. Emory. 1992. *The Poverty Debate: Politics and the Poor in America* (Westport, Connecticut: Greenwood Press).

CBS News 2008 (November 25).

CBS News 2008 (March 7).

Ehrenreich, Barbara. 2001. *Nickel and Dimed: On (Not) Getting By in America* (New York: Metropolitan Books).

Ehrenreich, Barbara. 2005. *Bait and Switch: The (Futile) Pursuit of the American Dream* (New York: Metropolitan Books).

Gans, Herbert J. 1995. *The War Against the Poor: The Underclass and Antipoverty Policy* (New York: Basic Books).

Gilbert, Dennis, and Joseph A. Kahl. 1987. *The American Class Structure: A New Synthesis,* third edition (Chicago: the Dorsey Press).

Gudrais, Elizabeth. 2008. "Unequal America," **Harvard Magazine** (July-August).

Harrington, Charles, and Susan K. Boardman. 1997. *Paths to Success: Beating the Odds in American Society* (Cambridge: Harvard University Press).

Henslin, James M. 2007. *Sociology: A Down-to-Earth Approach.* (Boston: Allyn and Bacon).

Jaret, Peter. 2008. "Going Hungry in America." **AARP Bulletin** (September).

Jargowski, Paul. 1997. *Poverty and Place: Ghettos, Barrios, and the American City* (New York: Russell Sage Foundation).

Newman, Katherine S. 1988. *Falling From Grace: Downward Mobility in the Age of Affluence* (Berkeley: University of California Press).

Rank, Mark Robert. 1994. *Living on the Edge: The Realities of Welfare in America* (New York: Columbia University Press).

Rank, Mark Robert. 2004. *One Nation, Underprivileged: Why American Poverty Affects Us All* (New York: Oxford University Press).

Regnier, Pat. 2007. "Is it Time for a *New* New Deal?" *Money* (February): 94-100.

Shipler, David K. 2005. *The Working Poor: Invisible in America* (New York: Vintage Books).

20/20. 2007. CBS News (January 19).

UNICEF. 2007. "Child survey has U. S., Britain last." **Dallas Morning News** (February 15): 17A.

Yates, Michael D. 2005. "A Statistical Portrait of the U. S. Working Class." *Monthly Review,* Vol. 56 (April): 1.

Employees at Mariano's restaurant, Dallas.

Chapter 9: RACE AND ETHNICITY

I went to high school and college in the 1950s in Birmingham, Alabama. As I grew up in that deep-South city with about 45 percent black population, I found that I never came into contact with a black person on any level of equality. I might speak to the black janitor as he came in to clean a room, or pass some black people on the street, but that was about it. What existed at that time was a rigid segregation of the two major racial groups in almost all areas of life.

Going to a northern state to attend theological seminary, I was assigned a black roommate for my first semester, and he became my first black friend. I also learned what I dimly knew already, that racial inequality and segregation were major contradictions not only to all major world religions but to the democratic principles our country presumably fostered.

Much of our lives in American society involve racial and ethnic relationships and conflicts. This issue was the most important domestic issue of the 20th century and continues to be important as the 21st century progresses. Many would assert that problems stemming from race and ethnicity are the most severe, persistent, and intractable facing the society (Macionis 2000: 6). Sociology can contribute greatly to our understanding of this challenge of our life as Americans.

Throughout the world, we have witnessed groups trying to kill each other. We have seen bombings, mass killing bordering on genocide, ethnically allied armies ready for battle. Such populations as the old Yugoslavia, Burundi, Protestants and Catholics in Northern Ireland, the Arabs and the Jews in the Middle East, and the Tutu and Hutus in Rwanda, have experienced conflicts, suggesting that ethnicity is a volatile force in human affairs (Turner 2006: 232).

The United States is somewhat unique in its history. The Native peoples, erroneously called "Indians," were conquered, Mexican territory was annexed, blacks were brought as slaves or indentured servants who eventually became slaves, and immigrants have come from almost every part of the world. Minorities predominate in major cities across the country. The thesis of a book by Ronald Takaki is that "Americans originated from many shores, and all of us are entitled to dignity" (Takaki 1993: 15).

The United States has more people of Irish descent than there are in Ireland, more Jews than in Israel, and more African Americans than in many African nations. Hispanics recently became the largest minority group, and Asian Americans are the most rapidly-growing group. Immigration continues as a highly controversial topic.

Approximate numbers and percentages of the total population of the major groups are:

Whites	239 million	80.1 percent of the population
Hispanics (of any race)	44.2 million	14.8 percent
African American	38.3 million	12.8 percent
Asian American	13.1 million	4.4 percent
Native Americans	2.2 million	1.4 percent
Native Hawaiian and other Pacific Islanders	0.52 million	0.2 percent
Two or more races	4.7 million	1.6 percent
		(*Time* 2006)

A slightly more recent estimate claims that minorities in this country exceed 100 million. The number of African Americans was given as 40.2 million and Asians 14.9 million (CBS News, 2007).

The Concept of Race

Many people assume that "race" is a self-evident concept: it refers to the physical or biological features, such as skin color and hair texture, of groups of people in largely exclusive categories. Some go further and argue that on the basis of genetic inheritance, some groups are innately superior to others. The physical traits people display, according to this view, are intrinsically related to their culture, personality, and intelligence. Finally, the differences among various groups are thought to be innate and not subject to change.

The reality is that there is no scientific basis for these assumptions (Turner 2006: 233). Human beings around the world are members of a single biological species. There is no agreement on which traits should be used in defining races; someone considered black in the United States might be classified as white in Brazil. Differences among individuals of the same group are greater than those found between groups. "Pure" races do not exist today, and some question whether they have ever existed. What racial categories there are form a continuum of gradual change, not a set of sharply demarcated types (Marger 2000: 19; Schaefer 2002: 12; Eitzen and Zinn 2007: 295).

The categories and guidelines for placing people into a race are often vague and contradictory. Colin Powell is the son of Jamaican immigrants with African, English, Irish, Scottish, and Jewish ancestry. Tiger Woods' mother is from Thailand and is one-half Thai, a quarter Chinese, and a quarter white. His late father was half black, a quarter Chinese, and a quarter American Indian.

Race is important, to be sure, but primarily because people attach significance to the concept and consider it a real and important division of humanity. It is a social construction: the belief system of a society and institutional practices provide its significance. Race is a label we use to describe perceived biological characteristics. It remains a widely used term for socially defined groups in popular discourse (Hirschman 2004).

Most social scientists reject the notion that any category of people is smarter than any other. There is little consensus regarding the very meaning of intelligence and how it can be adequately measured (Marger 2000: 20). It is not established if IQ tests measure innate potential, ability to think abstractly, or acquired cultural knowledge. Recent research shows that differences in intelligence scores between blacks and whites are virtually eliminated when adjustments are made for social and economic characteristics. "Biological deficiency theories are generally not accepted in the scientific community" (Eitzen and Zinn 2007: 306).

Ethnicity

An *ethnic group* shares a common national origin and/or a common culture (language, food, music, religion, etc.). While Jews do not necessarily have a common national origin (they may be from many countries), they are considered an ethnic group because they have a consciousness of kind, an awareness of close association (Marger 2000: 12). Not only have Jews endured hostility historically, but they have consciously sought to preserve their group identity. Hispanics (or

Latinos) are considered an ethnic group because a Hispanic person may be of any race.

Some people feel an intense sense of ethnic identity, while others feel little or none. "If your group is relatively small, has little power, looks different from most people in the society, and is an object of discrimination, you will have a heightened sense of ethnic identity" (Henslin 2007: 265). Others wonder why it is such a big deal.

Those classified as "white" can identify with a number of ethnic groups (Italian, Irish, German, Polish, etc.). Blacks, although they may be from Haiti, Jamaica, Kenya, or another country, experience social pressure to identify as black. Until the civil rights movement, many blacks were denied historical knowledge and educational opportunities to identify and explore ethnic pride.

Minorities

A *minority group* is a people singled out for unequal treatment and who regard themselves as objects of collective discrimination. Their physical or cultural traits are held in low esteem by the dominant group, which treats them differently, thus they tend to develop a sense of identity and common destiny (Henslin 2007: 263).

In addition, minorities receive unequal amounts of the society's valued resources—wealth, prestige, and power. Some get more than others and are treated more favorably (Marger 2000: 9). They tend to have poorer jobs, receive an inferior education, and exercise less political power. The *majority group,* also known as the *dominant group,* is the group in power, the one that owns or controls the dominant resources of the society.

Minority groups can be distinguished from the majority group, hold inferior political and economic status, and tend to be treated as members of a category. Note that a minority group could be larger in numbers than the dominant group, as illustrated by blacks in South Africa. Though not considered in this chapter, women and gays are sometimes considered to be minority groups.

Prejudice

Prejudice is a rigid and usually unfavorable judgment about a minority group that loosely applies to everyone in that group. It is an arbitrary belief or feeling towards a group or its individual members.

It is at attitude or a feeling (or both), not a behavior. It can range from mild aversion to outright hostility.

Emory Bogardus studied the effects of culturally rooted prejudice for more than 40 years. He thought prejudice was so widespread that it cannot be explained as merely a trait of people with prejudiced personalities. He believed everyone in the United States expresses some bigotry because we live in a "culture of prejudice" that has taught us to view certain categories of people as better as or worse than others (Macionis 2004: 278).

Theories of Prejudice

Sociology tends to see prejudice and discrimination as conforming responses to social situations in which people find themselves. "It is to individuals' social environment—the groups to which they belong, the cultural and political norms operative in their society and community, and the processes of socialization—that prejudice and discrimination can be traced" (Marger 2000: 92).

Prejudice comes from people around us. It does not depend on negative experiences with others. (Growing up in Alabama, it seemed to me that the most prejudiced people had had the *least* personal contact with blacks; they learned their prejudice from other whites.) Further, people who are prejudiced against one racial or ethnic group tend to be prejudiced against others (Henslin 2007: 266).

As suggested earlier, when there are prejudice and stereotypes about a group, a self-fulfilling prophecy may emerge. A group may begin to display the very traits attributed to them. They may find that they are allowed to hold only low-paying jobs with little prestige or opportunity for advancement. As a result, the false definition becomes real (Schaffer 2002: 21).

Conflict theorists stress how current arrangements benefit those with power, those with superior technology, weapons, property, or economic resources. Discrimination provides the privileged with advantages in the social, economic, and political spheres. Management can use fear of minority groups to pit worker against worker and weaken labor's bargaining power. Minorities come to see themselves as able to make gains only at the expense of the other groups (Henslin 2007: 271).

This approach views prejudice and discrimination as emerging from historical instances of intergroup conflict. Discrimination serves as a means of injuring or neutralizing minority groups that the dominant group perceives as threatening to its position of power and privilege. Historically, the white middle class realized substantial gains from the subordination of blacks. Studies have concluded that prejudice and discrimination against blacks continue to benefit at least some segments of the white population (Marger 2000: 100).

Exploitation theory sees prejudice against blacks and others as an extension of the inequality faced by the entire lower class. The Japanese were looked on favorably until they were seen as competitors (for jobs) by the whites. Historically, it is clear that much prejudice is economically motivated. In Florida and parts of the Southwest, the perception that Cubans, Mexicans, and other Hispanics are taking jobs from Anglos has touched off racial tensions.

Stereotypes

Prejudices are based on *stereotypes,* exaggerated generalizations about people. They are simplistic beliefs about a group, generally acquired second-hand and resistant to change. They prevent us from viewing other people as individuals. Stereotypes may be sustained despite numerous individual cases that clearly refute their validity. Some people may view all black teenagers as violent, or see all Native Americans living on reservations (only about a third do).

Racial and ethnic labels are powerful. People have used many words to belittle ethnic groups. Some stereotypes not only justify prejudice and discrimination, they even produce the behavior depicted in the stereotype, as a kind of self-fulfilling prophecy (Henslin 2007: 272). The greater the *fear,* the more negative the stereotype, which could result in more discrimination.

Discrimination

Discrimination is a behavior that denies valued goals, such as education, jobs, or health care, to other groups. Unlike prejudice, it is a *behavior* which treats other people unequally. It is interesting that discrimination can occur without an awareness of both those doing the discriminating and those being discriminated against; it can be a subconscious matter (Henslin 2007: 269).

Discrimination is stoked by fears, whether real or imagined. The fears may be the loss of jobs or high wages because others will work for less, the loss of cultural traditions, loss of political power, the loss of neighborhoods, even violence. The more threatened people feel, the more intense and severe the discrimination. Each wave of new white immigrants to America threatened the previous wave who had just begun to feel secure: the Germans against the Irish, the Italians against the Germans, the Polish against the Italians, and all against the blacks (Turner 2006: 237).

In an experiment on housing rentals by Douglas Massey, it was found that blacks were less likely to get to talk to rental agents, and if they did, they were less likely to be told an apartment was available, were more likely to pay an application fee, and more likely to be asked about their credit history (cited in Henslin 2007: 284).

At Texaco Oil Company, audio-tapes were released that showed senior company executives plotting to destroy documents demanded in a discrimination suit and using racial epithets in discussing black employees. Texaco, facing a threatened nationwide boycott, agreed to pay $126 million in compensation for outstanding grievances and complaints concerning racial discrimination (Schaefer 2002: 96-97).

Sociologist Joe Feagin, who made an extensive study of this subject, claims that over the course of a lifetime, a typical black man or woman likely faces *thousands* of cases of blatant, covert, or subtle discrimination at the hands of whites (Feagin 2001: 143, emphasis in original).

Institutional Discrimination

Institutional discrimination refers to discrimination that is a part of established practices or the customary ways that institutions behave. It suggests something woven into the fabric of society, a bias inherent in the operation of society's institutions. A certain bias prevails in the laws, customs, religious beliefs, and stable arrangements through which things get done. Patterns of employment, education, the criminal justice system, housing, health care, and government operations tend to maintain the social significance of race and ethnicity.

Discrimination is firmly incorporated in the society's normative system. Members of a group are legally or customarily denied equal access to various life chances. An example is that most new jobs are now being created in outlying and suburban areas, where transportation lines are more accessible, and where taxes are lower. This handicaps blacks who might qualify for them but who reside mainly in central cities (Marger 2000: 85-86).

Another example of institutional discrimination is bank lending. Studies found that even when applicants were identical in credit history, blacks and Hispanics were 60 percent more likely than whites to be rejected (Henslin 2007: 268). Another bank failed to provide lending services to minority neighborhoods because of race. Not one of its 34 branch offices was in a minority area. An apartment complex in Los Angeles would tell blacks there were no apartments available for rent.

Racism

When the basis of discrimination is someone's perception of race, it is known as *racism*. This is the belief that there is something in the makeup of an ethnic or racial group that explains and justifies lower status. It claims a connection between physical traits such as skin color and such things as personality and intelligence. Some observers object to the term racism, but it remains a serious social problem everywhere as people still contend that some racial and ethnic categories are better or worse than others (Macionis 2004: 278).

Some racist beliefs, more subtle than in the past, are still firmly rooted in American thought, though in modified form. To give a recent example, researchers sent out 5,000 resumes in response to help wanted ads in the Boston and Chicago papers. The resumes were identical except for the names. Lakisha and Jamal, usually perceived as black names, were given as well as Emily and Brandon, presumably white names. The white-sounding names elicited 50 percent more callbacks (Henslin 2007: 283).

Black and white Americans still differ dramatically in how they view discrimination. Most whites believe race is not much of a problem anymore, while most blacks believe that without affirmative action they would be denied equal opportunity.

In the mid 1990s, Pennsylvania researchers found that 80 percent of blacks thought inequality in jobs, housing, and income stemmed mostly from discrimination, while the majority of whites viewed this inequality as resulting from blacks' lack of motivation. Recent polls reveal the same pattern (Feagin 2001: 123-24).

As examples of extreme racism, there have been numerous hate crimes and bias-motivated incidents in the last several years. In a study of some of these in 1999, race was the apparent motivation for the bias in 56 percent of the reports (Schaffer 2002: 43). The Southern Poverty Law Center identified 762 hate groups in 48 states and the District of Columbia in 2004. Violence is the driving force of racist music (Eitzen and Zinn 2007: 314). In 2000 there were at least 254 U. S. internet sites disseminating extreme racist views (Feagin 2001:240).

Assimilation

Assimilation is the process by which ethnic and racial distinctions between groups disappear, or at least become minimal. The groups are absorbed into the mainstream culture and eventually would face no prejudice or discrimination. Under most definitions, they would no longer be minority groups.

One type of assimilation is *melting pot* assimilation, where the groups accept many new behaviors and values from one another. A new cultural system emerges that is a blend of the previous systems. Despite its popularity, there is little evidence that America has become a melting pot. Some have found the image of a "tossed salad" more appropriate, in that all the groups have something to contribute to the whole (see pluralism below).

Some scholars reject the concept of assimilation because it implies that it is the minority group that must do all the changing. But the word can mean an incorporation or acceptance of the group(s) in question, suggesting that not only has the minority group altered its attitudes, but the dominant group has becoming more accepting. Irish Americans, for example, used to face strong prejudice but they have now become assimilated, not only because they have changed but the majority group has come to accept them.

Pluralism

A word drawing considerable attention in the last generation is *pluralism,* a state in which peoples of all races and ethnicities are distinct but have social parity. They differ in their heritage but share social resources roughly equally (Macionis 2004: 280). Pluralism emphasizes the contributions of various cultures to the diversity and vitality of the larger society. This approach is sometimes referred to as *multiculturalism.*

Switzerland provides an outstanding example of multiculturalism. The Swiss population includes four ethnic groups: French, Italians, Germans, and Romansh. They have kept their own languages, and they live peacefully in political and economic unity. None of the groups could be called a minority (Henslin 2007: 274). Belgium is also organized along pluralistic lines.

Segregation

Segregation is the physical and/or social separation of categories of people (the standard practice when I was young in Alabama). Neighborhoods, schools, occupations, hospitals, restrooms, and even cemeteries can be segregated. Segregation allows the dominant group to maintain social distance from the minority and yet to exploit their labor as cooks, housekeepers, nannies, and the like.

Although the civil rights movement ended legal segregation, the United States is still segregated; most white citizens and most citizens of color live largely separate lives in neighborhoods and in the workforce. Schools in the United States have become increasingly segregated in recent years. Minority schools tend to be understaffed and underfunded, and have limited access to important resources (Eitzen and Zinn 2007: 313).

The most evident, persistent, and consequential forms of racial discrimination in American society are found in the area of housing. Patterns of discrimination are direct and deliberate. Several research studies have shown that all metropolitan areas in both the North and the South have a high degree of racial segregation. Housing segregation includes a range of white discriminators—landlords, homeowners, bankers, realtors, and government officials (Feagin 2001: 153-155). Less progress in breaking down racial barriers has been made in this sphere of social life than in any other.

Housing determines the schools people attend, the jobs they have access to, the benefits they receive from public institutions, and the commercial establishments they have access to. Continued segregation in housing prevents whites and minorities, especially blacks, from interacting at personal levels, thus reinforcing racial attitudes. According to Marger (2000: 261), the present pattern of housing in the U. S. is the chief obstacle to progress in all other aspects of racial and ethnic relations.

Studies have shown that even where average rents paid by blacks and whites are equivalent, little racial integration is evident. Class factors do not significantly account for concentrations in central cities. That the segregation is due mainly to group preferences is also not supported by research evidence (Marger 2000: 264-65).

The present segregation of blacks cannot be dismissed as wrongs committed in the past. Blacks are no more likely to have white neighbors today than they were in 1990 (Eitzen and Zinn 2007: 310). Research shows that many whites continue to avoid neighborhoods where blacks live. *Hypersegregation,* where residents have little contact of any kind with people in the larger society, applies to about one-fifth of blacks but only a small percentage of poor whites (Macionis 2004: 281).

Genocide

Genocide is the attempt to eliminate a hated or feared minority group. The attempt of Adolf Hitler to eliminate the Jews through various means may be the best-known example, but there have been others. Before the 20th century, there were persistent and concerted attempts to eliminate Native Americans. In Rwanda, the attempt by the Hutus to slaughter the Tutus, mentioned earlier in this chapter, is an example of massive genocide. A few years later, the Serbs in Bosnia massacred thousands of Muslims, giving us the name "ethnic cleansing."

African Americans

African Americans, or blacks (there is not complete agreement on the term) are the only group that entered the society as involuntary immigrants, and no other group was subsequently victimized by two centuries of slavery. They have been the central, most visible minority throughout our country's history, and they have been at the cutting edge of the civil rights movement (Takiki 1993: 7).

A full history of blacks in America takes us beyond the scope of this chapter, but their status in this country was scarcely improved following slavery, as many went into sharecropping and often faced terrorism. Later many moved to cities, especially in the North, where some found work but conditions proved very difficult. Systematic segregation and discrimination were their lot until at least the middle of the twentieth century.

The Supreme Court outlawed segregation in public schools in a landmark decision in 1954, and the civil rights movement gradually ended legal segregation. The Montgomery bus boycott of 1955-56 and mass demonstrations in Birmingham and other cities were highlights. Laws prohibiting discrimination in public facilities (1964) and ensuring voting rights (1965) went on the books. Martin Luther King, Jr. (whom I heard speak in 1963) was the best-known of many civil rights leaders.

Substantial improvement in the economic status of blacks in the '60s slowed significantly in the '70s and '80s. Economic progress helped create a substantial black middle class but had little impact on blacks at the bottom of the economic scale (Marger 2000: 246). The result has been a persistence of black poverty, increasing unemployment for young blacks, and a dramatic rise of female-headed families.

Today, income for blacks is about 61 percent of whites. Poor blacks, many of whom are trapped in inner-city ghettos, are worse off than poor whites. There are large gaps not only in income but in educational attainment, infant mortality, poverty rates, and unemployment. One study found that minorities tend to be concentrated in jobs that have shorter career ladders, less decision making authority and more vulnerability to shifts in labor market demand.

Between 1990 and 2004, the percentage of blacks in management and professional occupations increased from 17 percent to 26 percent. In 2001, 48 percent of blacks earned more than $35,000 a year, and 33 percent earned $50,000 or more. But most blacks are still working class or poor. Blacks predominate in service jobs such as cleaners, cooks, security guards, and hospital attendants (an exception: college-educated women). Black unemployment among teenagers in many cities exceeds 40 percent (Macionis 2004: 286; Marger 2000: 250).

Even with a college degree, blacks and Hispanics have had more difficulty in jobs than their white counterparts. Minorities, regardless of level of education, are underpaid compared with whites of similar education. Black and Hispanic men earn 30 percent less than white men with similar education. Further, there are "job ceilings" that separate them from executive suites and boardrooms (Eitzen and Zinn 2007: 314-15).

Further, blacks control only a tiny fraction of the nation's income-producing assets, and they seldom own their own businesses. There is a striking absence of blacks in banks, insurance companies, and other financial institutions (Marger 2000: 259).

William Julius Wilson (1996) has documented the devastating effects that joblessness and the disappearance of blue-collar jobs have in our urban ghettos. Blacks have become locked in the inner city by economic and technological changes—crime, family dissolution, and welfare are all connected to the structural removal of work from the inner city. Male joblessness encourages nonmarital childbearing and undermines the foundation of black families. Adaptation to these structural conditions leaves black women disproportionately divorced and solely responsible for their children (Eitzen and Zinn 2007: 319).

There is a common notion that there are jobs available for the inner-city black poor but they just do not seek them out. However, an analysis of jobs advertised in *The Washington Post* found that only 5 percent of these jobs were open to people without skills and experience. Interviews disclosed that an average of 21 people applied for each position, which typically was filled within three days of when the ad appeared. This counters the popular view that there are plenty of jobs for the underclass (Schaeffer 2002: 81).

Although Hurricane Katrina disproportionately affected poor blacks, many residents of minority neighborhoods said that they were not aware that they could seek state help. An Associated Press analysis showed that white homeowners were three times as likely as minorities to appeal insurance settlements (Bass and Callimachi 2006).

Blacks have made remarkable educational progress since 1980. The share of adults completing high school rose from half to almost three-fourths. The share of blacks with a college degree rose from 8 percent to more than 16 percent. But they still are at just over half the national standard when it comes to completing four years of college (Macionis 2004: 287).

Some blacks transferred from segregated schools in St. Louis to integrated ones in nearby Clayton in 2004. It was found that only one-half of one percent of black kids in the integrated school dropped out, and 94 percent graduated, compared to at least a 12 percent dropout rate in the St. Louis schools (Kozol 2006).

Blacks, like other minorities, report frequent problems with the police. A New Jersey dentist was stopped by the police more than a hundred times in a four-year period as he drove from home to office in his expensive car. The targeting of black Americans is common practice for many law enforcement agencies across the nation (Feagin 2001: 1). Most blacks see a justice system that treats blacks differently from whites.

Blacks comprised 42 percent of jail inmates in 2000 (Schaefer 2002: 261). Their arrest rate is higher, and it is harder for them to post bail. Black men ages 12-24 are especially likely to be victimized at a rate double that of whites. They receive longer sentences. Blacks are 37 percent of those arrested for drug offenses but 65 percent of those sent to prisons for drugs.

Compared with whites, blacks have higher death rates from diseases of the heart, pneumonia, diabetes and cancer. Death rates from strokes were twice as high among blacks. Part of the reason is higher poverty rates, but part of the picture is prejudice and discrimination (Schaefer 2002: 264). They are more likely to use the emergency room as a primary source of care. White males live seven years longer than black men. On virtually every measure of health, blacks (and Hispanics) are disadvantaged. Black babies are nearly twice as likely to die within their first year as white babies (Eitzen and Zinn 2007: 316).

Environmental racism is the disproportionate exposure of some racial groups to toxic substances. Hazardous waste facilities are much more likely to be built in or near minority communities, and evidence is that race and not social class is the significant factor.

Once largely disfranchised, blacks are voting in large numbers and their vote is an important swing factor in many elections. There has been a sharp rise in the number of black elected officials, particularly at local and state government levels. As of 2008 there were 42 black members of the House (9.7 percent of the total) and one black member (Barack Obama) of the Senate (Infoplease 2008). Overall, however, blacks comprise only about two percent of all public officials. The election of Barack Obama as president in 2008 was widely viewed as a positive development.

The mass media have persistently presented stereotyped pictures of blacks. There has been considerable improvement, but there is still a tendency for the media to exaggerate the role of blacks in poverty, homelessness, drug use, and drug crime. As Feagin (2001: 116) points out, black youth are *less* likely than white youth to use marijuana or cocaine, smoke cigarettes, or drink alcohol, and rates of drug abuse (and child abuse) are higher for single-parent white families than for similar black families.

Hispanics

Hispanics, or Latinos, include those of Spanish heritage and language. The most common Hispanic groups in the United States come from Mexico (25 million), Puerto Rico (3 million), Cuba (over one million), and Central or South America (over 5 million). Most identify themselves not as Hispanics or Latinos but as members of their specific nation such as Mexican or Cuban (Henslin 2007: 278).

Most Mexican immigrants to the United States are *mestizos*, a physical type combining European and Indian traits. Although sociologists refer to Hispanics as an ethnic group, not a race, most are physically distinct enough to be perceived by many Anglos in racial terms (Marger 2000: 283).

Hispanics are heavily concentrated by region. Mexican Americans live mainly in the five southwestern states of California, Texas, Arizona, New Mexico, and Colorado. Almost 80 percent are in California and Texas alone. But in recent decades, there has been dispersion throughout the United States, particularly cities of the Midwest such as Chicago. Puerto Ricans live heavily in New York City, Chicago, and northern New Jersey, and Cubans in the Miami area (Marger 2000: 293).

Today Hispanics are more urbanized than the general population. The most "Mexican" cities are Los Angeles-Long Beach, San Antonio, San Francisco-Oakland, El Paso, Albuquerque, and Phoenix. They are relatively young and rapidly increasing, having recently passed blacks as the nation's largest minority group. They tend to have larger families and women are less likely to work outside the home.

Mexican influence in the Southwest is strong: this may be seen in the names of hundreds of places, in architecture, food, the arts, music, and of course language. Salsa and Latin jazz are now standard musical genres (Marger 2000: 315). The Mexican American experience has been unique, for most of them live close to their homeland, a proximity that has helped reinforce their language, identify, and culture (Takiki 1993: 8).

Hispanic influence in the history of the Southwest is not always acknowledged. Settlers from Spain established a permanent colony in 1598, 22 years before the Pilgrims arrived. There were Spanish settlements in Texas in the early 1700s. Peace-loving Mexicans lived there harmoniously with the Indians for the most part. Their culture included folk opera, dramas, instrumental musical productions, and extensive art, particularly in New Mexico and California. Mexicans were the father of agriculture in the Southwest and were the first cowboys.

Mexico lost more than half of its territory in the Mexican War. The United States acquired what are today the states of California, Colorado, New Mexico, Nevada, Utah, and most of Arizona, in addition to Texas, which had been annexed previously (Marger 2000: 206). Mexicans who remained became a minority, different in language, custom, and race from the growing Anglo population. They were confined to the lowest economic positions, including some who had been upper class.

A pattern of second-class treatment for Mexican Americans ensued. Many were forced into segregated schools of inferior quality, and subject to harassment by the Border Patrol and the police (Turner 2006: 244). The Anglo system of property ownership began to replace the Hispanic system. Anglo cattle ranchers gradually pushed out Mexican American ranchers. The suspicion in which Anglos have held Mexican Americans has contributed to mutual distrust between the two groups.

There have been periods in our history when Mexican labor was eagerly sought. The bracero program in 1942 allowed Mexicans to work legally in the United States. After World War II, it was extended several times as a labor supplement. The program ended in 1965.

An important chapter in the history of Hispanics in this country happened when Cesar Chavez organized migrant farmworkers, forcing growers in California and the Southwest to recognize his United Farm Workers. Chavez became something of a folk hero to Mexican Americans, and his charisma thrust him into the forefront of the Mexican American movement (Marger 2000: 288-289; Schaefer 2002: 301).

Substantial income disparity continues between Hispanics and Anglos. Mexican Americans and Puerto Ricans are disproportionately found among America's poor. Over one-quarter of all Hispanic families are below the poverty line (Marger 2000: 296). There has been a strong tendency to steer Hispanic workers into the most menial, arduous, and low-paying jobs.

The role of Hispanics in leadership positions of the American economy is limited. The 1,000 largest United States corporations have only a few dozen Hispanics on their boards of directors and less than 200 at the vice-presidential level or above. Hispanic-owned firms, while growing, are small (Marger 2000: 305).

Among Hispanics over 25, only 55 percent have four years of high school, and about 25 percent have less than five years of schooling. Dropouts, especially in Texas, are high (Marger 2000: 298). A report indicted southwestern schools for having consistently failed to provide equal educational opportunities. Their culture and language are often ignored. As the number of Hispanic children has increased, many schools have become re-segregated (Schaeffer 2002: 315).

Language preference and proficiency has been a controversial issue in recent years. Spanish-speaking pupils are judged less able to compete until they learn English. Twenty-six states have passed laws that declare English their official language. While bilingual education programs might help these children learn the culture of both groups, it is employed sporadically and inconsistently (Schaefer 2002: 275-276). Hispanics tend to be absent from higher education.

Although a minority of Hispanic Americans speak only Spanish, and most of these are first-generation immigrants, as they move to the second and third-generation, English becomes their primary language. (Many Hispanics do not speak Spanish at all.) Over 90 percent of Hispanics supported the proposition that citizens and residents of the United States should learn English. So contrary to a common perception, most Hispanics prefer English and support its usage (Marger 2000: 312-313).

Hispanics are locked out of the health care system more often than any other racial or ethnic group. A third has no medical insurance or coverage, and the rate is higher for those born outside the United States. Many wait for a crisis to seek care, and few are immunized (Schaefer 2002: 317).

Along with other minorities, Hispanics report problems with the police. Commonplace police brutality of indifference in dealing with Mexican Americans has been repeatedly affirmed (Marger 2000: 310). While efforts have been made to improve this picture, genuine concerns remain.

Hispanics are vastly underrepresented at all levels of government. As of 2008 there were 24 Hispanics in the House (5.5 percent) and three in the Senate (Infoplease 2008). But their young and growing population is becoming more significant as a political force. (About two-thirds of Hispanics voted for Barack Obama in 2008.)

Puerto Rico became a territory of the United States in 1808 and inhabitants of the island were given American citizenship in 1917. New York City is the center of Puerto Rican life in the continental United States and is home to about one million Puerto Ricans. One-third of this community is severely disadvantaged. They have a higher incidence of women-headed households than other Hispanics, and are more likely to speak Spanish at home. This pattern puts them at greater risk of poverty (Macionis 2004: 292.

Cubans came largely by voluntary immigration, but initially they were impelled mainly by political rather than economic motives. Their status is easily the highest of all Hispanics. In Miami, Cubans are president of the city's largest bank, owner of the largest real estate developer, managing partner of the largest law firm, and publisher of the largest newspaper (Marger 2000: 305).

Despite their problems, Hispanics today radiate a sense of pride and hope for the future. Students are being taught to be proud of their Mexican and Indian heritage. They have an important role in the U. S. economy; they take pride in their families and in their country. Steady if slow progress has been made in closing the gap between Hispanics and Anglos. Hispanics are moving into greater participation in the society's mainstream economic and political systems (Marger 2000: 315).

Asian Americans

Asian Americans make up almost four percent of the population, but one that is rapidly growing not only in numbers but in economic and cultural significance. Today they are the fastest-growing ethnic minority in the United States, accounting for almost half of all immigration to this country. The Chinese remain the largest component of the Asian American population, yet Filipinos are almost as large. The Asian-Indian and Korean groups have also continued to grow steadily (Marger 2000: 331).

There are huge variations among those classified as "Asian." In addition to those named above, there are those from Japan, Malaysia, Pakistan, Siberia, Thailand, Vietnam, and others. The culture and language of these groups are very different.

Asian Americans are most heavily concentrated in five states: California, Hawaii, New York, Illinois, and Washington. Almost half the Asian American population is found in just four urban areas: Los Angeles, New York, San Francisco, and Honolulu, and many are living in suburbs (Marger 2000: 332).

Among voluntary immigrants to American society, none suffered more severe prejudice and discrimination in their settlement experiences than Asians. They were constant targets of all forms of social and physical abuse (Marger 2000: 342). An 1882 law actually prohibited further Chinese from entering the country. The term "yellow peril" was applied to Asian immigrants and their customs. As recently as 1996, 534 suspected and proven anti-Asian incidents were reported (Schaefer 2002: 331).

The most blatant and unlawful action against an Asian American group occurred in World War II, when 110,000 Japanese Americans, most of them citizens by birth, were interred in concentration camps. Only in 1988 did Congress pass a bill with a formal apology and a modest payment to each of the survivors of these camps (Takiki 1993: 401).

Asian Americans rank higher than most ethnic groups in family income, occupational prestige, and level of education. About 43 percent have completed college, and some one-third of Asian-American males are in managerial and professional occupations (Marger 2000: 335). While their family income tends to be high, they live mostly in states with a higher cost of living.

Despite their success, Asian Americans are not found in the corporate hierarchy on a par with European Americans. At the very top managerial levels, their numbers are very few. Less than one percent are found on the boards of the nation's 1,000 largest corporations (Schaefer 2002: 328).

Recent Asian immigrants vary considerably by social class. Many came as educated middle-class professionals with highly valued skills and some knowledge of English. Others, such as the Indochinese, arrived as uneducated, impoverished refugees.

Many Chinese immigrant women have no choice but to work as seamstresses. They have become a major source of labor for New York's garment industry, and in San Francisco and elsewhere, Chinese women are found in sweatshops (Schaefer 2002: 361).

Among the Asian groups, the Japanese seem to have experienced the most assimilation. They have been in this country for several generations and have formed close associations with non-Japanese, including frequent intermarriage. Chinese Americans are also moving rapidly in the direction of full assimilation (Marger 2000: 325, 351). Korean Americans are the most likely to form their own businesses, but still report some serious problems.

Asian Americans have been slow to achieve political clout. In Congress in late 2008, there are six Asian American members of the House and two in the Senate. Yet they should be a future political force in the United States. There seems no doubt that people of Asian ancestry will play a central role in United States society in coming decades.

Jews

The United States has the largest Jewish population in the world, about 6 million. Basically, a Jew in contemporary America is an individual who thinks of himself or herself as a Jew (Schaefer 2002: 386). They are concentrated in metropolitan areas such as New York City, Los Angeles, and Miami.

By the middle of the nineteenth century, a majority of America's 20,000 itinerant traders were German Jews. They commonly established clothing and dry goods or general stores. Many familiar department store names such as Macy's, Bloomingdale's, Saks Fifth Avenue, Sears, and Neiman-Marcus, stem from German-Jewish founding families (Marger 2000: 200).

Those Jews who came after 1880 tended to be poorer and less educated. Most came from eastern Europe, particularly Russia and Poland. Most remained in a few large cities, especially New York, where they were concentrated in lower-class ghettos. Many labored in garment factories, called sweatshops, where they worked long hours for poor wages. On the famous Lower East Side, 350,000 people a square mile were jammed into squalid rooms and apartments (Marger 2000: 201).

In the 1930s, German Jews were subjected systematically to an almost complete expulsion from every phase of the society's life. Later, Jews were compelled to leave Germany through a terrorist campaign. Finally, Nazi policies established death camps. On the notorious "Night of Broken Glass" in Berlin on November 9, 1938, some 90 Berlin Jews were murdered, hundreds of homes and synagogues were set on fire and ransacked, and thousands of Jewish store windows were broken (Schaefer 2002: 390).

American Jews have gained notable success in education and business and are strongly represented in the upper-middle class, but are still subject to discrimination in housing, membership in private clubs, college fraternities, and even sectors of the economy (Turner 2006: 247). Contrary to a common perception, Jews are dramatically *under* represented in management positions in the nation's leading banks (Schaefer 2002: 388).

Despite a perception that Jews hold great economic power, they are found in every class level, including the very bottom. Research since 1930 has found that Jews are actually underrepresented in the higher executive positions of the most powerful American and multinational corporations (Marger 2000: 214). They are denied total assimilation in the United States, and many individual Jewish families are trapped in poverty.

Historically, Jews have identified with other minority groups such as blacks. Most Jews supported the civil rights movement of the 1960s. But in recent years a certain tension between Jews and blacks has emerged. Many Jews view affirmative programs as discriminatory in that they favor blacks.

Jews have traditionally placed emphasis on education. Jews have founded graduate schools of medicine, education, social work, and mathematics (Schaefer 2002: 398). Jews are also among the most urbanized of American minorities. About three-fourths of the entire Jewish population in the United States is found in 12 large urban areas.

Arab Americans and Muslims

The Arab American and Muslim communities are among the most rapidly growing minority groups in the United States. (In Dearborn, a suburb of Detroit, Arabs make up over 20 percent of the city's population.) Westerners often confuse the two groups. Arabs are an ethnic group and Muslims are a religious group. Many Arabs are not Muslim, and most Muslims are not Arabs (Schaefer 2002: 61). Both groups have been stereotyped as different and dangerous. For more on Jews and Muslims, see chapter 12.

There has been stereotyping of Arabs and Muslims by Westerners, and simplistic views of their beliefs and behavior are widespread. Some citizens have found themselves under special surveillance due to "profiling" at airports. Fearing terrorism, some airlines have established criteria involving people's appearance or names which have caused Arab Americans to be taken aside on domestic flights (Schaefer 2002: 63).

Native Americans

No group has suffered more in U. S. history than Native Americans, inasmuch as they were stereotyped and treated very poorly by the conquering Europeans. They are the one group in America whose subordination came about wholly by conquest. Thousands died in a forced march (the famous "Trail of Tears") from the Southeast to Oklahoma in 1830. From a population of several million, they shrank to about 250,000 by 1900. But because of a high birthrate, Native Americans now number a little over two million (Henslin 2007: 288).

The isolation of about a third of Native Americans on reservations reduces their visibility and they face severe problems of low income, high unemployment, poor education, poor housing, and health concerns. Most have now moved to cities such as New York, San Francisco, Oakland, Seattle, Minneapolis, Chicago, and Los Angeles (Takiki 1993: 418).

They have recently reasserted pride in their cultural heritage. The Native American middle class is growing in cities. Many Native American tribes have built casinos and now control 20 percent of all U. S. gambling, though this has proven to be a mixed blessing (Macionis 2004: 284). There is only one Native American in the House and none in the Senate.

Immigration

Immigration has been a matter of intense debate in recent years, and undoubtedly race and ethnicity are factors in the controversy. There appears to have been a rising hostility toward foreigners in recent years. The concern is that "too many" immigrants will change the character of the United States. Proposition 187 in California, cutting social services, including schooling, to illegal immigrants, was passed in 1994. Since then, voters have mandated that all children learn English in school (Macionis 2004: 295). An attempt to overhaul the country's immigration policies in 2007 did not succeed.

Much of the vitality and energy of this society has come from immigrants anxious to work and build a better life. According to Schaefer (2002: 124), research supports the view that immigrants adapt rather well and are an asset to the economy. Immigrants generally pay more in taxes than they receive in welfare and health benefits. But it is possible that in some areas, such as California, heavy immigration may drain a community's resources, leaving the state with a large bill.

Affirmative Action

Affirmative action means programs intended to open educational and job programs to minorities. Employers and educators were instructed to carefully monitor hiring, promotion, and admissions policies to eliminate discrimination against minorities.

There has been wide support for the goals of affirmative action but disagreement about means. The courts seem to be saying that striving to achieve racial diversity is laudable, but rigid quotas are unacceptable (Henslin 2007: 292). Recent Supreme Court decisions seem to question certain affirmative action policies.

Many indirect policies tend to perpetrate nonwhite disadvantage in employment and higher education. Institutions have consistently given preference to children of alumni, veterans or athletes, and employers to those with strong recommendations from friends. And if discrimination is woven into the fabric of U. S. society, it still seems that more aggressive measures to ensure equal rights are appropriate. .

Corporations understand that recruiting more minority managers is simply good business in an increasingly diverse society as a well as a global economy. They recognize that minority groups will supply much of their labor in the future. At least 75 percent of top firms have diversity programs aimed at attracting and retaining minority workers (Marger 2000: 367. For more on affirmative action, see "Society and Government" at the end of chapter 10.)

Summary

Race and ethnic relations is a critical issue in contemporary America and even around the world. *Race* is an important concept because people attach significance to the concept and consider it an important division of humanity. There is no agreement on what traits should be used in defining race. An *ethnic group* shares a common national ancestry or a common culture. A *minority group* is singled out for unequal treatment by the dominant (majority) group, and develops its own sense of identity.

A *prejudice* is a rigid judgment about a minority group, a feeling or an attitude. Prejudices are based on *stereotypes,* exaggerated generalizations or simplistic beliefs about a group of people. *Discrimination* is a behavior that denies valued goals to other people. In its *institutionalized* form, it can become part of established practices or customary behavior.

Segregation refers to the physical or social separation of people. Its opposite is *assimilation*, the process by which distinctions between racial and ethnic groups disappears, or at least become minimal. *Pluralism* occurs when the various groups maintain a certain distinction but have social parity, as in Switzerland. This is sometimes called *multiculturalism*.

As noted earlier, racist beliefs are still firmly rooted in American thought, though in modified forms. There is ample evidence that blacks and whites, for example, do not see the same reality with regard to the current status of blacks or the nature and cause of black problems (Marger 2000: 267).

Recent history has challenged the common wisdom that laws could not change prejudice in people. Laws and court rulings that have equalized the treatment of blacks and whites have led people to reconsider their beliefs about what is right and wrong (Schaefer 2002: 63).

Research has found that intergroup contact between people of equal status in harmonious circumstances will cause them to become less prejudiced. Another key factor in reducing hostility is the presence of a common goal. Bringing people of diverse backgrounds together to share a common task has been shown to reduce ill feeling. Today, multiracial organizations continue to work at national and local levels to fight and eradicate racist beliefs and institutional racism (Eitzen and Zinn 2007: 320).

As Feagin (2001: 7) says, people are entitled to equal concern and treatment because they are human beings, not because they are members of a particular society or nation. As the world's people of color become more influential in international politics and economics, still other pressures will likely be put on the United States to treat all people of color with fairness and justice.

References

Bass, Frank, and Rukmini Callimachi. 2007. "Race Disparity seen in Katrina insurance appeals." *The Dallas Morning News* (February 1): 1A.

CBS News, May 17, 2007.

Eitzen, D. Stanley. 2007. *In Conflict and Order: Understanding Society,* eleventh edition (Boston: Allyn and Bacon).

El Nasser, Hoya. 2007. "American Muslims Reject Extremes." *USA Today* (May 22).

Feagin, Joe R. 2001. *Racist America: Roots, Current Realities, and Future Reparations* (New York: Routledge).

Henslin, James. 2007. *Sociology: A Down-to-Earth Approach, Core Concepts,* second edition (Boston: Allyn and Bacon).

Hirschman, Charles. 2004. "The Origins and Demise of the Concept of Race." *Population and Development Review,* Vol. 30: 1.

Infoplease. 2008 (November 11)

Macionis, John. 2004. *Sociology: The Basics,* seventh edition (Upper Saddle River, New Jersey: Prentice-Hall).

Marger, Martin N. 2000. *Race and Ethnic Relations, American and Global Perspectives,* fifth edition (Belmont, CA: Wadsworth).

Miller, Lisa. 2007. "American Dreamers: Islam USA." *Newsweek* (July 30): 24-33.

Schaefer, Richard T. 2002. *Racial and Ethnic Groups,* eighth edition (Upper Saddle Rivers: Prentice-Hall).

Takaki, Ronald. 1993. *A Different Mirror: A History of Multicultural America* (Boston: Little, Brown, and Co.).

Turner, Jonathan H. 2006. *Sociology* (Upper Saddle River, New Jersey: Prentice-Hall).

Wilson, William Julius. 1996. *When Work Disappears* (New York: Vintage Books).

A federal building in Dallas

Chapter 10: ECONOMICS AND POLITICS

Chapter 1 introduced the concept of institutions, structures created to meet basic human and organizational needs. Two of the most important institutions, which are related to each other, are *economics* and *politics*.

Economics is the social institution that organizes a society's production, distribution, and consumption of goods and services (Macionis 2004: 302). *Goods* are commodities ranging from necessities like food and shelter to luxury items like swimming pools. *Services* are tasks performed by people, such as the work of teachers and physicians. Economics is fundamental to civilized life, and some argue the prime mover of society.

Different methods are used to allocate goods and services. Economics involves basic human concerns: making choices, the dynamics of our transactions with others. People acting individually or collectively through government must choose which methods to use to allocate different kinds of goods and services, given that goods and services are scarce in society (Lopos et al. 2003).

The *political system* is the institution that organizes and regulates the power that is essential to realizing local, regional, or international interests. *Government* is the structure that directs people's involvement in the political and economic activities of a country or some other territory (Ferrante 2006: 386-388).

Students often consider subjects of economics and politics to be dull and unrelated to their practical lives. Yet some of the most pressing issues of the day play out through these institutions: work, unemployment, taxation, corporate monopolies, welfare, political leadership, and legislation that affect millions of people in their everyday lives.

In thinking about these institutions, some history would be instructive, looking at the development of the United States in a formative period in its history, the late nineteenth and early twentieth centuries.

Following the Civil War, the nation faced a host of problems. The war had decimated the old social and political order as well as the economic landscape, leaving much ill will behind. The economic future of the nation seemed uncertain. The nation, while largely agricultural, was becoming urban with the growth of large cities. Immigration accelerated and cities were brimming with people of diverse social and economic backgrounds.

The late nineteenth century became a period of great economic growth. Iron and steel production mushroomed. In 1865 the typical New England mill employed only 200 or 300 people. By 1915, the first Ford Motor plant employed at least 15,000. Between 1870 and 1900 the nationwide rail network grew from 53,000 to 193,000 miles. The standard of living improved substantially, as manufacturing and transportation surpassed farms in employment.

However, the wealth was not evenly spread. The gap between rich and poor and the gap between the skilled and unskilled laborers both widened. In 1896, by one estimate, 1 percent of the population owned more than half of all wealth, while the 44 percent of families at the bottom owned only 1.2 percent. This disparity raised questions about the meaning and viability of democracy.

The "Gilded Age" was the time of the concentration of wealth and the growth of large corporations. Names such as Andrew Carnegie, John D. Rockefeller, and J. P. Morgan symbolized this growth. Corporate organization decimated many occupations, such as small merchants, while creating new ones, such as the industrial worker. Between 1897 and 1904 the first great wave of corporate mergers in American history swept over Wall Street, creating many new corporations.

While the "robber barons," as the financiers were known as, acquired unprecedented wealth, most Americans had little protection against railroad exploitation, expensive credit, and price deflation. The new industrial trusts stifled competition and transformed economic power into political power. Unorganized, workers were dependent on wages set by corporate bosses. Industrial strife was marked by labor disturbances, riots, and strikes with their revelation of social injustices. In 1886 alone there were more than 1,500 labor disputes involving at least 600,000 workers. Worker safety was a major issue.

The ideology of the Gilded Age was social Darwinism, survival of the fittest with little or no interference by government. Stock manipulation, speculation, fraudulent manufacturing, and the adulteration of food, were among the practices arousing public concern. Many believed that an exaggerated individualism rode roughshod over human rights. The age boasted "self-made" economic success, by releasing the untrammeled pursuit of wealth without regard to the demands of social justice. Many worried that industrial capitalism was destroying the fabric of a democratic society (Bellah et al. 1985: 43).

The depression of 1893-1897 devastated both business and labor. In 1893 alone, more than 500 banks failed, 30 percent of the railroads were in bankruptcy, and over 15,000 businesses failed. Gold reserves fell to unacceptable levels. Social discontent rose and the mood of the country was turning ugly (Geisst 2000: 55-56). Problems of day crime, violence, disease, urban squalor, and political corruption intensified.

Urban degradation became a grave problem. Bursting cities were industrial wastelands: centers of vice, poverty, and rampant disease; full of dark, crowded slums; and corruptly administered. Child labor was common: in 1900 nearly one-fifth of children under 15 earned wages in nonagricultural work, and uncounted millions of others worked on farms. Crime surged in cities; whole neighborhoods were congested, filthy, and foul. Consumption, pneumonia, bronchitis, tuberculosis, and diarrhea were epidemic in cities.

Political organizations known as "machines" engendered some beneficial effects, especially in providing political access for urban immigrants. Still, bribery, graft, and malfeasance ruled urban politics. City machines offered patronage to the urban poor. Rake-offs and corruption were rampant, as with Boss Tweed of New York City (adapted from Putnam 2000: 359-378).

By the turn of the 20th century, a sense of crisis in the country, inspiring grassroots and national leadership, produced an extraordinary burst of social inventiveness and political reform. Most of the major community institutions in American life today were invented or refurbished in that period of civic initiative known in American history known as the Progressive movement.

Social reformers began to see society's ills as societal and economic causes, not individual moral failings. Social evils could not remedy themselves. Rugged individualism seemed increasingly unrealistic in the new, more complex and interdependent circumstances that might be called an organic conception of society.

The challenge lay in reforming our institutions and adapting old habits to secure the enduring values of our tradition. What occurred was a massive new structure of civic organizations the late 19th and early 20th centuries. An unprecedented number of associations—fraternal, religious, ethnic, labor, professional, civil, and the like, rose sharply. Social and mutual aid networks among the poor increased widely.

Religion played a substantial role in civic revitalization. A movement in the churches known as the "social gospel" sought to relate the teachings of the faith to civic, economic, and other social issues. Many ministers and other religious leaders were strongly involved in this movement.

Organized labor became a serious force in American life. From 1897 to 1904 union membership rose from 3.5 percent of the nonagricultural workforce to 12.3 percent. Women assumed new public roles, demanded the vote, got advanced education, and increasingly worked and played alongside men.

Progressives were responsible for the most thoroughgoing overhaul of public policies and institutions in American history. Playgrounds, civic museums, kindergartens, and public parks were established. Popular initiatives and referendum, presidential primary elections, the city manager system, the direct election of senators, and women's suffrage moved to the forefront of state and local politics and gradually spread nationwide.

Landmark legislation passed in this period included the Federal Reserve, the income tax, the Bureau of the Budget, consumer protection, the Federal Trade Commission, a national forest system, the national park system, the Departments of Commerce, Labor, and Agriculture, strengthening anti-trust regulations, child labor laws, an eight-hour day, workmen's compensation, regulation of the communications industry, federal campaign finance regulation, trade liberalization—hardly an area of public policy was untouched by Progressive initiatives (Putnam 2000: 382-399). (For more on 20th century, see "Society and Government" at the end of this chapter.)

Several tentative conclusions can be drawn from this history. First of all, *capitalism,* an economic system in which natural resources and the means of producing goods and services are privately owned (Macionis 2004: 306), increased economic growth, as measured by a higher gross domestic produce (GNP). But unrestrained capitalism led to significant social problems, especially maldistribution of wealth. While management at the very top will be handsomely rewarded, workers at the bottom and possibly in the middle may not be.

Second, the system of the corporation raises a set of issues different from an economy based on individual or family ownership. While a *monopoly,* the domination of a market by a single producer, is illegal (but has still occurred in our history), *oligopolies,* where a relatively few corporations produce a particular good or service and control the market, are more common. Corporations try to avoid competition by buying out their competition, or by merging, in ways that allow them to control a large segment of a market (Turner 2007: 274).

Beginning in the late 1970s, antitrust forces have been plainly less enthusiastic in pursuing alleged monopolists. Concentrations that would have been frowned on before World War II were now seen as economically healthy and as posing no threat to the political or economic order (Geisst 2000: 2).

The role of the government in the economy invites controversy. Conservatives typically press for a minimal role for the government and liberals for a more activist one.

There is general agreement, however, that the government has an important role in safeguarding its citizens, regulating business, protecting the environment, and providing for the destitute (Johnson 2006).

Socialism is an economic system in which natural resources and the means of producing goods and services are collectively owned (Macionis 2004: 306). It limits the rights to private property, especially property used to generate income. The government controls such property and makes housing and other goods available to all. The People's Republic of China and several other nations in Asia, Africa, and Latin America have socialist economies, with almost all wealth-generating property under state control. It has declined in recent years as countries in

Eastern Europe and the former Soviet Union have moved toward a market system.

While some socialist ideas motivated the Progressive reformers, they instituted relatively moderate changes in a basically capitalist system. But after the New Deal under Franklin Roosevelt, the country appeared to be headed toward what could be called *welfare capitalism.* This refers to a market-based economy that also offers broad social welfare programs. The government owns some of the largest industries and services, such as transportation, the mass media, and health care. Most industry remains in private hands but is subject to external government regulation. High taxation funds a wide range of social welfare programs (Macionis 2004: 307). The aim is to use governmental agencies to enable everyone to compete with roughly equal chances of success and to aid those who lose out.

Some nations in Western Europe, including Sweden and Italy, have a market-based economy but also offer broad social welfare programs. In the middle of the 20th century, it appeared the United States was headed in this direction, but more conservative trends in the latter part of the century have greatly slowed this movement.

A final conclusion from a review of this history regards grassroots involvement of the citizens in social networks and associations as important, if a healthy and democratic society is to endure. The Progressive movement showed that concerned citizens can clean up government and use it for positive purposes. In that period, most of the major community institutions in American life today were invented or refurbished in that period of civic innovation in American history (Putnam 2000: 368).

The earliest societies were hunters and gatherers living off the land. When people harnessed animals to plows some 5,000 years ago, agriculture began. The resulting surplus meant that not everyone had to produce food, so many people took on specialized work: making tools, raising animals, and building dwellings. Soon towns and later cities sprang up.

Industrialization, introduced in chapter 1, was the shift from human and animal power to machines. This change moved work from farms and homes to factories. People in factories turned raw materials into finished produces. Superseding artisans who made products from beginning to end, laborers repeated a single task over and over. They became wage earners who sold their labor (Macionis 2004: 302).

The Postindustrial Economy

While the Industrial Revolution made a huge change in the economy and the culture, it is giving way to what is called a *postindustrial economy*, a productive system based on service work and high technology. Automated machinery and robotics reduced the role of human labor in production, while expanding the ranks of clerical workers and managers. White-collar jobs came to outnumber blue-collar work. Service industries, such as public relations, health care, advertising, banking, and sales, employ most working people in this country (Macionis 2004: 303).

Today, computers and technologies can store, retrieve, and send information at incredible speeds. They accelerate the productivity in professional white-collar jobs.

On the Internet, one might send or receive information on an incredible variety of subject; web pages advertise places, products, and services of all kinds, and compact discs enable one to interact with what one is seeing. Some see this trend as so important they consider this an *Information Revolution*, while others see this as simply a trend in the postindustrial economy.

One development spurring economic growth has been the systematic progress of creating basic scientific knowledge and using it to advance technology. Once science became the foundation for technical change, the rate of technical change accelerated. Information production has come to play a central role in modern advanced economies because we have learned to develop ideas more productively (Johnson 2006).

There has been a huge increase in the manipulation of numbers, words, images, and other symbols. Jobs for computer programmers, technical writers, financial analysts, educators, market analysts, advertisers, and customer service representatives are growing. They utilize the skills of communication, reading, writing, and calculating (Ferrante 2006: 373). (See chapter 13.)

Different Approaches in Economics

The field known as classical or orthodox economics is attributed to Adam Smith and was articulated by the late Nobel-prize winning economist, Milton Friedman. It starts with the individual and his or her choices in a free market. Consumption is assumed to be the end of all economic activity, with production simply a means to that end. Competition will ensure that private interests ultimately serve the public interest. Friedman saw profit maximization as the proper goal of the business firm. However, he did not favor the unbridled pursuit of self-interest by any means possible, such as polluting the environment and defrauding investors (Champli and Knoedler 2004).

Looking at U. S. history of a hundred years ago shows that capitalism has the advantage of producing strong economic growth and raising the standard of living of the country as a whole. Except for some periods of depression (as in the 1930s) and recession, most of the nation's history has experienced improved economic growth, even though the distribution of wealth might not be what most of us would desire.

Classical economic thought sees economic activity as subject to its own inbuilt constraints, and these, by implication, neutralize political power. If the economy worked automatically and well, there was no cause for intrusion by the state (Galbraith 1994: 43).

Many economists acknowledge the problems with an unbridled capitalism, but believe that a market economy, properly understood, offers safeguards against the excesses. When corporations work together to produce an oligopoly, the free market is negated. When we have clear violations of the law occur, as in the Enron and WorldCom cases, the free market is not failing. Classical economy stresses competition, and a free market emerges from real competition. These economists believe that a market economy, which increases economic growth, in cooperation with a limited government, is the most promising course to follow.

In the case of monopoly, the state must limit its power—either dissolve or regulate it. The classical system not only allowed state intervention to this end but in a very real sense demanded it (Galbraith 1994: 47). A free market relies upon a watchful government to keep big business in check (Geisst 2000: 320).

A modified approach would recognize more important functions for government. Government has a role in providing for an infrastructure, such as transportation systems, that make modern business possible. It can establish and enforce rules against unfair and illegal acts. It properly invests in the research and development that is not profitable for the market-oriented business firm (Galbraith 1994: 199). It also can ensure that certain public needs, such as education, are taken care of.

Other writers take a more critical view. John M. Clark claimed that orthodox economics produced an "economics of irresponsibility." It led to an excessive individualism and a denial of responsibility for the public interest. Instead, we need an "economics of responsibility" in which business recognizes and accepts its responsibility for the public interest and in which society as a whole works toward that end. A greater social control of business serves the broader interests of the community rather than the narrower private interests of individual businesses or persons (Champli and Knoedler 2004).

Relying on the market to eliminate anti-social behavior is not effective, but to rely on the government to curb business excesses may not work either, because where government and business become business partners, the public interest ceases to be a primary concern of either business or government. Needed is a mobilization of public opinion to establish norms of behavior for both business and government (Champli and Knoedler 2004).

Nobel-prize winning economist Joseph Stiglitz recommends a balance between the government and the market. Government plays an important yet limited role not only in correcting failures and limitations of the market, but also in working towards greater social justice. Markets, he argues, do not always work well by themselves and do not solve all problems. At the heart of every successful economy is the market, but successful market economics requires a balance between the government and the market (Stiglitz 2003: xi, 283).

Markets, claims Stiglitz, produce too much harm, like air pollution, and not enough of good, like investments in education, health, and knowledge, and they fail in self-regulation. Unemployment and other social and economic costs often increased. The United States was experiencing a slow economy in early 2008, as people were spending less and states were struggling. As many as 18 states have deficits, totaling

$14 billion in the current budget, and 20 states forecast spending shortfalls for 2009 (Welsh-Huggins 2008).

Government regulation, if used sparingly and with care, often plays an important role in making markets work better, in limiting the scope, for instance, of the conflicts of interest that repeatedly appeared in accounting, business, and finance (Stiglitz 2003: 12, 15). Regulation can help ensure that markets work competitively. The Savings and Loan debacle of the 1980s illustrates the high costs to the public of failing to regulate.

In the late 20th century, some of our investments went into wasteful private expenditures, such as the dot-coms and fiber optic cables that were not needed. Too little investment went to address vital public needs, in education, in infrastructure, and in basic research. Eventually, underinvestment in the public sector will hurt returns to investment in the private. (Stiglitz 2003: 18, 53).

A rather recent, minority movement in this field is known as "social economics," which is more focused upon the wholeness of social life, of the good and just society, than simply material progress and economic growth. The quality of work, the values of community, solidarity, justice and beauty should count most.

This school of thought quotes Adam Smith, "No society can surely be flourishing and happy, of which the far greater part of the members are poor and miserable." Higher per capita income does not necessarily promote overall happiness. According to this view, capitalism has eroded many of the traditional community structures that enabled active and spontaneous social relationships.

It is not only materialistic values that we need, but self-actualization, belonging and esteem, as well as intellectual and aesthetic values. A less impersonal society invites more say in job and community, more say in government, more free speech, beautiful cities and nature. Institutions should channel human energies into those activities that best achieve desirable social goals (Wisman 2003).

Trends

New information technology is drawing the nations of the world closer together, creating a *global economy*, the expanding of economic activity with little regard for national borders. Different regions of the world are specializing in one or another sector of economic activity. The poorer countries are likely to specialize in agriculture, while the high-income countries in the service sector (Macionis 2004: 304).

A small number of corporations, operating internationally, now control a vast share of the world's economic activity. In the major industrial sectors, relatively few corporations control the market. On one estimate, the 600 largest multinational companies account for half the world's entire economic output (Macionis 2004: 304). Giant corporations composed of many smaller corporations are known as *conglomerates*.

Globalization will continue. The service sector will continue to accelerate, as goods and commodities move outside a country's borders in search of the lowest-priced labor. Mass marketing and retailing will continue driving small businesses into insolvency, but create niches for businesses that can meet people's needs for unique goods and services. Global corporations will continue to operate globally and will increasingly be out of the reach of governmental control and regulation in their home nation. (See chapter 13.)

National governments no longer control the economic activity that takes place within their borders. Money can now move in seconds in financial markets around the world. Vast quantities of goods are shipped in containers and offloaded by machines in hours instead of days. People fly about the globe in hours rather than months, selling, buying, and trading goods and services.

Labor and capital will continue to move about the world rapidly. The labor force is increasingly split between the better-educated, higher-skilled, and better-paid sector, on the one side, and the less-educated, poorly-paid blue-collar work on the other, with more inequality. This will put pressures on corporations and governments to find new, world-level forms of economic governance of markets and corporations (Turner 2007: 271-273).

As the recession of 2008 deepened, the sagging economy faced a real crisis, especially in the area of housing and finance. Close to two million jobs were lost in 2008. The government finally acted, and (after one failed attempt) proposed a bailout of the financial industry in the amount of $700 billion, passed and signed into law October 3. Some saw this as a necessary correction to restore confidence in the nation's markets, while others viewed it as a giveaway to Wall Street interests.

President Bush agreed to a loan package for the troubled American auto makers in December. Congress passed a major stimulus package in February 2009.

As fewer workers are needed in factories, blue-collar work declines. Robots are replacing hands on assembly lines. Factory work is often exported to poor nations. As a consequence, there are not enough jobs for all who need them.

Taken together, small firms control roughly half of the assets in the U. S. economy. They are the major source of employment and the creation of new jobs, and they make up between a third and a half of all U. S. companies. Small firms can innovate more quickly and less expensively (Harper and Leicht 2007: 106).

The government becomes a larger employer, as growth makes it is necessary to coordinate and control activities in a complex society through police, laws, courts, and regulatory agencies, and to build and staff public school systems. More administrators and support personnel will be needed (Turner 2007: 209). Because the need for government services is constantly expanding, a significant portion of the workforce is involved in providing government services.

Credit has eased its way into market transactions, allowing people to buy when they do not have all the money (or, in some cases, none of it). Today the credit card, or "plastic," drives the economy as people mortgage their future earnings by buying on credit. Unfortunately, many find themselves in excessive debt with high interest rates. Demand in the marketplace is manipulated by advertising so that people's needs for goods never wane. New appetites translate into demands (Turner 2007: 270).

A *profession* is a prestigious, white-collar occupation that requires extensive formal education and credentials to perform certain kinds of work. Members agree to abide by certain principles. They have certain theoretical knowledge, are usually self-employed, follow a code of ethics, advise clients, and serve the community instead of merely seeking income (Macionis 2004: 310).

However, professional work is increasingly bureaucratized in larger corporations. For example, Health Maintenance Organizations (HMOs) have changed the way hospitals and doctors work. When an HMO owns a hospital, it operates as a business, assessing care against cost. They provide only so much money for a procedure, forcing compromise in health care. Accounting scandals are the result of big accounting firms compromising professionalism in the name of profits (Turner 2006: 275-276).

Self-employment is on the increase: this refers to people who do not work for an organization. It could be professionals like lawyers and physicians, but most self-employed are small business owners, farmers, plumbers, carpenters, many writers, artists, and long-distance truck drivers. The majority are in blue-collar occupations (Macionis 2004: 311).

Factories and increasingly places where modules made in other factories are put together into a final product. There is still a need for manual labor not only in factories but in janitorial work, taking orders, cooking hamburgers, and the like. Much of manual work, however, now pays very little, with increasing inequality for those who get stuck in such types of work (Turner 2007: 270).

Much service work, including sales, clerical, and work in hospitals and restaurants, yields little of the income and prestige of white-collar professions, and offers fewer financial rewards than factory work. Hence many jobs provide only a modest standard of living, and these jobs are disproportionately held by women and minorities (Macionis 2004: 309). (See chapter 8.)

Labor unions, organizations that seek to improve wages and working conditions of workers, have declined over the years. In 1950, over one-third of nonfarm workers were unionized, and almost 25 million workers were in unions by 1970. Today the figure is about 16 million men and women, or about 13 percent of nonfarm workers. About 37 percent of government workers are unionized, but just 9 percent of workers in the private sector (Ferrante 2006: 383).

Because many corporations are trying to unburden themselves from the costs of health care and retirement for their workers, workers are now assuming greater risks for their future retirement and health care. These issues will be major concerns in the future (Turner 2007: 275-276).

The gap between white-collar workers and blue-collar workers is likely to grow. This is due to the relatively low level of taxes on corporations and individuals, the decline in union membership, the exporting of jobs, and a general lack of sympathy for the poor in our society (Macionis 2004: 311).

Every society has some unemployment, but it is a real issue in the United States. The official figure, about 6.5 percent in 2008, is somewhat misleading. It is much higher in West Virginia and certain other states, and is extremely high among young blacks in the inner city. The figures do not count those who have given up and are no longer looking, nor do they count part-time workers who would like a full-time job. The economy itself is largely the reason: jobs disappear as occupations become obsolete, businesses close, and companies downsize to become more profitable.

There will be a big increase in blacks and Hispanics in the workplace over the next several years. This should create an incentive for companies to welcome social diversity. Only about 4 percent of Fortune 500 top executives are women, and just 1 percent are minority women. There will be pressure to provide more child care in the workplace (Macionis 2004: 312).

Politics

This chapter began by defining the *political system* and *government*. Some students tend to view government in an abstract way, doubting it has much influence in their lives. In actuality, the government can grant a building permit, license an occupation, determine how many fish someone can catch, how many pets one can have, and can take children into custody. Government regulates and stabilizes the economy and provides social programs (Harper and Leicht 2007: 111).

Power is the ability to achieve one's will even against opposition. *Authority* is legitimate power considered just and proper. Society believes leaders are entitled to give orders (Ferrante 2006: 386-387).

Democracy is a system of government that vests power in the people and gives citizens a voice directly or indirectly in the decision-making process. Power is given to the people as a whole (Macionis 2004: 317). The authority is in the hands of leaders who compete for office in elections.

According to Charon, democracy is difficult to achieve: it allows for dissent as well as majority rule, and fed as much by civic action as by voting. No society is perfectly democratic, but certain social conditions make it possible, and certain patterns support it.

Under a true democracy, the individual is free in thinking and action. Political and economic power is limited by people throughout society; the government and large economic social organizations are effectively regulated. Human differences are respected and protected; diversity is respected and even encouraged. The people have equal opportunities to make decent lives, with equality before the law and in educational opportunity, and the chance for material success (Charon 2007: 310-311).

All societies have to work out a balance between order and freedom. Durkheim pointed out that there can be no freedom without society, for a basic agreement over rules must precede the exercise of freedom. Bellah and colleagues (1985: 256) believe that the tension between competitive private enterprises and the public good has been the most important unresolved problem in American history.

Social inequality, discussed in chapter 8, is of primary importance to understand the possibility for a democratic society. There are many forces that create inequality. If large numbers of people must expend all of their energy to barely survive because of their poverty, where is their freedom, their right to improve their lives?

A democratic society requires not only limited government but also limitations on the military, the upper class, the corporations, and narrow interest groups. Limited government brings freedom to the individual, but also unlimited power for economic elites in society, which then threatens or diminishes individual freedom (Charon 2007: 315).

Authoritarianism is a political system that denies popular participation in government. It is usually indifferent to people's needs and offers them no voice in selecting leaders. A person or group (such as a party or the military) holds all power (Macionis 2004: 319). *Totalitarianism* is a similar system with centralized political power, generally a party that regulates people's lives. There is an official ideology which is professes to hold. It operates in an atmosphere of isolation and fear.

America's civic life has weakened in recent years, and our society has focused more on the individual than the community. There has been a loss of what Putnam calls "social capital," networks such as extended family, friends, clubs, associations, and group ties of all sorts (Putnam 2000).

Fewer voters show up at the polls in America than in most other democracies. Our turnout rate ranks us just above the cellar (though it was up in 2008). Participation in presidential elections and in off-year elections has declined by roughly one fourth over the last 50 years. Men and women vote at about the same rate, but people over 65 are at least three times as likely to vote as college-age adults. Whites vote slightly more than blacks, and both significantly more than Hispanics. Generally speaking, people with a bigger stake in the society, homeowners, people with good education and good jobs, are more likely to vote (Macionis 2004: 323). An encouraging sign is the registration of new voters in the primaries of 2008.

The last several decades have witnessed a serious deterioration of community involvement among Americans from all walks of life. Fewer Americans follow public affairs. Fewer are working for a political party. There has been a decline in membership in unions, church groups, fraternal and veterans' organizations, civic groups, and charities.

There are two competing views about political power in America. *Pluralists* believe that power is dispersed rather than concentrated. Different groups have different goals. Such interests as labor, oil, coal, steel, automobile manufacturers, environmentalists, groups such as the American Medical Association and the National Rifle Association, organize to bring pressure on the president and Congress on issues that affect them. Diversified interest groups are meant to check and balance each other in influencing political decisions (Turner 2006: 291).

Politics is an arena of negotiation. Organizations operate as veto groups, realizing some of their objectives while keeping opponents from achieving their ends. The political process relies heavily on forging alliances and compromises between numerous interest groups. According to this view, all people have at least some voice (Macionis 2004: 323). More conservative social scientists tend to support this model.

The alternative view is the *power elite* model, which sees power as concentrated among a relatively few people at the top. A small number of people in lofty positions of leading institutions make decisions that have consequences affecting millions of people. To put it somewhat bluntly, power is concentrated among the rich.

C. Wright Mills argued that there is a power elite in three major sectors of the United States: the economy, the government, and the military. Corporate executives and their major stockholders, the top officials in Washington, and the highest-ranking officers in the U. S. military comprise this elite (Macionis 2004: 324).

A majority of national political leaders enter government from top corporate positions, and most return to the corporate world later on. According to this view, the concentration of wealth and power is too great for the average person's voice to be heard.

Studies in New Haven, Connecticut, tended to support the pluralist model. A major study in Atlanta tended to support a power elite position. In any case, the U. S. political system is far less democratic than most people think. The major political parties typically support only positions acceptable to the most powerful segments of society (Macionis 2004: 325).

A political elite decided that a permanent war industry was needed to contain the spread of communism. Those involved in this industry became deeply and intricately interrelated in hundreds of ways, resulting in a triangle of power. The social, economic, and political lives of the elites are interwoven (Turner 2006: 291).

In addition to those at the very top, there are other interest organizations that exert political influence: some unions, professional groups like teacher associations and lawyers, those in academia, environmental groups, government employees, gun owners, and others who are not elites. Many political decisions are not highly relevant to elites, and here is pluralism in action.

Towards a More Democratic Society

Thoughtful observers argue that the country needs a renewed set of institutions and channels for a reinvigorated civic life that will fit the way our people have come to live. Perhaps we should reinvent the 21st century equivalent of the Boy Scouts or settlement houses or United Mine Workers or the NAACP. Like those in the Progressive Era, our generation needs to create new structures and policies, public and private, to facilitate renewed civic engagement (Putnam 2000: 401).

As Putnam says, we need many more Americans to participate in the public life of our communities—running for office, attending public meetings, serving on committees, campaigning in elections, and even voting, if America is to stay democratic. Voluntary associations are the buffer between the individual and government, acting as essential watchdogs and advisors to community-guaranteed services.

Campaign reform, and campaign finance reform, should be aimed at increasing the importance of social capital, and decreasing the importance of financial capital, in our elections, federal, state, and local. A person without huge resources can have no hope of running for national office in this country.

The country is better off when citizens pay the taxes they owe. The legitimacy of the tax system turns in part on the belief that citizens do their share. My willingness to pay my share depends crucially on my perception that others are doing the same. In a community rich in social capital, government is "we," not "they."

Liberals should be ready to transfer government authority downward as compassionate conservatives should be ready to transfer resources from have to have-not communities. Decentralization of government resources and authority to neighborhood councils has worked in such cities as Minneapolis, Portland, and Seattle (Putnam 2000: 413).

It is a false debate whether government is the problem or the solution. It can be both. Many of the most creative investments in social capital in American history—from county agents and the 4-H to community colleges and the March of Dimes—were the direct result of government policy. While government is not our sole salvation, it is hard to imagine that we can meet the challenges for America today without using government.

This became more obvious at the end of 2008. (See article by Frank Mensel at the end of this chapter.)

As Bellah and his colleagues (1985: 211) point out, we must strengthen all those associations and movements through which citizens influence and moderate the power of the government, revitalizing politics. We cannot simply write off "big government" as the enemy. We need to bring a sense of citizenship into the operation of government itself. We need to increase the prestige of government, not derogate it

In the United States, the election of Senator Barack Obama as president in November of 2008 signaled a significant change for a country that had become dissatisfied with the direction the nation was moving. While opinions differed as to the approach he would take in office, many hoped that his administration would move towards a more democratic country and towards more collaboration with other countries on the world scene.

The best alternative may be a government-business-labor coordination in a free economy. This calls for a restoration of the spirit in which the republic was founded, the spirit of commonwealth, of the public good, of the public welfare. The tradition that the late historian Arthur M. Schlesinger calls "affirmative government" is quite as authentically American, quite as expressive of American ideas and character, as the competing tradition of self-interest and scrambling private enterprise (Schlesinger 1986: 254-255).

Schlesinger believed the nation went through cyclical patterns every 30 years or so, reflecting an inevitable tension between unfettered capitalism and democracy (Schlesinger 1986). The Progressive movement in the early 20th century was largely replaced by a conservative movement, followed by an activist movement of the 1960s and later, than conservatism in the latter part of the century. Schlesinger suggests it may be time for another progressive movement to take hold.

Summary

Economics is a social institution that organizes a society's production, distribution, and consumption of goods and services. Different methods are used to allocate these goods and services.

The political system organizes and regulates the use of an access to power. *Government* is the structure that coordinates people's involvement in political and economic activities.

A review of American history in the late 19th and early 20th centuries shows that this was a time of great economic growth but maldistribution of wealth. Corporations grew in size while the plight of workers worsened. Urban degradation and child labor were other problems. The Progressive movement helped address these problems through a more effective government, landmark legislation, and organized labor.

Capitalism, a system where goods and services are privately owned, tends to increase economic growth but can lead to social problems. Monopolies and particularly *oligopolies*, a domination of a few corporations, represent concerns. The government can have an important role, as can the involvement of citizens.

The *post-industrial society* is based on service work and high technology. An increase in computers and technology led to the Information Revolution.

Classical economics stressed consumption and inbuilt constraints. Various views of the role of capitalists and the government are discussed. The role of public opinion is important, as is a balance between government and markets.

Globalization, interdependence among businesses and countries, discussed in chapter 13, is likely to continue and accelerate.

A *profession* is a white-collar occupation requiring formal education and specific credentials. Self-employment is on the increase and unemployment remains a concern.

A *democracy* vests power in the people and gives citizens a voice. There is always a need to balance order and freedom. In the United States, participation in civic life has been weakened.

Pluralists believe that power is dispersed among several competing groups. A *power elite* model believes that power is concentrated among a few at the top, such as the government, corporate world, and the military. In any case, the society is less democratic than most people think. What may be needed is a government-business-labor coordination in a free economy.

SOCIETY AND GOVERNMENT: THE AMERICAN CENTURY

By Frank Mensel

Government and society. Society and government. Each has a deep and persistent influence on the other in every nation, and on its culture. Their interaction was amply illustrated among nations in the 20th century. In few, if any, was it more freely at play than in the United States, which rose in less than three generations from a frontier culture in which, irrespective of the Constitution's 14th Amendment promise of equal protection, women were denied the vote to the top of the industrial world, its expansion propelled substantially by arms production for two World War wars, and by women, finally empowered to vote, assuming a steadily growing role in the workplaces outside the home.

The elixir fueling the interaction of society and government is politics. History suggests that their intervention is more persistent, more pronounced, and more progressive in democracies than in nations ruled by force, with notable exceptions wrought by extreme force, civil war or revolution. Imperial dynasties and dictatorships typically resist social progress because their rulers fear losing control. Their rule of force is ordinarily threatened by change. They typically form lines of succession, usually within a family tree, to mitigate the potential threat that accompanies installation of the next ruler. They rely on large and highly visible armies to perpetuate their power, which ironically puts them at risk of a military coup.

Various imperial dynasties and dictatorships were ousted by military coups or revolution during the 20th century, replacing one form of rule by force with another. Among the examples, the Russian Revolution had perhaps the most sweeping impact on the 20th century. Centuries of serfdom and imperial plundering by the dynastic line of tsars came to a bloody end at the hands of the Bolsheviks. In the name of communism, the royal lineage was replaced by the new line of one-party tyrants who gained and tightened much of their power by ruthless genocide, burying countrymen in numbers that became the most extreme of the century. In human terms, the serfdom that had pervaded Russia changed merely in degree, form, and hands, which were taken by a government that called itself the Union of Soviet Socialist Republics. It gathered disparate peoples in an iron grip over an unequaled land mass.

Closer to home is the rule by force of Cuba for half a century by the communist government of Fidel Castro, who handed the levers of power to his brother Roall. The world will be watching closely as to how this example of a change of rulers within the family pans out and what its impact will be on Cuban society.

Two Wars

More towering still to the century as a whole were the two World Wars. Each produced sweeping changes to the world and its cultures from economics to railroads, from deadlier armaments to education and the arts. Each ironically spurred bold advances in medicine, science and technology. World War I was the first to test aircraft in battle, bringing the Air Age into bloom first in domestic and soon thereafter in international transportation, with profound consequences for both society and government. World War I also opened the eyes and conscience of the world to the black abyss of chemical warfare, prompting nations to adopt an international convention against it.

It was World War II that produced the most dramatic changes in United States society and culture, catapulting the nation from the Great Depression to preeminence in almost every field of human endeavor, from economics and finance to education and research that provided cures to such global scourges as polio, tuberculosis, and venereal diseases. At the war's end, the military, long segregated by racial lines, was declared wholly integrated by the stroke of President Truman's pen.

The combination of the Great Depression and World War II in particular accelerated what could easily have been the century's most profound change in American society as a whole: the evolving role of women. Gathering steam for half a century, the drive in which the suffragettes secured the vote for women, by the 21st Amendment to the Constitution, meant, as many a male chauvinist predicted, "life would never be the same." As the stock market crash of 1929 triggered job losses for legions of men, women began mixing homemaking and employment in larger numbers, typically as office or sales clerks or housekeepers. (See chapter 13.)

The war accelerated this gender upheaval. As millions of men were drafted or volunteered for military service, their places at work had to be filled with women (child labor was not about to be revived). Women were enlisted for jobs they had never tried before: Rosie the Riveter became the gender's poster face for the war effort. If there was a pause in this upheaval after the war, it was short-lived. The appetite of women for the financial independence that came with jobs outside the home continued to grow, as did their desire for the higher education that could lead to better jobs: so much so that by the end of the century women were outnumbering men in earning college degrees. Women were being leveraged in this pursuit by government, through such programs as Pell Grants, Work-Study, college loans, and employee educational assistance. Still, ironically, by the end of the century men continued to draw higher pay than men for like jobs, though the gap is narrowing.

Rails and Cars

The interplay of society and government was clearly at work in various landmark turns of the century. Before 1900, competing railroads, whose development had been spurred by generous grants of federal land, had completed a national transportation system that paved the way for the rapid transformation of an agrarian economy into a manufacturing one, with the attendant concentrations of labor in emerging urban centers. The continent had been spanned by connections among such prospering carriers as the Pennsylvania Railroad, the Baltimore and Ohio, the New York Central, the Union Pacific, the Santa Fe, and the Burlington. Regional lines made possible the hourly movement of foodstuffs and people in and out of the cities. Bedroom communities, later more popularly known as the suburbs, formed rings around the larger cities, with breadwinners commuting to and from the city by rail.

At nearly the same time, the automobile was emerging as an invention of vast economic and social consequences that grew inexorably throughout the century. In fact, in the prosperity that followed World War II, automobiles soon became the standard by which most Americans gauged their quality of life. President Eisenhower put the government behind the plan that would crisscross the nation with an interstate system of limited access highways that in one way or another changed almost every American's way of life. The immediate postwar slogan of "a chicken in every pot, a car in every garage" was short-lived because families had little trouble convincing themselves that two or more cars were a necessity. That demand fed a proliferation of paved roads and highways, funded mainly by the collaboration of local, state and federal government, whose maintenance looms as one of the larger infrastructure challenges of the 21st century.

Acts of Change

The myriad legislative acts on which federal, state and local governments are built, and affirmed as rule of law by the courts, come largely from the interplay of society and government. The people and the leaders of the 13 founding states, uncomfortable with leaving the States largely responsible for their separate destinies, convened the Constitutional Convention in Philadelphia, at which General Washington presided and his fellow Virginian, James Madison, supplied the working draft of the eventual Constitution. Even upon initial adoption, it faced immediate change with the addition of the Bill of

Rights. Though somewhat varied in form, state and local governments are largely patterned after the federal model and strive for similar balance, knowing that as they go about their business, they too must ultimately conform to the Constitution as interpreted by the courts.

FDR

The misgivings of traditional conservatives notwithstanding, the presidency of Franklin Delano Roosevelt became the 20th century model of activist government. He saw his office as a partnership with society that he would use to blunt the Great Depression through public works that expanded public payrolls. Jobless Americans, then constituting roughly a fourth of the potential labor force, lined up in droves for the federally subsidized work of building livable communities: more airports, dams and other waterway improvements, new municipal water and sewer systems, better hospitals, more libraries. The Civilian Conservation Corps, like the Army, clothed and fed its young enlistees on modest wages to build parks and mountain trails, among other recreational works. His grand plan took the name New Deal, and the press popularized him by his initials, FDR.

FDR changed the United States—its government, its economy, its way of life—more than any other leader of the 20th century. His election to four terms validated the voters' fondness for his idea of society and government's interacting as partners. That partnership primed the nation's unprecedented surge of industrial output that armed and propelled the Allies' victory over the ruthless Axis' powers, whose atrocities would haunt survivors and free people for generations. Remnants of the New Deal remained the underpinning of interaction between society and government for the remainder of the century.

The GI Bill

Short of formal acts of war, the legislation implemented in the first GI Bill of Rights seems unrivaled in the sweep of its impact on American society. Led by the waves of returning veterans, the doors of higher education were opened almost overnight to virtually everyone with a high school diploma who chose to enroll. The intention of the bill's framers in Washington was chiefly concerned that legions of veterans leaving the services would swamp the job markets, possibly reviving the Depression. Better to divert many of them into college, at least for the short term.

The results, however, soon astounded the nation. Before World War II, college attendance came more from privilege than choice. Unless high school graduates were fortunate to reside near a college, they were unlikely to leave home for college unless their family could cover most or all of the costs, and that was no small challenge even to more affluent families in the Depression.

The GI Bill literally rewrote both student and institutional expectations. As veterans flooded the colleges, President Truman became concerned that distance from campus would keep many veterans from using this benefit, so he convened the Truman Commission on Higher Education to explore options for broadening access. The president wanted the college experience to become no more than an hour's commute for every potential student. From the Commission's 1947 report, the nation began to embrace a new phase in higher learning—the community college, which before the end of the century would become the largest sector of undergraduate enrollment.

Academy Reborn

The waves of returning GIs inevitably affected the whole academic landscape. Older, highly motivated students who had not dreamed of college before the war were using college as "catch up" for their years in military service. They were not only knocking down bachelor's degrees but also competing successfully in graduate schools, and becoming doctors, engineers, lawyers and educators. The institutions used liberal tuition increases made possible by GI Bill income to fund the new faculty, staff and facilities necessitated by rising enrollment. The federal dollars flowing into campus coffers sweetened both campus pay and the competition for better faculty, as they also opened new vistas in graduate study and research. The example of GIs competing successfully in college prompted younger siblings to think college was their right too. The elite colleges and universities were becoming more selective, favoring better prepared students as much as the offspring of alumni, in the new streams of applicants.

The impact rippled positively into the public schools too. Before WWII, elementary schools were liberally staffed with classroom teachers holding only two-year degrees, from the so-called normal colleges. The late Professor Ted Bell, who served President Reagan as Secretary of Education, started his career as a graduate of the then two-year College of Southern Idaho at Albion. After the war, the bachelor's degree quickly emerged as the standard of K-12 teaching, with many veterans earning four-year degrees to become teachers.

Among the ripple effects, the GI Bill contributed heavily to the emergence of American universities as "graduate school to the world." Paradoxically, the first generation schooled on the GI Bill produced in turn a new generation of "privilege," many of whom by ability or family advantage or both succeeded their parents in the front ranks of business, government, the professions, and the military.

Affirmative Action

President Truman's postwar order erasing the color line in the military did possibly as much as Jackie Robinson's sea-change conquest of major-league baseball to spur integration in college athletics. By the early 1950s, southern universities were as busy as their northern rivals in blending black recruits into basketball and football teams. (Unfortunately, no data was kept on the number of minority "walk-ons" who were able to make varsity teams because they had enrolled on the GI Bill.) As the controversy and court jousting over affirmative action favoring minority applicants in college admissions has simmered on into the 21st century, the recruitment and success of black athletes in intercollegiate competition has proven an undeniable force in affirmative action and integration, and an ironic contradiction of historic proportions to both higher education and society.

The education components of President Lyndon Johnson's Great Society agenda also drew impetus from the GI Bill. The president knew that the leveling up of opportunity promised by the Civil Rights Act of 1964, which he had spearheaded, would sputter without better schools. The Elementary-Secondary Education Act (ESEA) and the Higher Education Act (HEA) of 1965 opened a larger partnership between the federal government and the States in education.

The Pell Grant

Chiefly through the leadership of Rep. Edith Green, the Oregon Democrat who chaired the postsecondary subcommittee in the House, the HEA initiated direct federal Educational Opportunity Grants (EOG) to better students with financial need. In the 1972 amendments to the HEA, Sen. Claiborne Pell, the Rhode Island Democrat who chaired the Senate's education subcommittee, was driven by the belief that universal access to education through the 14th year was vital to the nation's economic future. He prevailed in a two-year campaign to turn the EOG into the Basic Educational Opportunity Grant (BEOGG), thus making the direct grants potentially available to all students who could benefit from college courses.

Quickly the Pell Grant grew into the most popular federal program in the history of postsecondary education, carrying strong bipartisan support through successive Congresses. To the pleasure of both public and private colleges, Pell Grants were a spur to both enrollment and diversity. Before the end of the century, a far larger number of students had earned college credits and degrees on Pell Grants, many leveraging their job skills in the process, than had gone to college on the four successive GI Bills. (The GI Bill was strengthened in 2008.)

Unquestionably, the Pell Grant has played an important role also in broadening affirmative action, as has another historic act of the last generation—Section 127 of the federal tax code, which allows employers to pay for college courses to upgrade employee job skills, without that benefit becoming taxable income. Pell Grants and the employee educational assistance (EEA) alike have leveraged upward mobility for women and minorities in their pursuit of degrees and better jobs. Research is needed to more fully document the impact of both on society.

Summing Up

Government plays an indispensable role in the quality of American life, from city hall and the county courthouses to the state capitols and the myriad federal agencies. The lifestyles that characterize cities and suburbs could not have developed, nor be sustained, without the diversified tax base that builds water and sewer systems, schools and hospitals, roads and highways, airports and parks.

Universal access to publicly supported education through high school, augmented by broadly based access to college and lifelong learning, including the popular tax-free Employee Educational Assistance (EEA) that the federal code allows employers to provide their personnel for job-related training, has long been considered essential to national progress. Ironically, global economic competition today is raising concern about whether the nation is pushing schools and colleges hard enough to endure that the U. S. workforce is more than equal to advancing international standards. The answer may lie in heightened collaboration of society, the private sector, and government.

References

Bellah, Robert N., Richard Madsen, William M. Sullivan, Ann Swidler, and Steven M. Tipton. 1985. *Habits of the Heart: Individualism and Commitment in American Life* (New York: Harper and Row).

Champli, Del P., and Janet T. Knoedler. 2004. "J. M. Clark and the Economics of Prosperity." *Journal of Economic Issues,* Vol. 38.

Charon, Joel M. 2007. *Ten Questions: A Sociological Perspective,* sixth edition (Belmont, CA: Thomson Wadsworth).

Ferrante, Joan. 2006. *Sociology: A Global Perspective,* sixth edition (Belmont, CA: Thomson Wadsworth).

Galbraith, John Kenneth. 1994. *A Journey Through Economic Time: A Firsthand View* (New York: Houghton Mifflin).

Geisst, Charles. 2000. *Monopolies in America: Empire Builders and Their Enemies from Jay Gould to Bill Gates* (New York: Oxford University Press).

Harper, Charles L., and Kevin T. Leicht. 2007. **Exploring Social Change: America and the World**, fifth edition (Upper Saddle River, New Jersey: Pearson).

Johnson, William R. 2006. "The Economics of Ideas and the Ideas of Economists." *Southern Economics Journal,* Vol. 73.

Lopos, Jane S., John S. Morton, Robert Reinke, Mark C. Schug, Donald R. Wentworth, Richard D. Western. 2003. "Is Economics Your Worst Nightmare?" *Social Education,* Vol. 67.

Macionis, John J. 2004. *Society: The Basics,* seventh edition (Upper Saddle River, New Jersey: Prentice-Hall).

Putnam, Robert D. 2000. *Bowling Alone: The Collapse and Revival of American Community* (New York: Simon & Schuster).

Schlesinger, Arthur M., Jr. 1986. *The Cycles of American History* (Boston: Houghton Mifflin).

Stiglitz, Joseph E. 2003. *The Roaring Nineties: A New History of the World's Most Prosperous Decade* (New York: W. W. Norton).

Turner, Jonathan H. 2006. *Sociology* (Upper Saddle River, New Jersey: Prentice-Hall).

Welsh-Huggins, Andrew. 2008 (Associated Press, February 24).

Wisman, Jon D. 2003. "The Scope and Promising Future of Social Economics." *Review of Social Economy,* Vol. 61.

A family in front of Christmas tree, Dallas.

Chapter 11: FAMILY

Every known society in history has had some form of family, though the term is difficult to define precisely. *Family* can be understood as a group or social network whose members are linked by blood, marriage, or adoption (Ferrante 2006: 408). A broader definition, which not all would accept, is "everyone who lives under one roof and expresses love and solidarity." A legal definition is "people whose living arrangement is recognized under the law as constituting a family."

The *extended* family, more common in earlier periods, is a family unit that includes parents and children as well as other kin (Henslin 2004: 337). Extended families are widespread in most regions of the world outside of Europe, North America, and Oceania (Therborn 2004: 107). Industrialization, increased social mobility, and migration gave rise to the *nuclear* family, a family unit composed of one or two parents and their children. Although many members of our society live in extended families, the nuclear family is most common in the United States.

There have been numerous changes in family life since World War II. At any given time, only 30 percent of U. S. households fit the description of a working husband, homemaker wife, and their young children (Macionis 2004: 336). High divorce and remarriage rates have made stepparents more important in family life than they were in the past. In the United States, there are at least 11 million families in which at least one spouse was married before. Family violence, including spouse and child abuse, has received increased attention. The increasing numbers of working women and a shift in gender roles have changed the family in significant ways (see chapter 13).

A Functionalist View of the Family

Functionalists ask the questions of what need or vital tasks a social structure (such as family) meets. The major functions a family fulfills include the regulation of sexual behavior, replacing the members of a society, socializing the young, providing care and emotional support, and the conferring of social status (Ferrante 2006: 410-411).

While norms relating to sexual practice vary enormously around the world, every society regulates sexual behavior in some way. The *incest taboo* is a norm forbidding sexual relations or marriage between certain relatives, and is found everywhere in the world. While many taboos about sex have disappeared, the new openness has not taken away longings for deep, lasting, and exclusive emotional bonding (Therborn 2004: 314). If a society does not replace its members, by natural means or immigration, it will eventually die.

Chapter 4 discussed the importance of socialization, or nurturing the new members of society in the proper ways of the culture. The family is the first and most important setting for child rearing. Early interaction with parents is basic. Rules learned from parents shape the way children, and later adults, coordinate meaning with others (Vangelisti 2004: xiv). An increasingly important function of a family is providing care and emotional support in times of stress and difficulty; the family can be a "haven in a heartless world."

A final function of the family is conferring of social status. A functionalist argues that as each new family member starts life with the social status of its parents, stability of the society is enhanced. From a conflict perspective, some are critical of this function, arguing that starting with the status of one's parents is unfair to thousands of people and limits their future achievement.

A Conflict View

The conflict perspective also points out the differences in power and authority between men and women, creating tensions that could erupt into conflict (Turner 2006: 303). Throughout human history, strong patriarchal traditions have kept women at a disadvantage. Resentment of their subordination has always been present, which have recently been forcing a rebalancing of power relations in the household. Finally, conflict theorists note that family conflict often erupts in violence in the family, a subject discussed later in this chapter.

Conflict theory is critical of *patriarchy*, the authority of males in the family and in society as a whole. Although a type of *matriarchy* (authority of the female) may be found in areas where husbands are absent, no truly matriarchal society has existed (Henslin 2004: 339).

However, in industrial societies such as the U. S., more egalitarian families are evolving as the share of women in the labor force goes up.

The principle of patriarchy has been widely challenged. But it is still strongly entrenched, and in many parts of the world, husbands control not only all major family decisions but also whether the wife may leave her house or not. While violence against women has become an issue in Africa and Asia, wife-beating is still legitimate in many social milieu (Therborn 2004: 107).

Symbolic Interaction and Communication

The interactionist perspective explores the meanings people give to their lives, examining the ways they shape and experience family life. Ideally, family living offers an opportunity for *intimacy*, or the building of social bonds. Family ties often include sharing confidences as well as turning to one another for help with daily tasks and responsibilities (Macionis 2004: 340).

Communication is the vehicle through which family members establish, maintain, and dissolve intimate relationships. Once a family is formed, members continue to relate to each other through communication. Spouses employ communication strategies to maintain their marriage. These communication patterns change significantly by the time of adolescence. Family relationships are also terminated using communication (Vangelisti 2004: xiii).

There is evidence that income and education influence communication. Highly educated parents are more likely to use complex reasoning and less likely to use commands than are less educated parents when interacting with children. Middle-class parents are more likely to use discrete interrogative questions when talking with their children (Anderson and Umberson 2004: 641).

Mate Selection

In the United States, powerful beliefs about romantic love dominate mate selection (Turner 2006: 305). Most Americans are socialized to believe that one chooses a mate based on whether or not the two are in "love." This is not at all a universal view; in fact, relatively few societies consider love a basis for marriage. *Arranged marriages,* alliances between two extended families of similar social standing (Henslin 2004: 341), have been extremely common, though declining today. Parents still have a major say regarding their children's marriage in at least half of the populations of Asia, in many parts of Africa, in pockets of Europe, and among Native peoples of the Americas (Therborn 2004: 107).

Endogamy refers to norms that people of the same social standing marry (Henslin 2004: 337), particularly in terms of age, race, and social class. There are usually strong pressures for endogamy, as people tend to marry someone similar to themselves in important respects. This tendency of people to marry some similar to themselves is known as *homogamy*.

There is also a norm, known as *exogamy*, which encourages marriage to someone of a different social group (Henslin 2004: 337). A simple example is that people go outside their immediate family to find a mate. Or a person might be encouraged to find a mate from a higher social class.

Monogamy is a marriage that unites two partners. Many lower-income countries, especially Africa and South Asia, permit *polygamy*, marriage that unites three or more people. By far the most common form of polygamy unites one man with two or more women, a union, though illegal, that is occasionally found in the United States. (In April of 2008, a polygamous sect in Texas received widespread attention.) Marriage of one woman to two or more men is quite rare, though it may be found in parts of Tibet (Henslin 2004: 337).

Cohabitation

Living together before or instead of marriage, known as *cohabitation*, has been on the increase in most Western societies. Estimates are that cohabitation has increased six fold since 1970, numbering 5.5 million couples in the U. S. (Henslin 2004: 349). Partners are usually under the age of 35 and have never been married. For most, cohabitation is a stage en route to marriage. At least one partner expects to marry in 90 percent of cohabitations. Within eighteen months of moving in together, most couples either get married (60 percent) or break up (40 percent). There is no evidence that living together before marriage increases the likelihood of a permanent marriage. In fact, cohabitation may actually discourage marriage because it is a low-commitment relationship.

Children born to cohabiting couples are half as likely to grow up with parents in the home as children born to married parents.

When cohabiting couples with children separate, the involvement of both parents, including financial support, is far from certain (Henslin 2004:349).

Successful Marriage

Numerous studies have shown that, on average, married people are happier than single people. Married people tend to have better health, physical and mental, than single people (Galvin 2004: 684). Marriage usually enhances the sex lives of the partners. The married have more economic resources (income, financial assets, equity in their primary residence) than the unmarried. Married people are more likely to live in a safe neighborhood, experience more quality in leisure and the good things of life (Eitzen and Zinn 2007: 442).

A recent study found that about three of every five married Americans report that they are "very happy" with their marriages. Husbands consistently are happier with their marriages. Jeanette and Robert Lauer interviewed 351 couples who had been married fifteen years or longer and found that 300 of them considered their marriages happy. These couples think of their spouse as their best friend; like their spouse as a person; think of marriage as a long-term commitment; believe that marriage is sacred; agree with their spouse on aims and goals; believe that their spouse has grown more interesting over the years; strongly want the relationship to succeed; and often laugh together (cited in Henslin 2007: 325).

Other traits found in successful marriages include few conflicts, agreeing on major issues, enjoying the same interests in leisure time, and gaining confidence in and showing affection for each other. Still other variables related to happy marriages include happily married parents, parental approval of the union, knowing the person at least two years, a long engagement, shared traditional values, the same religion and race, both with a college education, good health, a happy childhood, emotional stability, and adaptable personalities.

Divorce

While there is no question divorce rates are very high in America and the Western world, it is a myth that divorce is steadily increasing. Rates increased dramatically from the 1950s to about 1980, but then leveled off and have remained steady or increased only slightly since then. The oft-reported statistic that one marriage in two will end in divorce is misleading if not inaccurate (Henslin 2007: 317: Turner 2006: 306). Harper and Hirsch (2007: 92) state, "We found several compelling reasons for thinking that today families and households on the whole are doing at least as well as and often better than in the past."

A study of almost 11,000 women between the ages of 15 and 44 found that 20 percent of marriages ended in the first five years, with the rate jumping to 43 percent by 15 years. The divorce rate was roughly twice as high among low-income couples, and blacks had a significantly higher rate than whites, Hispanics, or Asians (cited in Turner 2006: 307).

Some scholars are not alarmed at the large number of divorces. "A high divorce rate is the price for allowing people to escape from unhappy, tyrannical, and sometimes brutal relationships" (Harper and Leicht 2007: 91). Although divorce may provide escape from a miserable marriage, it generally brings new problems. Mental illness, depression, and suicide are common results. The economic impact, usually on the woman (and children, if any), may be very harsh (Corsaro 1997: 227; see Single Parents, below).

Many reasons have been offered for the high divorce rate. The rise of individualism emphasizes personal happiness over the well-being of families and children. Romantic love often subsides, and a new relationship promises renewed excitement and romance. In the complex world of today, the stress of two or more family members holding jobs may leave less time and energy for family life (Henslin 2004:346-347).

Two important reasons for high divorce rates include the changing role of women and the reduced stigma of divorce. As women become more educated and more career-oriented, they are less dependent on a man. This opens up more choices and means that their staying in an unhappy marriage is less likely. The greater number of divorces has reduced the stigma, meaning that divorce is more likely to be considered in problematic marriages. One influence has been the reform of divorce laws, especially the adoption of no-fault divorce. Longevity is also a factor: life expectancy has increased by almost 30 years in the last century (Ferrante 2006: 437), thus enlarging the possibility of divorce.

Younger couples face a much greater risk of separation and divorce. Forty-seven percent of women marrying before age 18 ended the marriage within ten years, compared to 19 percent of women marrying at age 23 or later. Other factors include a low educational background, a cohabitation history, and a spouse who had been married previously (Martin et al. 2004).

It is possible to identify a number of additional factors that are associated with a high divorce rate, though they are not necessarily *causes*. Those who are pregnant when they marry, and those who marry without the approval of parents or close friends, are more likely to divorce. Those who knew each other a short time and who married with no engagement or a short engagement face a greater likelihood of breaking up. Couples who have a great difference in age, race, or social class divorce more frequently. Couples without a religion or from conflicting religions are more likely to divorce (Henslin 2006: 319; Ferrante 2006: 437-438).

Spouses who are distressed generally express more negative affect, less positive affect, and more reciprocity of negatives than those who are not distressed. Studies have demonstrated that the quality of parents' communication can affect children's problem-solving skills as well as children's ability to relate with peers. Parents' tendency to engage in certain types of conflict is associated with distress in children (Vangelisti 2004: xiv).

Children of Divorce

The effect of divorce on children has elicited extensive research. Divorce affects more than one million children in the United States each year (Wolchik et al. 2002), and they are undoubtedly affected by the experience. Often the children are unprepared for the divorce, and many take it personally, feeling they were at least partly in fault. In one study done five years after their parents' divorce, 29 percent of children were doing reasonably well, 39 percent were still depressed, and 34 percent were thriving.

Children of divorce are more likely than children reared by both parents to experience emotional problems, both during their childhood and after they grow up, and more likely to become juvenile delinquents.

They are also less likely to complete high school, to attend college, and to graduate from college. And they are more likely themselves to divorce (cited in Henslin 2007: 320). While most appear to make an adequate long-term adjustment, there is no doubt that many are seriously affected.

These children often have to relocate to smaller homes or rented apartments, have less money for their basic and leisure needs, and spend less time with both their fathers and mothers. External effects included aggression, disobedience, and lying. Internal disorders included depression, anxiety, or withdrawal. Boys in high-conflict families tend to show more aggression and antisocial behavior. Girls usually do better after marital disruption, but may develop disorders that become apparent years later (Corsaro 1997: 229-230).

Other problems of children appear in poor academic performance, school drop-out, poor peer relationships, drug and alcohol abuse, early sexual behavior, and adolescent pregnancy. For some children effects are mild and short lived; for others, divorce leads to clinically significant and lasting adjustment problems during childhood and adolescence. Longitudinal studies show elevated rates of mental trauma in adults who experienced parental divorce as children.

Divorce often engenders increased fights between parents, exposure to parental distress, changes in residence and schools, involvement with parents' new partners, and loss of time with one or both parents. It has been shown that changes in parenting, such as decreased warmth and affection, poorer communication, and erratic discipline, commonly follow divorce.

Children, like adults, need to be part of a caring and stable social group. Divorce can cause a pervasive sense of vulnerability for children as the protective, nurturing aspects of the family diminish. For many children, time with one or both parents is reduced markedly by custody arrangements and longer work hours needed to meet the added costs. A high-quality relationship with the primary residential parent reduces this threat. Improving mother-child relationship quality is helpful. Children may benefit from explicit reassurance that the mother-child relationship will endure over time (Wolchik et al. 2002).

Children who feel close to both parents make the best adjustment, and those who feel close to one parent make the next-best adjustment. They adjust well if they experience little conflict, feel loved, live with a parent who is making a good adjustment, and have consistent routines. It helps too if a second adult, preferably the father or perhaps another relative or friend, can be counted on for support (Henslin 2007: 320).

Single Parents in the U. S.

The number of single parents in this country has greatly increased, largely from those who divorce but from those who never marry, and whose partners died or were institutionalized. By 2000, single-mother families accounted for 22 percent of all families with children, up from 6 percent in 1950 (cited in Eitzen and Zinn 2007: 440).

Among women under 30, half of all pregnancies occur out of wedlock. Half of the children will live with a single parent at some time before reaching age 18. About one-third of women in the U. S. become pregnant as teenagers. Slightly more than 50 percent of black families are headed by a single parent. On average, children growing up in a single-parent family start out poorer, get less schooling, and end up with lower incomes as adults (Henslin 2004: 349).

> New reproductive technologies and women's increased independence mean that husbands are less of a necessity. Still, families headed by a single parent run a high risk of being poor because they lack the economic resources of dual-parent families. Furthermore, single-parent families are usually headed by women, who are at great risk of economic hardship. The earnings gap bound in all occupations makes female-headed households especially vulnerable (Eitzen and Zinn 2007: 441).

The present system of child support often puts an enormous economic burden on women in periods of separation and following divorce. Women who were unemployed before a divorce often find they must enter a job market for which they have limited skills or training. Most who are employed find that their meager incomes are insufficient. Many women and their children must live near or below the poverty line following divorce, as mothers work longer hours or combine work and further education and job training (Corsaro 1997: 228-229).

Courts award child support in 59 percent of all divorces involving children. Yet in any given year, half of children legally entitled to support receive partial payments or no payments at all. Some 3.3 million fathers fail to support their youngsters. Federal law now requires employers to withhold money from the earnings of parents (Henslin 2004: 347).

Most single-parent families must deal with a great deal of strain in their households. For the less affluent, economic strains always supercharge family relations and destroy the myth of romantic love, whereas for the more affluent, they can afford to buy help to relieve domestic strains. Cultural traditions such as religion and extended family are also very important in explaining these differences (Turner 2006: 308. For more on economic problems of single parent families, see chapter 8.)

Remarriage

Four out of five people who divorce remarry, most within five years. Nationwide, about half of all marriages are now remarriages for at least one partner. Men are more likely to remarry, possibly because they gain more from marriage than the woman (Henslin 2004: 348). Remarriage often creates *blended families*, usually requiring major adjustments. An only child may now have siblings in the home. Discipline problems may be acute ("I don't have to listen to you; you're not my real father").

The probability of remarriage and its success is affected by four important variables: age, social class, race, and religion. The age of women is crucial, with younger women much more likely to remarry than older women. The remarriage prospect of younger women with children is less than it is for younger women without children. The more money a divorced man has, the more likely he is to remarry, but the reverse is true for women. Blacks and Hispanics remarry at lower rates than whites (Eitzen and Zinn 2007: 446-447).

Dual-Career Families

Among the most important changes in U. S. families is the increase in married-couples where both are in the labor force. Since 1960, the rise of women's participation in the labor force has been dramatic: the percentage of women in two-parent families with children under six years of age who are in the workplace increased from around 19 percent in 1960 to 64 percent in 2003 (Eitzen and Zinn 2007: 448). Higher material aspirations have encouraged women to enter the workforce.

Surveys reveal that couples have a strong desire both to embark on a career and form a family, including having children. But to combine them is a difficult task (Therborn 2004: 314). The full-time position of homemaker, common until the 1950s, is less a reality in today's society.

Studies in the 1970s and 1980s revealed positive outcomes of maternal employment to child development. Children appear to have higher self-esteem, make better grades in school, enjoy more positive family and peer relations, and show less gender-stereotyped beliefs (Berk 2004: 9).

Childcare has become an important and popular service in reconciling work and family. A strong argument can be made that employer-provided on-site childcare, with government support, can broaden availability, affordability, and quality (Ghosheh 2005).

However, long hours in child care during infancy in the preschool years are linked to less favorable parent-child interaction. In one study, the more time children spent in child care, the less positive and responsive their mothers' behavior toward them. Children experiencing less positive interaction were less engaged with their mothers, more negative in mood and less affectionate. But where there was minimal child care in the first year or so, if mothers schedules regular times to devote to their children, negative influences were minimized (Berk 2004: 8-9).

Psychologist Rosalind Barrett and journalist Caryl Rivers conducted extensive interviews with 300 dual-earner couples in the Boston area and found that despite stress at work and at home, most were highly satisfied and found child rearing to be manageable and pleasurable. In a survey of 6,000 employees at DuPont, nearly half—and only slightly more women than men—turned down upward career moves to remain in jobs that allowed for more family commitment (Berk 2004: 8).

The demands of the family intrude more on women's work roles than on men's. If an emergency arises, the family role usually takes priority over the work role for mothers. When there is a child crisis in school, it is the working mother, rather than the working father, who will take initial responsibility. For fathers, the relationship is reversed. The work role takes priority over the family role. Many fathers take work home with them or use their time at home to recuperate from the stresses they face in the work role (Eitzen and Zinn 2007: 448).

Gender Roles

There has been a significant shift of attitudes regarding appropriate roles of men and women in marriage, family, and work. How society defines what it means to be a man or a woman has shifted towards a more egalitarian view, as the number of women in the workforce has reached unprecedented levels. The attitudes of men and women toward the equity of gender roles are often related to marital satisfaction (Martin et al. 2004).

A study of college students found strong agreement that childrearing and household chores should be divided between parents. Young people are leaning to more flexible gender roles, and want more options in terms of marriage and family life and their roles in these relationships. However, male adolescents often describe themselves as egalitarian but express traditionalism in their behavior.

Despite the increasing number of women in the U. S. labor force, domestic equality between men and women has not been achieved. In most marital relationships, women are still responsible for the bulk of domestic labor. In a study in Australia, men remain largely peripheral to the domestic sphere. Men in most cultures are "compliant helpers" in the household rather than being equally responsible. Women continue to shoulder the greater burden in looking after the household (Singleton and Maher 2004).

Jane Lewis argues that women are obstructed in their development as individuals by the unequal distribution of care (nurturing) work between men and women, the lack of affordable care in the formal sector, women's presumed moral obligation to provide care, and their unequal status in the labor force. Lewis suggests that the society needs to place added value to care work (Kaiser 2004).

Interracial Marriage

Marriage between partners of different races was illegal in 16 states until 1967, though it has increased since. The actual proportion of mixed marriages is now 2.9 percent. Most U. S. teens claim they have dated someone of another race (Macionis 2004: 345). The number of black and white transracial married couples almost doubled since 1967. Over 4 percent of U. S. children are of mixed race and that figure is rising rapidly (Galvin 2004: 678).

Surrogate Motherhood

One development that has affected ideas about family is surrogate motherhood. Experts estimate there were about 1,000 surrogate births in the United States in 2007. Technology has made the process safer and more likely to succeed. In the past five years, four states—Texas, Illinois, Utah and Florida—have passed laws legalizing surrogacy, and Minnesota is considering doing the same. Many military wives have taken on surrogacy to supplement the family income, some while their husbands are serving overseas. Even though the cost to the intended parents, including medical and legal bills, run from $40,000 to $120,000, the demand for qualified surrogates in well ahead of supply (Ali and Kelly 2008).

Young Pregnancy

The United States has higher teen pregnancy, abortion, and birth rates than almost all other developed nations. There is a big difference of nonmarital births for teens in this country and in other countries. Teen birthrates are highest among mothers of greatest economic disadvantage. However, pregnancy rates for teenagers have not increased dramatically since the 1950s, and in fact are down slightly (Corsaro 1997: 234).

Sexually Transmitted Diseases (STD)

STD infection and transmission are higher in the United States than in any other industrialized nation, with adolescents and young adults representing the largest-growth group. More than half of sexually active adolescents do not use any form of birth control (Martin et al. 2004).

At least one in four teenage girls nationwide has a sexually transmitted disease, or more than three million teens, according to the first study of its kind in this age group. A virus that causes cervical cancer is by far the most common STD among teen girls aged 14 to 19, while the highest prevalence is among black girls (Tanner 2008).

New Family Forms

New marriage and family forms include the dual-income couple; the deliberately childless couple; the only-child childhood; empty-nest middle-aged couple; the single elderly person household (Therborn 2004: 314); and the household headed by one or more homosexuals.

Massachusetts in 2004 became the first state to legalize same-sex marriage (California followed in 2008), which continues to be controversial. One argument is that same-sex marriage denigrates marriage and abandons the basic building block of the family. The other side claims that gay couples should have the same rights as heterosexual couples in social security, health care, pensions, and asset ownership. The United States trails Canada and several European countries on the issue of gay rights (Eitzen and Zinn 2007: 444).

Among gays, about 22 percent of female couples and 5 percent of male couples have children from a previous marriage. Lesbians are concerned about issues of custody, adoption, and the right to be parents. One study of gay couples found that their concerns paralleled the concerns of heterosexual couples. They are more likely to break up than heterosexual couples, which could be an argument for allowing same-sex unions (greater legitimacy of the union could increase the odds for stability). There is no evidence that children raised by gay parents are more likely to be gay themselves.

Family Violence

The family can be a haven from an uncaring, impersonal world. But it also has a dark side; it is a common context for violence in society. Sociologist Richard Gelles, an authority on this subject, claims that except for the military, the family is the most violent social group in American society. The home may be more dangerous than a dark alley. "People are more likely to be killed, physically assaulted, sexually victimized, hit, beat up, slapped, or spanked in their own homes by other family members than anywhere else in our society" (Gelles 1995: 450).

Most family violence goes unreported. Still, the U. S. Justice Department estimates that well over 800,000 women are victims of violence each year, and 20 percent of the homicides against women come from their spouse or ex-spouse. Well over 1,000 women a year die from domestic violence (Turner 2006: 308). In the first year-long nationwide study of infant abuse and neglect, over 905,000 children were victims (October 2005 to October 2006). Over 10 percent of these were one year of age or younger, and almost one-third of those were one week old or younger (CBS News 2008).

Recent estimates of assaults between adult partners in the U. S. witnessed by resident children range from 9 to 30 percent. Over 10 percent of U. S. children experience severe violence at the hands of their parents year to year. Evidence suggests that an even larger number of children suffer from neglect than from physical abuse (Anderson and Umberson 2004: 629).

Some of the major contributing factors to family violence include severe economic stress; a parent who was abused as a child; poor communication; a "macho" male attitude; inappropriate and excessive discipline of children; severely authoritarian family norms; and some social and cultural support for violence. The intimacy of the family, which elicits strong emotions, and its privacy, which suggests secrecy, contribute to violence. Mental illness and drug abuse have been found to be relatively minor factors, although alcohol may be significant in many cases. While the incidence is somewhat higher in lower social classes, violence occurs at all class levels.

Family violence used to be considered a private matter, with only rare intervention from authorities. Widespread publicity has changed this picture: today the law gives victims more options. A woman can obtain court protection from an abusive spouse. Communities in North America have established shelters to provide counseling, temporary housing and relocation for women and children driven from their homes by domestic violence (Henslin 2004: 348; see "A Closer Look" below).

For important changes in family life, see chapter 13.

The Family in China

Overall changes in China are discussed in chapter 13. Family, the bedrock of Chinese society, is changing today, as more children are leaving their hometowns—even the country—in search of jobs. This generation is the first to grow up under the one-child policy, rolled out in 1979. "As adults, children of this generation lack the inclination to support their parents," says demographics expert Cai Feng. Forty-two percent of Chinese families in 2008 consisted of an old couple living alone.

Young parents are rethinking the meaning of family in China. Historically, a healthy brood of boys was considered the best form of social security, which is still generally true in the countryside. But in China's cities, many young couples now say they prize daughters over sons for their loyalty. Many believe girls are more thoughtful, especially towards their parents. In a recent poll, respondents who preferred a daughter edged out those who wanted a son (Liu 2008).

Others are hoping to increase the odds against abandonment in creative and sometimes illegal ways. Some wealthier urbanites simply ignore the one-child policy and pay fine for having an extra kid. Others give birth abroad, or pretend their first child was born handicapped (a loophole that allows them to have another legally). There is speculation that China might phase out the one-child policy (Liu 2008).

A Closer Look: Family Violence

Violence is motivated by a desire to communicate a message—often a demand for compliance—to the victim. Parents and intimate partners use violence to gain control, to express anger and frustration. Men's violence against partners is often linked to a general pattern of controlling behavior, including monitoring partners' activities and regulating their friendships. Violence can also be motivated by fear, shame, or a desire for revenge or recognition.

Women and children suffer the most detrimental consequences of family violence. The physical punishment of children by their parents is considered a legitimate disciplinary tool in many nations. Because children lack power within and outside of the family system, they are particularly vulnerable as targets of physical and sexual abuse. Girls are approximately three times more likely to be sexually abused than are boys. Although women and men report similar rates of violence against spouses or partners, women are much more likely to suffer injury and depression as a result of violence than men. A context of gender inequality places women at a disadvantage within relationships marked by violence.

Violence within families has been associated with deficits in members' communication skills. A number of studies find that partners in violent marriages or dating relationships lack problem-solving and positive negotiation skills. In one study, violent couples were more likely to use vague language, to be oppositional and interfering, and to express complaints and despair. Family violence has also been associated with defensive communication patterns such as blaming, interrupting, invalidating, and withdrawing.

Members of violent families have limited opportunities to witness and practice positive communication skills. Among adults, the experience of abuse at the hands of a loved one often leads to a loss of self-confidence and undermines the victim's ability to form and sustain healthy social relationships. Survivors of child sexual abuse report experiencing poor communication with their intimate partners as adults. Communication skills may be adversely affected by violence because victims lose self-confidence or learn to be fearful, secretive, and distrustful of others because of abuse.

A number of studies found that abuse between spouses is linked to negative interaction patterns between parents and children. Violence between parents is linked to a number of negative parenting practices. Abusive parents often have rigid expectations for their children's behavior that they attempt to enforce through punishment. Fathers who were abusive toward their wives were controlling in interaction with their sons.

Abusive parents interpret their children's actions as hostile or threatening. They are more likely to experience annoyance and irritation in response to their children's behavior. Individuals who engage in violence against family members (spouses or children) often read negative intentions into the victim's actions. Violent men, in particular, are more likely to attribute hostile intent to their female partner's actions.

Several studies have shown a significant association between women's experiences of sexual abuse during childhood and alcohol problems in adulthood. Higher levels of mother's physical and psychological aggression were significantly associated with a higher likelihood of alcohol dependence (Downs 2004).

Violence has detrimental consequences for family members' ability to learn positive forms of communication. Violence undermines the self-esteem and confidence of its victims, it teaches victims that aggression and controlling styles of interaction are normative, and it isolates victims from other people. Victims learn to be fearful, anxious, and insecure in their relationships with others (adapted from Anderson and Umberson 2004: 634-639).

Nonetheless, the impact of stressful life events and conditions, whether poverty, divorce, or abuse, can be mitigated. A close relationship with a parent, relative, or teacher, who introduces affection, assistance, and order into the child's life, fosters resiliency. This can encourage a mastery of cognitive and social skills that enable the child to withstand and even overcome adversity (Berk 2004: 27-28).

Summary

Family is a group or social network linked by blood, marriage, or adoption. The *nuclear* family refers to a husband, wife, and their children; the *extended* family to this group and also other kin. Many changes in the family include the increasing role of stepparents, families headed by gays, and working women and a shift in gender roles.

Major functions for a family are regulating sexual behavior, replacing members of a society, socializing the young, providing care and emotional support, and conferring social status. A conflict perspective emphasizes patriarchal norms that disadvantage women and increasing family violence.

Symbolic interactionism stresses the meanings of intimacy and social bonds provided by a family, and strategies for communication.

Mate selection can vary from a romantic view to arranged marriages. *Endogamy* refers to norms that encourage people to marry someone of a similar background. *Polygamy* is a marriage that unites three or more people. *Cohabitation,* meaning living together without being married, is on the increase.

Divorce rates in the U. S. increased dramatically until about 1980, then leveled off. Some reasons for divorce include individualism, the changing role of women, and a reduced stigma for divorce. About one million children a year are impacted by divorce, and may suffer depression, emotional problems, and other negative results. The best results are found when children are still close to at least one parent.

The number of single parents has increased significantly. They often face a series of problems, especially economic hardship. Four of five divorced people remarry, creating a number of *blended families.*

Some positive outcomes for working women have been identified. Child care is a major concern.

Young people are adopting more flexible gender roles, though women remain at a disadvantage. Issues such as young pregnancy and sexually transmitted diseases were discussed.

The family is a common context for violence. Some reasons for this are economic stress, having been abused as a child, poor communication, a "macho" male image, authoritarian norms, and cultural support. The relationship between family violence and communication practices was discussed in some detail.

References

Ali, Lorraine, and Raina Kelly. 2008. "The Curious Lives of Surrogates" (**Newsweek**, April 7).

Anderson, Kristin L., and Debra Umberson. 2004. "Violence and Abuse in Families" (pp. 629-641 in Anita L. Vangelisti (ed.), **Handbook of Family Communication** (Mahwah, New Jersey: Lawrence Erbaum Associates).

Berk, Laura E. 2004. **Awakening Children's Minds: How Parents and Teachers Can Make a Difference** (Oxford: Oxford University Press).

CBS Evening News. 2008 (April 3).

Corsaro, William A. 1997. **The Sociology of Childhood** (Pine Forge, California: Pine Forge Press).

Downs, William E., Thomas Capshew, and Barbara Brindels. 2004. "Relationships Between Adult Women's Alcohol Problems and Their Childhood Experiences of Parental Violence and Psychological Aggression (**Journal of Studies on Alcohol**, Vol. 65).

Eitzen, D. Stanley, and Maxine Baca Zinn. 2007. **In Conflict and Order: Understanding Society,** eleventh edition (Boston: Allyn and Bacon).

Ferrante, Joan. 2006. **Sociology: A Global Perspective,** sixth edition (Belmont, California: Thomson-Wadsworth).

Galvin, Kathleen. 2004. "The Family of the Future: What do we Face?" (pp. 675-688 in Anita L. Vangelisti (ed.), **Handbook of Family Communication** (Mahwah, New Jersey: Lawrence Erbaum Associates).

Gelles, Richard. 1995. **Contemporary Families: A Sociological View** (Thousand Oaks, California: Sage).

Ghosheh, Naj Jr. 2005. "The Economics of Work and Family" (**International Labor Review**, Vol. 144).

Harper, Charles L., and Kevin T. Leicht. 2007. **Exploring Social Change: America and the World**, fifth edition (Upper Saddle River, New Jersey: Pearson).

Henslin, James M. 2007. **Sociology, A Down-to-Earth Approach,** second edition (Boston: Allyn and Bacon).

Kaiser, Michael. 2004. "Jane Lewis, Should We Worry about Family Change?" **The Canadian Review of Sociology and Anthropology** (Vol. 41).

Liu, Melinda. 2008. "China's New Empty Nest" (**Newsweek,** March 10).

Macionis, John. 2004. **Society: The Basics,** seventh edition (Upper Saddle River, New Jersey: Prentice-Hall).

Martin, Paige D., Don Martin, and Maggie Martin. 2004. "Redefinitions of the American Family" (**Annals of the American Psychotherapy Association,** Vol. 7).

Richter, Rudolf. 2005. "Should We Worry About Family Change?" (**Journal of Comparative Family Studies,** Vol. 36).

Singleton, Andrew, and Jane Maree Maher. 2004. "The NewMan is in the House: Young Men, Social Change, and Housework" (**The Journal of Men's Studies**, Vol. 12).

Tanner. 2008. "One in four teen girls has sexual disease" (**Associated Press**, March 11).

Therborn, Goran. 2004. **Between Sex and Power: Family in the World** (London: Routledge).

Turner, Jonathan H. 2006. **Sociology** (Upper Saddle River, New Jersey: Prentice-Hall).

Vangelisti, Anita L. (ed.). 2004. **Handbook of Family Communication** (Mahwah, New Jersey: Lawrence Erbaum Associates).

Wolchik, Sharlene A., Jenn-Yun Tein, Irwin N. Sandler, and Kathryn W. Doyle. 2002. "Fear of abandonment as a mediator of the relations between divorce stressors and mother-child relationship quality and children's adjustment problems" (**Journal of Abnormal Child Psychology**, Vol. 30).

First United Methodist Church, Dallas

Chapter 12: RELIGION

Religion has developed in practically every society in the history of the world. It has been found in such varied forms that a definition is difficult. People of faith report that religion has been an inspiration in their lives, leading them to better understand their place in the universe, and challenging them to their best. Religion is one important way in which Americans get involved in the life of their community and society (Bellah et al. 1985: 219). Others consider religion to be a divisive force that engenders conflict and violence. Others consider it a wasteful evasion of reality that is hastening the end of humanity.

A perusal of any newspaper would indicate that religion is highly salient and visible in the events of the world. Protestants and Catholics in Northern Ireland have only recently come to agreement after years of conflict; the Pope arouses controversy with some of his public statements; the two major sects of Islam are in a near civil war in Iraq; American Protestants debate what should be taught in public schools; and in politics, the religious right debates the religious middle and left. For anyone interested in understanding society and history, religion cannot be ignored.

Polls of 2,013 national adults in the United States aged 18 and older were conducted in the fall of 2006. The results showed 39 percent of Americans label themselves "somewhat religious," 37 percent classify themselves as "extremely" or "very religious" and 23 percent say they are "not too religious" or "not religious at all" (News Briefs 2007: 29).

In a recent study by the Pew Forum on Religion and Public Life, disenchantment with organized religion was detected. About 44 percent of those raised in a particular religious faith now belong to another faith or to none at all. Some 78 percent of Americans are Christian, of whom 51 percent are Protestant (26 percent evangelicals and 18 percent mainline Protestant). About 31 percent were raised Catholic, of whom 24 percent are still practicing Catholics. Nearly four in ten of married couples are of different faiths. While 16 percent are unaffiliated, almost a third of them consider religion important (Weiss 2008).

Religion encompasses those human responses that give meaning to the ultimate and inescapable problems of existence—birth, death, illness, aging, injustice, tragedy, and suffering. Weber appears to have been right when he claimed that no single definition could capture the essence of religion (Ferrante 2006: 522). Religion, or faith, is one way people combat stress, overcome adversity, and analyze challenges (Berger 2001: 497).

Some sociologists, following Durkheim, define religion as belief in the supernatural, or realm beyond the everyday world, drawing a distinction between the *sacred* and the *secular.* That which is sacred refers to deep and absorbing sentiments of respect, mystery, and awe. Definitions of what is sacred vary according to time and place. The sacred could include objects, creatures, elements of nature, places, days, states of consciousness, past events, ceremonies, and the like (Ferrante 2006: 524).

There is more to the universe than the physical, more to a meaningful life than immediate pleasure, more to life than the everyday mundane affairs of the human being. That "more" is the sacred. Because it is special, universal, beyond our senses, beyond the immediate, it is to be honored, respected, and held in awe.

The sacred is created by human beings in their social life. A cemetery or a particular grave might be sacred to a family; certain elements used in religion (bread, wine, a cross) might be considered sacred; certain prayers, buildings, places, values, beliefs, and rituals could be held sacred. Certain life-cycle events--birth, baptism, bar mitzvah, marriage, death—are made sacred for some (Charon 2007: 249-250).

Religious *beliefs* articulate the nature of the sacred. Religious *values* are statements about what is right, wrong, good, and bad. Religious *ritual* is a patterned and stereotyped sequence of actions directed towards the supernatural. While these practices may be performed privately, they also are often performed collectively in the presence of others (Turner 2006: 313).

Such an understanding would not be applicable to all known religious forms. Certain expressions of Buddhism, for example, require no deity or other supernatural being; and neither does Scientology. And certain progressive religious groups, such as the Unitarian-Universalists, do not fully accept this understanding.

Sociologist Joel Charon has devoted much thought to defining religion in our day. After considering the views of such thinkers as Durkheim and Weber, he concludes that religion is "a view of the universe that through beliefs and practices identifies a special separate sacred world apart from our physical, mundane, profane, everyday existence. It is socially created, it is part of human culture, and it has an important impact on human action as well as the continued existence of community" (Charon 2007: 253).

The trend in religion over the past 1,000 years has been toward monotheism, or the worship of one God. Islam, Christianity, Judaism, and Confucianism clearly tend toward monotheism. Even the pantheon of deities in Hinduism is interpreted by many as simply manifestations of one spirit. Religious mythologies have declined and are simplified in more contemporary religions (Turner 2006: 315).

Functions of Religion

Functionalists enumerate important social functions met by religion.

According to Durkheim, in religion people celebrate the awesome power of their society. He claimed that religion unites people through shared symbolism, values and norms. Society also uses religious ideas to promote conformity. And religious belief offers the comforting sense that our brief lives serve some greater purpose. That is why we mark major life transitions—including birth, marriage, and death—with religious observances (Macionis 2004: 354).

Weber emphasized religion as a central part of a people's culture, as their way to understand their own lives in relation to their universe. Religion was an "ethic," a cultural view, a tool people use to understand their lives and to bring meaning to them (Charon 2007: 250).

In his most important work, *The Protestant Ethic and the Spirit of Capitalism,* Weber demonstrates that human beings are moved by religious values and ideals as much as they are by economic interests. Economic developments have been influenced by religious beliefs and practices. Capitalism in Western Europe and the United States, claims Weber, was built on a religious ethic, a Protestantism that taught that those who believed and acted in a certain way were among the elite: they worked hard, were successful at making a living, and invested in their values. The point was that ideas and values, not just economic interests, shaped human action and society (Charon 2007: 251).

Sociologist Peter Berger, following Durkheim and Weber, emphasizes the social essence of religion. He thinks religion is a way that people make sense out of reality. It helps make sense out of tragedy, find order in chaotic events. Religion helps to find a more meaningful, permanent, and sacred universe. The idea of *meaning* is central here. Religion, for Berger, helps us see our place in the universe as special and more than simply a profane physical existence (Charon 2007: 252).

One function of religion is to promote social solidarity. People can come to feel a part of a community through ritual—a wedding, funeral, or baptism. The community can be a few people, a group, a city, a whole society, or people scattered throughout the world. In a religious community, people become socialized into a morality that appears sacred. Religion teaches a view of justice that upholds that morality and interprets it as responsibility to the community.

Religion attempts to set norms for morality. It sets rules that may be actually socially derived, temporary, and situational. Society becomes a moral power. Religion controls individuals by teaching them to work cooperatively in the community instead of simply following selfish pursuits. Our actions will always have important consequences for other people and for the future of the community.

In a theocracy, a government controlled by religious leaders, democracy is unlikely to thrive. Yet religion can support the development and growth of a democratic society. Religion can inspire people to participate in government and help ensure that democratic government does not slip into a tyranny.

Finally, religion finds meaning in the universe. It helps make sense of the chaos we observe as we look at the universe. It helps give life purpose and fulfillment: to understand oneself in relation to the universe, to find importance in what one is and does, and to believe that life matters in some way (adapted from Charon 2007: 256-263).

A Conflict Interpretation

While religion typically teaches love and tolerance, it may also be used to justify oppression or even destruction of people who are outside the religious community. Religion has inspired people to do things that today we regard to be highly immoral: deadly sacrifice, slavery, expulsion from the community, silencing those who disagree. Some people obey without value analysis and discussion.

A serious stumbling block to democracy has been traditional, authoritarian, fundamentalist religion. Traditional religious beliefs and practices are sometimes contrary to freedom of thought and speech, respect for the individual, acceptance of minority differences, and human equality.

Religion may legitimize the status quo and divert people's attention from social inequities. In a famous quotation, Marx claimed that religion serves as "the opiate of the people." He meant that religion encourages people to endure exploitation and social and economic inequalities without complaint, while they look hopefully to a better world to come. That is, people should not protest their oppressed condition since they will be rewarded after death (Macionis 2004: 355).

Almost all the major religions are patriarchal. Judaism, Christianity, and Islam have traditionally given men dominance over women. Only in recent years has there been a noticeable change in this respect, with most religions offering women leadership roles, and some seeing God as gender-neutral (Macionis 2004: 355-356).

Which view is right? Does religion provide understanding, meaning, and motivation for personal and social fulfillment? Or does it encourage intolerance and support oppression? History has many examples of both. An answer seems to depend on the type of religion, and the political and cultural context in which it is found.

Roman Catholics

The largest religion in the world is Christianity, and the largest single form of Christianity is the Roman Catholic Church. It has a very long tradition and is found in virtually every country in the world. There are well over a billion Catholics worldwide, approximately one-sixth of the world's population. Many are attracted to the church by its tradition, its liturgy and pageantry, and for its cohesiveness.

All Catholics recognize the Pope and the Vatican in Rome. Despite this cohesiveness, however, there is considerable diversity among Catholics. Even within the United States, Catholics have not been molded into a single group. Religious behavior has varied somewhat for the various ethnic groups within the church. Influence of life in the United States has increased German and Polish involvement in the Catholic Church, while Italians have remained relatively inactive (Schaefer 2002: 153).

The American Catholic Church has embraced new members in large numbers from the Philippines, Southeast Asia, and particularly Mexico and Latin America. This large gain in members has diversified a church that for years was dominated by Irish, Italian, and Polish parishes. The most prominent subgroup now is Hispanics, who account for one-third of Catholic parishioners.

Second only to the public school system, the Catholic Church has been a potent force in assimilating immigrants. Ethnic diversity is expected to continue in the Roman Catholic Church (Schaefer 2002: 153-154). Catholic churches are much more numerous in urban than in rural areas.

The Catholic Church has been hurt in recent years by allegations of sexual abuse by priests and others in positions of authority, which has cost the church both members and money. They have also been hurt by a shortage of priests and nuns, though some middle-aged men have been turning to the priesthood as a second career (CBS Evening News 2008). In 1970 there were 58,000 priests in the U. S., but only about 41,500 in 2006. The shortage of priests is especially felt among Hispanic Catholics.

Traditionally, Catholics have tended to vote Democratic, perhaps because of the church position of supporting working people and the poor, as well as its international quest for peace. More recently, more Catholics are voting Republican, largely because of the traditional stand of the church opposing abortion and gay marriage.

Protestants

Protestants are Christians who, following Martin Luther, "protested" what they saw as abuses in the Roman Catholic Church in the sixteenth century. Since then, Protestants have exerted strong influence in such countries as the United States, but they have witnessed even more diversity than the Catholics. Protestants vary from what are called "mainline" denominations to small but growing sect-type churches.

Mainline denominations include Presbyterians, Lutherans, United Methodists, the United Church of Christ, and the Protestant Episcopal Church. These churches tend to be ecumenical (see below), belong to the National Council of Churches, and range from conservative to liberal in their theological and political views. Mainline Protestants have tended to lose members over the last fifty years.

The *Yearbook of American and Canadian Churches* for 2007 shows that only three US traditional Protestant churches now rank among the 10 largest churches in the United States. The United Methodist Church, ranked third, reported a membership of a little over 8 million. The Evangelical Lutheran Church in America ranked seventh with a membership of about 4,850,000, and the Presbyterian Church, USA, ranked ninth with a membership of about 3,100,000 (News Briefs 2007: 30).

The ecumenical movement, which has existed for over a hundred years, is an attempt to promote cooperation, if not actual merger, among the various denominations. Several American churches have merged in the twentieth century, and others, while maintaining separate bodies, emphasize cooperation and mutual understanding. Many have engaged in dialogue with Roman Catholics, Jews, and those of other religious backgrounds. The National and World Council of Churches are institutional expressions of the ecumenical movement.

Believing in a certain religion does not necessarily exclude the rules or truth of other religions. The truth of one's religion becomes plausible, not absolute; there is always room for more understanding. Any dominance by one religion is undermined as society becomes modern and diverse (Charon 2007: 272).

Fundamentalism is an important trend, not only in American churches but in worldwide religions. About a hundred years ago, a group of American Protestants established certain "fundamentals" they felt were essential to their belief system. While splintering into subgroups, the movement attempts to preserve a distinctive identity and to fortify themselves against what they believe are their enemies. Led by charismatic and authoritarian leaders, they emphasize rigid discipline. Revealed truth is valued, and the movement rejects modernization and tries to recapture the values and truths of the past (Charon 2007: 278).

The Southern Baptist Church is the largest single Protestant body, with a unique identity. It grew rapidly in the 20th century but has reported recent decline. While it is strongest in the South, it has churches in every state. The leadership of the church, in the last few decades, has moved toward fundamentalism in theology, and it tends to be conservative in other ways as well. However, there are diverse views among the membership and in many ways the denomination resembles mainline Protestants.

Two denominations that have experienced great growth deserve mention. The Church of Jesus Christ of Latter-Day Saints, commonly called the Mormons, pioneered the settlement of Utah and the Great Basin. While centered in Salt Lake City and in Utah, it has members across the country and around the world. The church believes there has been a special revelation to the peoples of this hemisphere. Two prominent Mormons are Mitt Romney, former governor of Massachusetts, and Harry Reid, Majority Leader in the U. S. Senate.

The other denomination with strong growth is the Pentecostalists, often known as Assemblies of God or holiness churches. The denomination appeals to those who want a more openly emotional expression to their religious faith. They believe in the infusion of the Holy Spirit into services and in religious experiences such as faith healing. Although the denomination is scarcely a hundred years old, it has experienced great growth not only in this country but in others, especially in Latin America.

A *sect* is a smaller church that has usually broken away from a denomination over one or more specific issues. A sect is more likely to hold distinctive beliefs, rely on charismatic leadership of one or a few people, be less inclined to institute a highly structured bureaucracy, and to be more critical of society and of mainline denominations. Some would consider Jehovah's Witnesses and Scientology to be sects, and Pentecostalists, mentioned above, were considered a sect when they first appeared. However, sociologists have noted the tendency of most sects to become more like mainline denominations over time.

In a work generally sympathetic to the church, the claim is made that mainline Protestant intellectuals have become more isolated from the general culture. They have failed to produce a Reinhold Niebuhr (the leading American theologian of the mid-twentieth century) who might be the center of fruitful controversy and discussion. The blandness of much of mainline Protestant religion at the local level cannot withstand the competition of more vigorous forms of religious individualism (Bellah et al. 1985: 238).

Catholics do not allow women to be priests (some have been ordained but Rome has not approved), and most Protestant denominations have only recently allowed women to become ministers. Despite some restrictions, there has been a notable rise in female clergy in the last 30 years. United Methodists permitted ordained women in 1956, and in 1980 elected their first woman bishop (the highest official in the church). Despite this progress, women face lingering sexism after ordination and find it difficult to land senior clergy appointments (Schaefer 2002: 157).

Religion and Politics

The influence of the Christian right has drawn widespread attention in the last two decades. Many Christians are drawn to conservative beliefs, particularly opposition to abortion, opposition to gay marriage, displeasure with certain coarseness in American life, and the loss of religious symbols, such as prayer in public life. Many believe the influence of the Christian right helped elect George W. Bush in 2000.

It is inaccurate, however, to assume that Christian and other religious groups will automatically vote in a conservative direction. Many opposed (or came to oppose) the war in Iraq and believe that religious people should work for peace. Many support the rights of working people and are sympathetic to the poor. Many Christians have taken up environmental issues such as global warming. Others work for gender equality and gay rights. The National Council of Churches, composed of most mainline denominations, tends to take progressive positions on most issues.

An important Christian evangelical in America, Jim Wallis, has argued for a different option in politics, following what he calls the prophetic religious tradition.

> It is traditional or conservative on issues of family values, sexual integrity and personal responsibility, while being very progressive, populist, or even radical on issues like poverty and racial justice. It affirms good stewardship of the earth and its resources, supports gender equality, and is more internationally minded than nationalist—looking first to peacemaking and

conflict resolution when it comes to foreign policy questions (Wallis 2005: 74).

Liberation theology is a liberal to radical movement in some Christian churches that emphasizes the oppression of the poor and marginalized, and argues for drastic reform in the lives of these people. It represents a fusion of Christian principles with political activism, often Marxist in character (Macionis 2004: 357). It has been particularly strong in Latin America. In Brazil, the world's most populous Catholic nation, many communities work for a type of liberation theology, with strong links to labor unions.

As mentioned earlier, Catholics have tended to vote Democratic until recent years, and American Jews have tended to be relatively liberal. The truth seems to be, then, that religious people in America, while tending to be conservative on many issues, differ among themselves politically and will be listening to more than one political party and one candidate (Charon 2007: 265).

Judaism

Next to Christians, Jews historically have been the most significant religious group in America. As mentioned in chapter 9, many families' department store name came from Jewish founding families. Today American Jews number about six million, the largest Jewish population in the world.

Not all Jews accept the religious principles of Judaism. An estimated one-third of adult Jewish Americans do not participate in religious services and are not a part of a temple or synagogue. A Jew in contemporary America is an individual who thinks of himself or herself as a Jew (Schaefer 2002: 385-386).

There are three main branches of Judaism: the Orthodox, which is the most conservative of the three, which tries to maintain the traditional Jewish practices; the Conservation, which also seeks to maintain these practise but is more flexible; and the Reformed, the most modern and liberal of the groups.

Jews still face stereotypes, that they are dishonest and unethical, clannish and conceited; power hungry, and intrusive. Chapter 9 found little if any actual support for these stereotypes, and noted that Jews are still subject to forms of discrimination.

Islam

Islam, whose adherents are known as Muslims, is the world's largest faith after Christianity: they comprise about one-fifth of the world's population. Some beliefs are held in common with Jews and Christians, but it is strongly influenced by the teachings of the Qur'an, the writings of the seventh century prophet Mohammed. Islamic believers are divided into a variety of sects, such as Sunnis and Shiites, who have experienced antagonism, especially in Iraq.

Muslims worship God or Allah and accept most of what Jews and Christians consider sacred writings. It is not widely reported among non-Muslims, but traditional Islam emphasizes brotherhood and peace. The September 11th terrorists violated essential Islamic principles; the Qur'an specifically prohibits the killing of innocent people. According to noted author Karen Armstrong, until the 20th century, Islam was a more tolerant and peaceful faith than Christianity (Armstrong 2006). A recent observer (Zakaria 2008) says that support for violence of any kind has dropped dramatically over the last five years in all Muslim countries.

The Qur'an strictly forbids any coercion in religion and regards all rightly guided religion as coming from God. According to Armstrong, the extremism and intolerance that have surfaced in the Muslim world in our day are a response to intractable political disagreements over oil, Palestine, the occupation of Muslim lands, authoritarian regimes in the Middle East—and not over an ingrained religious imperative (Armstrong 2006).

According to one expert, despite a rise in Islamic zeal, broad social and international trends in Islam give grounds for more optimism. In the Muslim world, millions of educated men and women have ended the monopoly that the clergy and its allies in the government enjoyed for centuries. Alternative sources of moral and international authority have reasserted themselves outside state structures, such as universities, cultural association, and unions. Further, many secular writers enjoy a growing audience across the Muslim world (Taheri 2007).

Many critics view the *hijab* (hair scarf) as the primary evidence that Muslim women are severely oppressed. Although women in Middle Eastern and other Islamic countries do not have the same rights as men, critics should not assume that the *hijab* is the source of oppression. It is the custom in their culture; many Western women look to the media as to how to look and behave (Ferrante 2006: 523). Some claim that most of the subjugation of women is cultural rather than religious.

There are some three million Muslims in the United States, of whom about 42 percent are African American, 24 percent South Asian, and 12 percent Arabs. There are more Muslims in the United States than either Presbyterians or Episcopalians (Schaefer 2002: 63).

A large number of American Muslims are foreign-born. There are few homegrown Muslim clerics in American today—and almost no institutions for training them. Prayer in many mosques in led by a scholar fresh off the plan from Lebanon or Saudi Arabia, someone with no connection to America and no affinity for its culture (Miller 2007).

According to a recent comprehensive survey, American Muslims hold more moderate political views than Muslims elsewhere in the world and are mostly middle class and willing to accept the American way of life. Most hold positive views of American society. They do have a much more negative view of the Iraq war and the war against terrorism than the U. S. public as a whole (El Nasser 2007).

Many jihadist sites on the internet are now published in English as well as Arabic, promoting rage against the West. While most American Muslims seem impervious to such propaganda, it is nonetheless true that 26 percent of Muslims age 18 to 29 believe that suicide bombing can be justified (Miller 2007).

As marginalized groups with virtually no power, Muslim Americans are vulnerable to prejudice and discrimination. Muslim women who choose to don *hijabs*, in keeping with their tradition to dress modestly, have faced harassment in the street or on the job (Schaefer 2002: 63). The Council on American-Islamic relations, an advocacy group, counted nearly 2,500 civil-rights complaints by Muslim Americans in 2006 (Miller 2007). (For more on Muslims, see chapter 9.)

Asian Religions

Major religions of Asian origin include Buddhism, Hinduism, Confucianism, Jainism, and Sikhism. It is impossible to generalize about all of these, but there is a tendency in Asian religions to emphasize contemplation, meditation, and the inner life of the individual, as well as world peace.

Fifty years ago, the U. S. population consisted largely of Protestants, Catholics, and Jews. Since then, there has been a considerable influx of non-Western religions, notably Muslims, discussed above, and Asian religions. Of these, Buddhism may have had the most influence on Jews and Christians, emphasizing as it does the contemplative spirit.

Buddhism may be traced to Siddhartha Gautama, later given the title the Lord Buddha, around 535 BCE. They have about 365 million followers, of whom about a million are in the United States. Four noble truths are central to Buddhism: existence is suffering; suffering has a cause, craving and attachment; cessation of suffering (nirvana) is possible; and the path to nirvana is through effort, mindfulness, and right concern.

Buddhist principles include selflessness, awareness, self-mastery, non-attachment, humility, compassion, and a peaceful mind (Columbia Encyclopedia 2007).

In the tradition of Eastern Buddhism, Zen Buddhism has developed a large following since the 1950s. For Asian American Buddhists, the temple plays a key religious, social, and cultural role in the community. Caucasian Buddhists focus on meditation. For some, Buddhism is more philosophy than religion.

There are some 837 million Hindus in the world; it is the dominant religion in India and Nepal and is generally regarded as the world's oldest religion. Hinduism may be unique in that it does not have a single founder, a theological system, a single code of morality, or a central religious organization. There are thousands of different Hindu religious groups in India. It is experiencing a revival not only in India but in other countries.

It is widely believed that Hinduism is a polytheistic religion, involving a large array of gods. Educated Hindus, however, consider the range of deities found in that religion to be but incarnations of one divine Spirit: *Brahman* is the God above all gods, the source of universal life. Orthodox Hindus accept reincarnation, or the Transmigration of the Soul. All creatures are in a process of spiritual evolution extending through limitless cycles of time. There are about 800,000 Hindus in the United States (Chakravarty 1978).

Sikhism originated some 500 years ago and claims some 20 million adherents today. Its founder, Guru Nanak, attempted to unify Islam and Hinduism around their shared devotional practices and belief in the unity of God. It stresses devotion and remembrance of God at all times, truthful living, the equality of mankind, and social justice. The emphasis is on disciplined, personal meditation. Most followers today live in the state of Punjab in India. The most significant religious center is the Golden Temple in Amritsar in Punjab (Sikhism home page 2007).

Confucianism, consisting largely of social ethics and moral teachings, has exerted tremendous influence on Chinese civilization down to the present time. There are about 6 million Confucians in the world, including 26,000 in North America. There are recent signs of a revival in mainline China. The cultures most strongly influenced by Confucianism include China, Japan, Korea, and Vietnam. Chinese Folk Religion has been practiced in China for thousands of years: it includes ancestor veneration, interest in the sun, moon, and stars, as well as animals. The end product is very colorful in appearance; one key religious icon is the Chinese dragon. Chinese Folk Religion could be a complementary adjunct to another religion, such as Buddhism or Confucianism (Ontario Consultants on Religious Tolerance 2004).

Shintoism, an animistic belief system involving the worship of *kami* spirits, was once the dominant religion in Japan. It began as a mixture of nature worship, fertility cults, divination techniques, hero worship, and shamanism (Ontario Consultants on Religious Tolerance 2004). While many in that country still practice Shinto rituals, less than 4 percent of Japanese people identify themselves as Shinto.

Modern Jainism was founded by Mahavira in the sixth century BCE. Jain monks believe in ahimsa, strict non-violence which prevents them from harming any person or animal. Jain teachings greatly influenced the thinking of Mohandas Gandhi, who influenced Martin Luther King. It teaches that one may rise above the cycle of rebirth only by total elimination of desire. Most of the 10 to 12 million Jains in the world live in India.

The Bahai faith began as an offshoot of Shia Islam, but it has attracted many Westerners. It believes in the unity of God and his family, and seeks to promote a tolerant, ecumenical attitude towards all religions. It teaches the harmony of science and religion and believes that truth is one. They claim over 5 million members around the world and have over 2,000 ethnic groups represented in their midst (The Bahais International website 2007).

Secularization

As modernization has increased in the world, so has *secularization*, the decline in the importance of religious institutions in society and in the everyday life of individuals. It stems in part from education which is increasingly critical, scientific, and goal-directed. People have more choices and may choose to minimize or abandon traditional religion in favor of practical and personal concerns.

There are two views about secularization. One holds that it is inevitable because of modernization and inevitably leads to the decline of religion. People are increasingly turning their time and energy to other interests. Sacred truths are not easily handed on to the next generation. This trend is pronounced today in European societies, where few people are actively involved in church (Charon 2007: 277).

Others believe that change may be inevitable, but not secularization. These observers argue that religion has changed but not declined in importance. People still seek meaning and community, and they still seek churches or a comparable group to give them these.

Interestingly, not all religious people bewail secularization. Theologian Harvey Cox (1965) claims that secularization is the fulfillment of a central Biblical theme: liberation from superstition and from animism (the belief that all material objects have spirits). A profoundly this-world orientation is deeply Biblical, he asserts. A number of liberal theologians concur with this view. An increase in secularization is not necessarily interpreted as a decline in religion (Roberts 1984: 380).

An interesting thesis is proposed by Thomas Luckmann. He argues that as society has become increasingly complex, and as institutions have become more specialized, traditional religions have had an influence over a decreasing range of human behavior and thinking. At the same time, technological, political, and economic changes have continued to occur rapidly. Luckmann maintains that this has caused traditional forms of religion to become irrelevant to the everyday experiences of the common person. But he denies that this represents a decline of religiosity: it has taken on new forms (reported in Roberts 1984: 395).

A movement in some religions, especially liberal Protestantism, thoroughly accepts modernization, including the main trends in secularization (though it still criticizes materialistic and hedonistic elements of the culture), and believes that religious faith must be modified to adapt to them. The best-known exponent of this view in American Christianity is retired Episcopal Bishop John Shelby Spong. The title of one of his books is revealing: *Why Christianity Must Change or Die.*

Some writers see religion as individualistic, meeting individual spiritual needs. No longer is religion simply a matter of maintaining the traditional religion we were born into. The search now includes traditional religion, a more liberalized established religion, and spiritualism without much church affiliation, smaller and stricter sects, and other options. There seems to be a search for individual fulfillment rather than a strong commitment to specific communities. There are a wide number of choices in modern society (Charon 2007: 275).

The Future of Religion

To predict the future of religion is hazardous because of the uncertainty of a clear definition and the difficulty of interpreting trends. A trend over the last decade or two may or may not be continued in future decades.

Some sociologists predict the continued decline of religion in this century. There does appear to be a recent reduction in traditional forms of religion and especially in institutional expressions of Christianity. This is most obvious in Europe but is also found among mainline Protestant denominations in America. Supporters of this view point to a decline of religious interest in the young, who would presumably not be supporting religion in their later years.

Others question this interpretation. Sociologist Peter Berger claims that more Americans than ever regularly go to religious services, support religious organizations, and describe themselves as holding strong religious beliefs (Berger 1992: 36). Except for Western Europe, the rest of the world is as religious as ever.

For those who see religion as a belief in the supernatural, religion may well be declining. For those who see religion as that which provides a sense of meaning in life, religion is changing but not necessarily declining. A move from a conservative stance to a liberal one would not necessarily mean a decline in religiosity (Roberts 1984: 380).

As for declining interest among the young, some point out that this is a normal development process most generations have experienced. Most people, by their 30s, join churches and see that their children get some religious training. Perhaps this generation will be no different (Roberts 1984: 382). Further, a larger percentage of Americans belong to churches today than was true in the early 1800s, an era sometimes considered the "golden age" of religion.

The likelihood is that religion will maintain a significant influence for large numbers of people for the foreseeable future, but the nature of religion will change.

Many religious functions will still be a part of human existence, but they may become more individualized, more varied, more unpredictable. While a fundamentalist, superstitious, or narrow religion may grow for a time, its long-range future is uncertain. But religion as a search for meaning and brotherhood, that is progressive and ecumenical, will surely continue.

Summary

Religion refers to human responses that give meaning to ultimate and inescapable problems of existence. It is one way people combat stress, overcome adversity, and analyze challenges. Religion is clearly salient and visible in the events of the world.

Durkheim stressed the distinction between the secular and the sacred, that with is spiritual, beyond our senses, honored and held in awe. There has been a clear trend in world religions towards monotheism.

Functionalists claim that religion reinforces the power of society, encourages conformity, and provides comfort. It is an attempt to make sense of tragedy and find meaning in the universe. Conflict theorists note that religion often justifies oppression, is almost always patriarchal, and tends to stifle freedom of thought and speech.

The Roman Catholic Church is the largest religious group in the world, with well over one billion members. In the United States it has been a major force in assimilating immigrants, and today Hispanics make up about a third of all American Catholics. It has been hurt by alleged sexual abuse by priests.

Protestants are Christians who broke from the Catholic Church and who have had numerous splits. Mainline denominations, who generally belong to the National Council of Churches, are somewhat more liberal but have been declining lately. The Southern Baptist Church is the largest Protestant group, and the Mormons and Pentecostals have shown great growth.

Much attention has been given to the relationship between religion and politics, with some claiming that the religious right has influenced elections. But moderate and liberal religious groups have been exercising more influence lately.

There are about six million Jews in the United States. While they have been an important part of the American religious scene for many years, they still tend to be victims of stereotypes (particularly concerning money) and some discrimination.

Islam, whose followers are known as Muslims, consists of one-fifth of the world's population. Traditional teachings of Islam are tolerant and peaceful. Extremism in Islam has largely been a response to political disagreements and authoritarian regimes. There are about 3 million Muslims in the United States, who tend to be middle class and who accept the American way of life.

Asian religions are on the increase in the United States. Buddhists, who have about one million adherents in this country, has probably had more influence on America than any other Asian religion. Hinduism, which claims to be the world's oldest religion, has about 800,000 followers in this country.

Secularization refers to the decline in the importance of religious institutions. There are different views on the future of secularization, but most scholars believe that religion is taking new forms today and that people have more choices than in the past. Some see religion as declining in the future, but others see it changing and adapting.

References

Armstrong, Karen. 2006. "We cannot afford to maintain these ancient prejudices against Islam." *The Guardian* (September 18).

Bahais International Website. 2007.

Bellah, Robert N., Richard Madsen, William M. Sullivan, Ann Swidler, Steven M. Tipton. 1985. *Habits of the Heart: Individualism and Commitment in American Life* (New York: Harper & Row).

Berger, Kathleen Stassen. 2001. *The Developing Person Through the Life Span*, fifth edition (New York: Worth).

Berger, Peter. 1967, 1992. *The Sacred Canopy* (Garden City, New York: Doubleday).

Chakravarty, Amiya. 1978. "Quest for the Universal One." Pp. 34-50 in *Great Religions of the World,* National Geographic Society.

CBS Evening News. 2008 (April 17).

Cox. Harvey. 1965. *The Secular City* (New York: Macmillan).

El Nasser, Haya. 2007. "American Muslims Reject Extremes." *USA Today* (May 22).

Ferrante, Joan. 2006. *Sociology: A Global Perspective*, sixth edition (Belmont, California: Thomson Wadsworth).

Macionis, John J. 2004. *Society: the Basics*, seventh edition (Upper Saddle River, New Jersey: Prentice-Hall).

Marger, Martin N. *Race and Ethnic Relations*, fifth edition (Belmont, California: Wadsworth Thomson).

Miller, Lisa. 2007. "American Dreamers: Islam USA." *Newsweek* (July 30): 25-33.

News Briefs. 2007. *The Progressive Christian* (May-June).

Ontario Consultants on Religious Tolerance. 2004-2006.

Roberts, Keith A. 1984. *Religion in Sociological Perspective* (Homewood, Illinois: The Dorsey Press).

Schaefer, Richard T. 2002. *Racial and Ethnic Groups*, eighth edition (Upper Saddle River, New Jersey: Prentice-Hall).

Spong, John Shelby. 1998. *Why Christianity Must Change or Die: A Bishop Speaks to Believers in Exile* (San Francisco: HarperSanFrancisco).

Taheri, Amir. 2007. "What Do Muslims Think?" *Dallas Morning News* (May 20): 1P, 5P.

Turner, Jonathan. 2006. *Sociology* (Upper Saddle River, New Jersey: Prentice-Hall).

Wallis, Jim. 2005. *God's Politics: Why the Right Gets it Wrong and the Left Doesn't Get It* (Harper San Francisco).

Weiss, Jeffrey. 2008. "Study Outlines America's Leaps of Faith." **Dallas Morning News** 1A (February 26).

Zakaria, Fareed. 2008. "The Rise of the Rest" (**Newsweek,** May 12).

OBAMA

CHANGE WE CAN
BELIEVE IN

A sign commonly seen during the 2008 presidential campaign.

Chapter 13: SOCIAL CHANGE AND GLOBALIZATION

Any young person who has talked with his or her grandparents, or even with his or her parents, is aware of enormous changes in the country in the last 30 or 40 years. Not only have science and technology changed the way Americans live, but attitudes and perceptions have shifted enormously. This is a worldwide phenomenon, but is most dramatic in such Western nations as the United States and the rapidly advancing economies of Asia.

Social change is any significant alteration, modification, or transformation in the organization and operation of social life (Ferrante 2006: 562). Sociology first emerged as a discipline attempting to understand social change, particularly the Industrial Revolution, which triggered dramatic changes in every area of social life.

Compare the United States in 1900 with the year 2000. The population went from 76 million to 281 million; the percentage of the population living in urban areas rose from 40 percent to 80 percent; life expectancy from 46 for men and 48 for women to 74 for men and 79 for women; household income, adjusted for 2000 figures, went from $8,000 to $40,000. People in 1900 spent 43 percent of their income on food, while those in 2000 spent 15 percent; one in 20 marriages ended in divorce in 1900, compared to 8 in 20 a century later (Macionis 2004: 443).

In 2004, in the U. S., 3.5 billion passengers traveled by air. The number of international passengers reached 760 million, up from an estimated 50,000 in 1950. International passengers are expected to increase to 1.6 billion by 2020. The movement of 1.34 billion travelers each year creates a logistical nightmare for airport security (Ferrante 2006: 566).

Innovation is the invention or discovery of something new—an idea, a process, a practice, or a device (Ferrante 2006: 564). Two technological innovations are largely responsible for the information explosion: computers and telecommunications. Both help people create, store, retrieve, and distribute large quantities of printed, visual, and spoken materials at mind-boggling speeds.

A single silicon chip only a quarter-inch thick can process millions of bits of information in a second. The chip has made possible the widespread use of the personal computer. Fiber-optic cables and satellites have replaced wire cables as the means of transmitting images, voices, and data. When the capabilities of fiber optics are exploited fully, a single fiber the diameter of a human hair can carry the entire telephone voice traffic of the United States and transmit the contents of the Library of Congress anywhere in the world in a few seconds (Ferrante 2006: 569).

The Internet began in the late 1960s to transfer information from one site to another quickly and efficiently in the event of war, and to create an information sharing system without central control. Today, the Internet comprises a vast network of computer networks connected to one another via special software and phone, fiber optic, or other type of lines that has the potential to connect billions of computers and their users on a global scale. The Internet has sped up both work and leisure, changed how students learn, and provides a vehicle by which the lives of people around the world will become more intertwined (Ferrante 2006: 575).

Theories about Social Change

In chapter 7, there was a long discussion of the way societies had moved from a "folk" society to an "urban" character, based on the theories of Robert Redfield and Emile Durkheim. Some of the important shifts were from a traditional mindset to one based on rationality; one oriented to the past to one oriented to the present and future; a homogeneous society to a heterogeneous one; one with generalized occupations to one with specialization; a patriarchal society to a more egalitarian one; one with strong primary relations to one based more on secondary relations; and one with a parochial outlook to one with a cosmopolitan view.

Rates of social change predictably increase as society becomes modern. The rate of change is normally determined by worldwide or societal trends—such as globalization, colonization, war, trade, and industrialization. Change is highly interdependent. When one part of society changes—such as education or trade—much of the rest of society changes, and the new rate of change increases (Charon 2007: 228).

Modernization theory refers to the process of social change begun by industrialization. This led to the decline of small, traditional communities, expanded personal choices giving people more control over their own lives, and an increase in social diversity seen in the mix of people, the growth of cities, and a growing bureaucracy. More optimism was evident in a growing awareness of time as something to be used (Macionis 2004: 442-443).

Although symbolic interactionism deals with the micro level of society, it has something to say about social change. As we have seen, it considers meanings and interpretations of social situations. Change begins when meanings or definitions of the situation become problematic. When they don't work, humans may discard, modify, or create symbols that are more satisfactory (Harper and Leicht 2007: 58).

For Max Weber, the unquestioned truths of an earlier time have been challenged by rational thinking, with its emphasis on calculation, efficiency, and goal-directed behavior. While Weber saw this change, largely brought on by science, as inevitable, he worried that science was carrying us away from more basic questions about the meaning and purpose of human existence (Charon 2007: 234; Macionis 2004: 445). Another writer claims that knowledge can be as much a curse as a blessing, and the most dangerous threats confronting us today are the results of the interaction of expanding human knowledge with unchanging human need (Gray 2004).

Postmodernism became a powerful theme among intellectuals in the 20th century. The claim was that modern technological society devitalizes life and robs humans of the subjective dimensions of experience found in myth, art, emotion, ritual, and community. Capitalism, science, technology, and bureaucracy have become instruments of social control by elites. Reality is being transformed so that people are reclaiming their subjective lives (Harper and Leicht 2007: 79).

Durkheim wrote about the growing division of labor, specialized economic activity that greatly changed society. He found a shift from *mechanical* solidarity, one of shared moral sentiments, to *organic* solidarity, based on mutual dependence: all of us must depend on others to meet most needs (see chapter 2). For Durkheim, modernization was not so much a loss of community as a change from community based on bonds of likeness (kinship and neighborhood) to community based on economic interdependence (Macionis 2004: 445).

One functionalist view speaks of the emergence of *mass society*, in which prosperity and bureaucracy have eroded traditional social ties. People may have more income, but kinship and other social ties have been weakened, so individuals often feel socially isolated. Face-to-face communication has been replaced by the impersonal mass media, large organizations, public education, and a formal criminal justice system. When the government assumes responsibility for more and more areas of social life, communities allow people little control over their lives.

Critics of mass-society theory say this view attracts social and economic conservatives who defend conventional morality but are indifferent to the historical plight of women and other minorities (Macionis 2004: 446-449). People seem to have less individuality in the world, yet shared norms and values seem strong enough to give most people a sense of meaning and purpose. And most people value the personal freedom modern society affords.

Gerhard Lenski developed a broad developmental theory of different types of societies where the transitions from one form to the next were caused by innovations in the technology of economic production that produced an ever larger and more certain surplus of food and material resources. At each stage, societies could support a larger population and grew in complexity (Harper and Leicht 2007: 25).

A conflict perspective argues that conflict, which is inevitable in social life, is both a consequence and cause of change. Any kind of change has the potential to trigger conflict between those who benefit from the change and those who stand to lose from it. Conflict can be a constructive force that prevents a social system from becoming stagnant, unresponsive, or inefficient. Self-interest, according to conflict thought, erodes the social ties of communities. People are treated as commodities. Capitalist corporations have reached enormous size and control unimaginable wealth as multinationals. Most people are still powerless (Ferrante 2006: 573; Macionis 2004: 449).

For Karl Marx, modern society was synonymous with capitalism. Marx believed that capitalism was the first economic system capable of maximizing the immense productive potential of human labor and ingenuity. But he thought that capitalism ignored too many human needs and that too many people could not afford to buy the products of their labor. The drive for profit takes no account of the health and the length of life of the worker unless society forces it to do so. While capitalism brought about sweeping changes in production, it would sow the seeds of revolutionary social change, leading to socialism. Marx imagined a future of human freedom, creativity, and community (Macionis 2004: 446; Ferrante 2006: 578).

Changes in the Workplace

Beth Rubin has written about a major shift in what she calls the *social contract* that underpins society. "Social contract" refers to the shared understandings that structure cooperation, as in the workplace or in a marriage. Market societies work, in part, through explicit and implicit social contracts underlying exchange, as between employer and employee (Rubin 1996: 3-26).

The idea of the "American Dream" developed in the 20th century. Stressing hard work, thrift, honesty, and community, this vision claimed that anyone who wants to can make it. People, including those not highly educated, were employed in industries or government, and usually represented by unions. Comfort and security seemed the norm. Through the 1960s the country experienced a period of economic growth, stable work, and a liberal state.

All this began to change in the 1970s as the economy slowed. Companies began to decrease the number of workers, replacing many of them with computers and robots, and moving jobs to other areas or other countries where production was cheaper. Many workers moved from manufacturing to the service sector, at lower average pay. Full-time workers began to be replaced with temporary and part-time jobs. Employers sought to rid the workplace of unions. These changes led to the insecurity and instability of many workers.

Workers can no longer anticipate long-term employment with a single company or even with a single industry. "The trajectory of education, job, and security…simply no longer exists for as many as it once did" (Rubin 1996: 181). Work no longer provides financial security for salaried and hourly workers. Most face intermittent job changes. The flexible economy is based on rapid change and adaptability.

Once centered on farms or factories, work has moved to offices and cyberspace, where computers communicate. The country has moved from an industrial economy to a global, flexible one. This transformation has eliminated the stable and well-paid jobs held by workers with only a high school diploma. Only about 35 percent of displaced workers have found work that equaled or surpassed their previous wages and benefits. Good-paying jobs today require at least a college diploma. But even a college degree and a big paycheck are no guarantee against unemployment (Rubin 1996: 3-9; Eitzen and Zinn 2007: 273).

In the United States, well over 90 percent of the workforce works for someone else's wages and salaries—up from 20 percent in 1800. Over half of employees work for organizations with 500 or more employees—of which there were none in 1800 (Perrow 2002). The household with two breadwinners worked an equivalent of seven additional weeks a year in 2000 compared to 1990, each person often working 50 or 60 hours. However, not everyone considers long working hours a problem because they often reflect worker preference (Perrons 2004: 16).

New innovations have led to a technological change that increases the demand and income of highly skilled and educated workers. New technologies allow a minority of superstars to capture a much larger share of the market. There has been a 2,500 percent increase in CEO income but a relative decline in blue-collar wages in the new century (Perrons 2004: 323).

In the U. S., inequalities have been widening between the very rich and all others, especially those at the lower end. Explanations for this widening inequality are that the wages of manual workers have been undermined by competition from low-wage regions, a decline in manufacturing, and the feminization of employment (Perrons 2004: 323). The new economy has led to increasing economic inequality and insecurity, along with intense competition and increasing risk and uncertainty for employers. A revolving door admits a few winners and casts out many losers (Perrons 2004: 16, 22).

Women who do caring (nurturing) work are rarely rewarded equivalent in monetary terms as, say, those in car maintenance. Pay for care for the elderly, despite the strength and patience required, is rarely much above minimum wage. Pay seems determined more by who does the job. Further, the proportion of women covered by collective bargaining is far lower than for men. Statistically women are likely to be poorer, earn less, and are underrepresented at higher levels in the employment hierarchy (Perrons 2004: 23; see Changes in Women's Roles, below.)

Changes in the Family

The meaning and definition of "family" are increasingly contested. Working mothers are now the norm, and latchkey kids are old news. Increasing numbers of universities are offering health insurance benefits to the gay partners of faculty and staff. In 1993, a judge in New Jersey allowed a lesbian couple to legally adopt a child that one of the women had borne (Rubin 1996: 2). Decline of fertility rates, a decline in teenage births since 1970, the rising number of lone parents, and couples in consensual union indicate major changes in family life (Richter 2005).

After World War II, marriage and birth rates soared. From 1946 to 1964 (the "baby boomer" years), women had on average 3.7 children. By the mid 1970s the number had fallen to less than 2.1 children per woman. During the 1950s half of all women who married did so in their teens and had children within 15 months of their marriage. In 1940, 70 percent of families were male-breadwinner and female-homemaker families. For the next 25 years, more than half of all families conformed to this norm, but that is diminishing today (Rubin 1996: 12).

Family life in the future will challenge and confound us. Some scholars foresee no one dominant family form at a time when there are gay and lesbian parents; single mothers by choice; males who take care of children or do household chores; and interracial adoptions and other non-traditional practices that transform the social landscape. For example, since the 1950s, over 100,000 Korean children and many Chinese children were adopted into American households (Galvin 2004: 677-678).

Western men are waiting until they are older before having children, and fewer are electing to become fathers at all. More men have flexible work arrangements. While women continue to bear the burden of housework, men are more involved as parents: men tend to see child-related tasks as contributing to an overall "engaged" involvement with their children (Singleton and Maher 2004).

Single householding is likely to go on increasing, but the phenomenon is much more circumscribed than is usually realized. It is largely confined to the rich world, and a couple of formerly rich countries in Latin America (Therborn 2004: 311). In one study, single mothers head approximately 50 percent of all U. S. households and are the fastest-growing, yet most underprivileged, group in today's society. Single or never-married parents are significantly younger, have fewer years of school, and lower levels of income (Martin et al. 2004).

Severe economic pressures can undermine partner interaction and impact parent-child communication. Children living in poverty are more likely to suffer depression, social withdrawal, and low self-esteem (Galvin 2004: 679). Children of single mothers often face more emotional, psychological and adjustment difficulties (Martin et al. 2004).

A high divorce rate means that many families are now *blended*. Families are increasingly composed of biological parents, stepparents, children from multiple marriages, and so on. More children in their twenties are returning to live with their parents (Rubin 1996: 19).

Population age structure in most industrialized nations has changed from a pyramid to a rectangle creating a family structure long and thin, with more family generations alive but with fewer members in the generation. This leads to more multigenerational bonds (Galvin 2004: 681).

Different rules and practices of marriage and sexuality have remained in the world. By and large they became more different in the last century. It is difficult to tell whether that divergence will continue, stop, or be reversed. But important differences are very likely to remain in the coming decades. Pre-marital non-commercial sex and informal pairing will become less rare (Therborn 2004: 315). The current generation is assuming more responsibility at an earlier age. Shifts in societal attitudes about premarital and marital living arrangements will affect the future attitudes and level of acceptance displayed by this younger generation (Martin et al. 2004).

Despite these changes, the core of romantic freedom and commitment in the modern family system is not broken, and is still there for the future. Marital happiness remains at a high level and married people have stayed much happier than non-married ones. In a large German survey in 2000, 70 percent of young people ages 12 to 25 held that one needed a family to be happy (Therborn 2004: 313). The vast majority of people will still marry at some point in their lives, and 71 percent of adults believe that marriage is a life-long commitment (Martin et al. 2004). Two recent scholars say, "We find several compelling reasons for thinking that today families and households on the whole are doing at least as well and often better than in the past" (Harper and Leicht 2007: 92).

Changes in Women's Roles

Married women are more involved in the paid labor force than previous generations. Some observers argue that housework is being transformed. The New Woman is being portrayed as seamlessly balancing tensions between career and motherhood, her identity far removed from the traditional, cloistered housewife role that belonged to her mother. Yet dramatic equality between men and women has not been achieved. In most cases, women are still responsible for the bulk of domestic labor. As the younger generation gets older, this situation will likely change (Singleton and Mohrer 2004; Martin et al. 2004).

A feminist consciousness has arisen among millions of U. S. women. During the 1960s and 1970s, this produced many changes in the roles of women and men. But periods of recession, high unemployment and inflation led to a backlash against feminism. A coalition of groups calling themselves profamily and prolife emerged, opposing feminist gains in reproductive, family, and antidiscrimination policies (Eitzen and Zinn 2007: 359).

Changes in Age and Population

Global population, only about one billion in 1800, reached 6 billion by 1999.

By 2050, United Nations demographers predict a population of about nine billion people on the planet, a 50 percent increase from the turn of the century. There will be more Africans and far fewer Chinese, Japanese, and Europeans than there are today. In 1900 Europe housed a quarter of the world's population; in 2000, one-eighth, and in 2050 it is predicted to harbor only one fifteenth of the human beings of the earth. Currently, the world is gaining 79 million people each year, with 96 percent of this increase in poor areas. Such growth increases the population pressure on food and economic resources of all sorts, and is a matter of urgent concern (Macionis 2004: 410; Therborn 2004).

Empowering women is the key to controlling population growth. As women are given more life choices, they will have fewer children. Women with access to schooling and jobs, who can decide when and whether to marry and who bear children as a matter of choice, will limit their own fertility (Macionis 2004: 413). Patriarchy has become officially illegitimate across the whole world, but is still entrenched in the poor parts of the world (Therborn 2004).

Perhaps two-thirds of all people who have every reached the age of 65 are alive today (Peterson 2002). Collective aging is forcing countries to face different political and economic choices. In the developed world today, the elderly (people over 65) amount to 15 percent of the population, and by the year 2030, the U. N. projects that they will be nearing 25 percent.

Major countries in East Asia—notably China, Taiwan, Singapore and South Korea—are projected to reach developed-world levels of old-age dependency by the middle of this century. Fifty years from now, the population in some developed countries may reach a median age of 55, 20 years older than the oldest median age of any country on earth as recently as 1970. By the 2030s at the latest, the total population of the developed world will peak and then start to decline. If fertility rates do not rebound, many developed countries will depopulate at an astounding rate. Italy, Spain, and Japan are on track to lose two-thirds of their population by the end of the century (Peterson 2002). By 2050 close to a third of China's citizens will be over 60—three times the current proportion (National Geographic 2008: 62).

Across the Middle East, from Morocco to Iran, birth rates are falling. Population growth is occurring not among children but in the ranks of the working age population (15 to 64). Middle Eastern states have pursued effective family planning policies (Laipson 2002).

Governments over the world have subscribed to millennium development goals. These goals relate mainly to poverty, hunger, primary education, gender equality, child mortality, and access to water and sanitation. On the basis of current trends, sub-Saharan Africa will not meet any of the targets while South Asia is set to meet all of them except enrollment in primary education and fewer numbers that are malnourished. Latin America will meet the targets and East Asia and the Pacific look set to exceed them (Perrons 2004: 320).

The United States is in a better comparative position to confront the aging challenge. It is the youngest of the major developed countries and is likely to remain so for the foreseeable future. But it has a low national savings rate, and a health care explosion without parallel in other countries. The U. S. spends twice as much per capita on doctors and hospitals as the typical developed economy (Peterson 2002).

The elderly, about 13 percent of the population, consume more than one-third of all health care in the United States. They are four times as likely as the nonold to be hospitalized. Medical expenses of the old are three times greater than those of middle-aged adults. A rapid rise in the number of the old-old (those 85 and over) inevitably exacerbates health costs (Eitzen and Zinn 2007: 221).

America is challenged to make aging both more secure for the old and less burdensome for the young. Only a higher birth rate will produce more children. Generous public funding for family allowances and investment in children, in the tradition of Scandinavia and France, along with more savings and investment, would be helpful (Peterson 2002).

Immigration has become a pressing concern. The number of foreign-born residents and children of immigrants has reached the highest level in U. S. history, numbering 56 million people, or 20 percent of the population. About 73 percent of those from Latin America have children under 18 (Galvin 2004).

Immigration challenged the hegemony of white Europe, creating incredible diversity in race, ethnicity, language, and culture, and leading, often, to division and hostility. The foreign-born population in the U. S. has risen from 19.8 million in 1990 to 34 million in 2004. Approximately one million annually set up permanent residence, and estimates of unauthorized foreign nationals residing in the U. S. range from 11 to 20 million. The majority of these are Hispanics and Asian (Eitzen and Zinn 2007: 204-205).

Immigrants weaken the wages of poorer, low-skilled workers, and they create an unfair burden on states such as California, New

York, Texas, and Florida, largely in health and education services. But they do society's dirty manual jobs that many poor U. S. citizens are unwilling to do. About 30 percent of recent foreign born arrivals over 24 hold a college, professional, or graduate degree. They are more likely than the rest of the population to be self-employed and start their own businesses, which in turn create jobs. An estimated 7 million undocumented workers pay $7 billion annually into social security and Medicare and are not eligible to receive the benefits (Eitzen and Zinn 2007: 209-210).

Over 80 percent of immigrants come to the U. S. legally, and illegals make up only about one percent of the total population. Immigrant demand for English classes far exceeds the number of available classes. Many studies show that immigrants do not cost U. S. citizens jobs, and their net effect is often to improve growing local economies, though they may cost the jobs of some low-skilled workers in slow-growing or stagnant economies. Immigrants have always caused controversy, but in the long run they have also been a source of richness and creativity (Harper and Leicht 2007: 83-84).

In the long run, according to several scholars, immigrants are a good investment for society. One study found that by the time a typical immigrant with a family dies, that person and his or her family will have paid $80,000 more in taxes than they receive in government benefits. Evidence is that immigrants are a fiscal burden for the first 22 years, mainly in educational costs. After that, the society benefits monetarily. Research also shows that legal and illegal immigration adds $1 billion to $10 billion a year to the U. S. gross domestic product (Eitzen and Zinn 2007: 210-212).

Population has been shifting to the Sunbelt, and 60 percent of the country's people now live there. In 1950, 9 of the 10 largest U. S. cities were in the Snowbelt (the industrial Northeast and Midwest); by 2000, 6 of the top 10 were in the Sunbelt. Since 1990, rural areas, especially those that offer scenic and recreational attractions, have been gaining population. Many prefer the slower pace, lower crime rate, and cleaner air found in the country and small towns. Many companies have relocated to rural counties as well (Macionis 2004: 417).

Urban and Environmental Change

Economic growth has brought considerable damage to natural systems and resources. Every major indicator of the earth's biophysical conditions shows this deterioration. Forests shrinking, croplands losing topsoil, fresh water becoming scarce, ozone layer continuing to thin, greenhouse gases accumulating, the number of plant and animal species diminishing, air pollution at health-threatening levels in several cities, damage from acid rain seen on every continent (Harper and Leicht 2007: 352).

Global warming has received enormous publicity in recent years. By 1995 the world's organized scientific bodies believed that the important evidence was in. There is vast scientific consensus that the earth's climate is warming and that human economic activity (particularly burning fossil fuels) is the main culprit. With about 20 percent of the world's people, the developed nations consume 50 percent of the total fossil fuels that are central to development and the key to global warming (Harper and Leicht 2007: 340).

Another concern is that urban areas are the major sources of carbon dioxide emissions from the burning of fossil fuels for heating and cooling, from industrial processes, and the transportation of people and goods. The vulnerability of urban populations, most often the elderly and poor, rises with heat waves, as seen in France and Spain in 2003. Future climate scenarios suggest greater risks in the future (Grimmond 2007).

Agricultural resources, especially soil and water, are under stress around the world. Right now, over a billion people lack adequate access to fresh water and 2.4 billion lack adequate sanitation. "By 2025, two-thirds of the world's population may be living in countries that face serious water shortages" (Harper and Leicht 2007: 344). Groundwater supplies are particularly critical in large areas of China, India, and the Middle East.

Changes in Education

American higher education is beset by major challenges in achieving equity, diversity, and access. They are due in part to retrenchment and reorganization of higher education in the late 1970s. Through the 1990s, budget cuts in public education and public health, with the growth of police and prisons, further narrowed educational opportunities. Today, class inequalities and educational tracking, combined with the rising costs of college, are making it almost impossible for poor students to move up the educational ladder (Anthony M. Platt, cited in Katz and O'Leary 2002).

According to Platt, a new market economy paradigm is driving the field of education. Local knowledge is devalued in contrast with corporate expertise. Memorization is favored over creative thinking. Needed is a democratization of education at the local, state, and national levels (Katz and O'Leary 2002).

Some 2.5 million college students were studying abroad in 2004. Today foreign students earn 30 percent of doctoral degrees awarded in the United States. They comprise 8 percent of undergraduates in the Ivy League institutions. In the U. S., 20 percent of newly hired professors in science and engineering are foreign born (N. A. 2006). Foreign students and immigrants account for almost 50 percent of all science researchers in this country. It is estimated that by 2010, 75 percent of all science Ph.D.s in this country will be awarded to foreign students (Zakaria 2008).

Change in Politics and Government

After World War II, government on every level increased in size and involvement in economic and social problems. Lyndon Johnson's "Great Society" was a recasting of FDR's New Deal, again driven by government help. Emphasis was given to the problem of poverty. Government took an activist cast and was seen as a source of redress for many social ills.

But later in the 20th century, faith in the government as a solution to social ills weakened. The American government has played an uncertain and vacillating role in international conflicts from Vietnam to Iraq. Political parties seem divided against themselves, amid growing doubt that either party could solve the nation's social problems. A reduction in resources available to the government hinders solutions. The tax base decreased. The growing national debt shrinks the budget that could be used to finance social programs (Rubin 1996: 20).

In America, there is a decreasing trust in national leaders and social institutions. The belief is widespread that the interests of people are not being honestly and completely served by leaders and social institutions

(Harper and Leicht 2007: 77). (The popularity of Barack Obama may stem, in part, from an awareness that he represents a different approach to leadership.)

Nation states currently display a very frail form of democracy because although everyone has an equal voice it is a weak one. Voting figures are often low in countries where democracy has a long history. There is generally a wide gulf between the elected and the electorate, with leaders only consulting the people in a cursory way at election time, and the electorate generally takes little interest in the day-to-day workings of the state (Perrons 2004: 326).

Sociologist Amitai Etzioni, among other scholars, argues that an individual's pursuit of self interest must be balanced by a commitment to the larger community. People, he says, have become too focused on individual rights. People expect the system to provide for them, but they are reluctant to support the system. Most people believe in the principle of trial by jury, but fewer and fewer people are willing to perform jury duty. The public is quick to accept government services but increasingly reluctant to pay for these services with taxes (Macionis 2004: 455).

Changes in China

The 2008 Olympics in Beijing called attention to changes in China. As the world's oldest civilization, China was for centuries resistant to social and cultural change. Today, China is at the cutting edge of economic, social, and political change that gives it an unprecedented influence in global affairs. The results could have profound economic, political and cultural consequences for the rest of the world.

China is expected to overtake the United States as the world's largest economy in ten years. The number of computers in China is doubling every two years, and it has the world's largest number of Internet users (220 million). Cell phones in China have grown from 87 million in 2000 to 432 million today. It consumes almost twice as much steel as the United States, as well as more grain, meat, and coal. It is well beyond the U. S. in the number of televisions and refrigerators. Along with Japan, it is the leading purchaser of U. S. treasury securities (National Geographic 2008: 62; Harper and Leicht 2007: 312).

China's GDP is growing by roughly 8.5 percent a year. For three decades the economy has grown at an average rate of nearly 10 percent

(Kessler 2008: 42). Seventy-two percent of U. S. shoes, 50 percent of U. S. kitchen appliances, 85 percent of U. S. artificial Christmas trees, and 80 percent of U. S. toys, are made in China (National Geographic 2008: 170). There has been a concern, however, about the quality of some of their exports.

Chinese schools have been remarkably successful at basic skills—the literacy rate is over 90 percent. But the curriculum depends heavily on rote memorization, and higher education is particularly weak (Hessler 2008: 176). Rural, female, ethnic, and migrants are falling further and further behind the mainstream of Chinese society, unable to compete for jobs but often no longer connected to their geographical and cultural roots. Despite significant reform, there is intractable inequality in education (Mohrman 2006).

The transformation of Chinese society is aptly portrayed by Hessler in National Geographic (2008: 176). He refers to the early industry of Lowell, Massachusetts, when John Greenleaf Whittier described the city as springing up, like the enchanted palaces of the Arabian tales.

Today it's the factory towns of China that seem to be conjured up from another world. The sheer human energy is overwhelming: the fearless entrepreneurs, the quick-moving builders, the young migrants. Virtually everybody has been toughened by the past; families remember well the poverty of the Mao period. Meanwhile most Chinese have seen their living standards rise in recent years, often dramatically. This combination—the struggles of the past, the opportunities of the present—has created a uniquely motivated population. It's hard to imagine another place where people are more willing to work.

But despite new prosperity, a huge gap remains between the rich and the poor. The gap is especially obvious between the coastal area and the western part of the country. Hundreds of millions live at the edge of survival. In some areas, a man makes three or four dollars a day chipping mortar, and a woman one or two dollars for the same work. There is considerable resentment over the income disparity, which is exacerbated with perceived corruption in the doing of business (Koppel 2008). The country was hit by a major earthquake in early 2008.

Sixteen of the 20 most polluted cities in the world are in China. China is the largest producer of sulfur dioxide emissions in the world.

Only 10 percent of China's 20 billion tons of city sewage is treated; the rest is dumped into rivers and lakes. By 2000 China had become the seventh largest importer of oil (Harper and Leicht 2007: 334). With so many new cars, traffic accidents have become a major concern.

There is now a Chinese middle class of some 100 to 150 million people. Ownership of both homes and cars is now common. People are now free to choose where to live, work, and travel. Yet with all the changes, there is a sense of unease at the sense of social change. Children are among the most pressured. Some observers see political change on the horizon: the generation of individualists will one day demand a say in how they are governed (Chang 2008: 80).

For changes in the Chinese family, see chapter 11.

Social Movements

A *social movement* is formed when a substantial number of people organize to change (or to resist or undo change) in some area of society. For a social movement to develop, there must be a condition some people object to, a belief that something needs to be done, and an organized effort aimed at attracting supporters and defining a strategy to remedy it. Examples of social movements are the environmental movement, the civil rights movement, and the women's movement (Ferrante 2006: 580).

Usually, individuals can do little to change society. Social movements have real potential when many people are working together. Change stems more from social conflict than from individual acts. Social movements protest the direction of other powerful groups, as when labor unions fight for workers' rights. To change society is to have enough power to influence those who defend society as it exists (Charon 2007: 227-231).

Lasting change results from social trends, driving far-reaching, general developments that affect various patterns in society. Once begun, these trends take on a life of their own and are difficult to turn around. Trends embody changes that arise from the actions of many individuals who deal with their everyday situations and act in a similar direction and produce a cumulative effect (Charon 2007: 233-234). Change is most likely when the social situation favors it. Martin Luther King was a key leader in the civil rights movement, but without favorable social circumstances, he would not have had the same impact. The individual makes a difference when social conditions are right.

Globalization

Globalization has become the subject of corporate and public policy think-tanks, academic conferences, TV programs, bestselling books, websites and papers of learned journals. It refers to the growing interconnectedness and interdependence among countries on a global scale. It encompasses not only the global circulation of goods, services and capital but also of information, ideas, and people. Fast modes of communication make it possible for money, ideas, goods, and people to flow around the world ever more quickly with significant implications for economic activities and employment (Perrons 2004: 1).

Exchanges of states, markets, communications, and ideas across borders are a leading characteristic of the contemporary world (Brysk 2002). Every part of the world is now tied into systems of markets; wholesalers and retailers can buy and sell with the click of a button (Turner 2006: 368). Chapter 5 introduced the concept of multinational corporations, enterprises that own or control production and service facilities in countries other than the one in which their headquarters are located. Across the world, the lives of all people are increasingly linked. Americans are no longer affected only by economic decisions made in New York and Chicago, but also by those made in Tokyo, Zurich, Frankfort, Beijing, and Shanghai (Harper and Leicht 2007: 69).

By the 1990s, practically every large American corporation was involved internationally in developing nations and less developed ones. Firms and banks in all nations are becoming so intertwined that as capital, parts, labor, and expertise flow across national borders it becomes increasingly difficult to distinguish between domestic and foreign products (Harper and Leicht 2007: 110). Labor is becoming redundant on a worldwide basis. Ford moved assembly plants from Michigan to Chihuahua, Mexico, replacing workers who made over $17 an hour with those making less than $3 an hour. They replaced a fully automated plant in Michigan with a semi-automated one in Chihuahua, requiring 700 Mexican workers to do what 400 Michigan workers used to do (Harper and Leicht 2007: 316).

The world economy is increasingly shaped by capitalism, a ceaseless search for markets. Firms and entrepreneurs are constantly seeking for new ways to lower the costs of production of existing products and to create markets for new ones. There is always a tension between how much goes to pay the employee and how much can be profit.

Different wage zones have been used to lower the costs of manufactured goods and also to lower costs in the service sector through the re-routing of phone calls for airline reservations, credit card inquiries and fast transactions (Perrons 2004: 2-10).

Positive Aspects of Globalization

While globalization has severe critics (see below), most observers find a number of positive aspects. Most economists claim that the movement toward a single global market for capital, goods and services, and labor has benefited the United States and the rest of the world. Living standards in the United States are higher by $1 trillion a year than they would have been without economic openness and trade, argues Robert Z. Lawrence, a professor of international trade and investment at Harvard University's John F. Kennedy School of Government (Fischer 2008).

Global transactions increase employment opportunities, transcend political hostilities, transfer technology, and promote cultural understanding. By utilizing low-cost labor, they help keep prices down. Savings may be invested in new products and services and in market expansion (Ferrante 2006: 38, 182).

Globalization can be viewed as the enemy of narrowness, parochialism, isolation, and war. It takes the cleavages of race, nation, and religion and turns them into a universalistic system of values and techniques (Harper and Leicht 2007: 364). Globalization has led to a homogenization of ideas, cultures, political and economic systems, and the vision of the global village.

It can also diminish "inefficient" forms of subjugation such as totalitarianism and gender oppression. It can improve security and political rights, and increase accountability for labor rights, social conditions, and environmental protection. Improved communication can aid human rights (Brysk 2002: 245). (Some observers question this.)

"Dependency theory" (see below) argues that globalization makes poor countries dependent on the richer nations. But many poor nations have never been dependent. Formerly dependent colonies such as Singapore, Hong Kong, India, and some Latin American countries, now enjoy considerable prosperity, perhaps as a result of investment by former colonial powers (Turner 2006: 375).

According to Fareed Zakaria (2008), America has benefited massively from globalization. It has enjoyed robust growth, low unemployment and low inflation, and received hundreds of billions of dollars in investment. U. S. exports and manufacturing have actually held their ground and services have boomed. Robert Samuelson (2008) points out that imports and foreign competition have raised incomes by 10 percent since World War II, according to some studies.

In 2006 and 2007, 124 countries grew their economies at over 4 percent a year. Over the last two decades, lands outside the industrial West have been growing at rates that were once unthinkable. The global economy has more than doubled in size over the last 15 years and is now approaching 54 trillion dollars. Global trade has grown by 133 percent in the same period. While wars and terrorism cause disruption, they eventually are doomed by waves of globalization (Zakaria 2008).

The experiences of China and India—along with Japan, South Korea, and Taiwan in earlier times—show that countries do not have to adopt liberal trade or capital market policies in order to benefit from enhanced trade and grow faster. Countries tend to become more open as they become richer (Held 2005). Russia and China are more integrated into the global economy and society than they have ever been (Zakaria 2008).

Contributing heavily to global capitalism are the new information and communication technologies. These have the potential for increasing productivity and raising welfare levels throughout the world. They have also increased and deepened the flow of information, which has widened people's horizons and increased their ability to challenge prevailing ideologies (Perrons 2004: 328).

Negative Aspects of Globalization

Many scholars acknowledge that globalization does have losers, both within and between countries. Incomes and standards of living of workers in some developing nations, particularly in Africa and Latin America, have declined, says Suzanne Berger, author of a five-year study of the impact of globalization. Some American companies and industries have struggled to compete internationally, which cost the jobs of workers here (Fischer 2008).

The outsourcing of jobs has sparked heated controversy. Capitalists will always seek the cheapest labor costs. A growing number of U. S. firms are exporting employment such as data entry, phone banks, and software design (Peterson 2002). Many manual jobs in shoes, clothes, toys, electronics, and other goods have also been exported (Turner 2006: 368). Commodity prices have soared.

Supporters of globalization claim that workers' income would rise, but the example of Mexico is not reassuring. American business came there, but many of the manufacturing facilities along the border have shut down, as companies moved their production to cheaper priced labor in Asia. Wages rose for awhile in Mexico, but many workers are now out of a job, forcing them into lower wage occupations or encouraging illegal immigration into the U. S. (Turner 2006: 368).

Economic globalization is often unequal and unfair. It has been argued that the debt crisis was used by western-dominated global institutions to remake the economics of debtor nations, especially in Latin America, Africa, and Eastern Europe (Ungar 2007). Unless there is a significant redistribution of global resources, our planet will become increasingly divided into industrial "haves" and nonindustrial "have-nots," struggling in vain to feed more and more people (Macionis 2004: 412). Devising policies to broadly distribute the benefits of globalization is a daunting prospect.

Africa is an example. Problems on this continent bear the imprint of decisions by local elites, in league with multinational corporations, to produce food and other products for export and externally controlled (and depressed) prices, and to import at inflated costs many of the staples needed for sustaining life (Franklin 2003).

Even as capital and manufacturers move about in search of lower cost labor, world-level inequality is increasing. The rich grow richer, as the poor in underdeveloped nations are becoming poorer. The sharp polarization of incomes means that many working people cannot afford to consume the goods and services they are producing (Perrons 2004: 12). Globalization moves capital and jobs around the globe, but, thus far, the world economic system has yet to help, not exploit, the poorest of nations. Inequality tends to breed revolution, war, and terrorism (Turner 2006: 370).

When what one segment of a population receives is seen by another of depriving them of their due, that can lead to violence. Terrorists strike at the developed and rich nations of the world because they see them, sometimes correctly, as implicated in the misery of people (Turner 2006: 272). "The world may currently be concerned with terrorism, but tackling the processes of inequality and injustice is probably more effective than building complex security systems" (Perrons 2004: 328-329).

Global inequality encourages the multinationals in developed nations to export labor and manufacturing costs to poorer nations with cheap pools of labor and unregulated manufacturing sectors. According to "dependency theory," the poorer nations come to depend on technology and capital of wealthy nations that can be moved to another poor nation (Turner 2006: 373). The dominant nations and their corporations gain control over significant segments of the economy and political system of poorer nations. Capital gains are not reinvested in ways to encourage broad-based development. This means that societies have little ability to modernize. The global domination exercised by rich capitalists is a form of colonialism, which perpetuates global inequality (Macionis 2004: 457-458). Globalization provides short-term benefits to the poorer countries, but it stagnates development in the long run because it does not encourage elites to develop economic structures that can employ all its citizens (Turner 2006: 373-374).

The most profitable product for a corporation may not be profitable for a society, because the society pays hidden costs associated with using, making, or disposing of a product that are not figured into the price. These costs include cleaning up the environment, medical treatments for injured workers, consumers, or other victims (Ferrante 2006: 188).

Robert Samuelson, who acknowledges advantages for globalization (noted above), fears that an economy plagued by financial crises, interruptions of crucial supplies, trade wars or violent business cycles could halt or reverse the advantages. "This is globalization's Achilles' heel" (Samuelson 2008).

Corruption is clearly an important issue. Developing countries engage in free trade on disadvantageous terms. The rules of free trade are unevenly applied and resources move from the poor to the rich countries (Perrons 2004: 325). Corruption abounds in the drug traffic in North America.

Major concerns have been voiced about human rights. Analysts of globalization have found that states' international integration improves security rights, but increases inequality and threatens the social rights of citizens. Economic development in and of itself does not improve human rights. The presence of multinational corporations has challenged labor rights throughout Southeast Asia, along the Mexican border, and beyond. Some of the neediest victims, such as the illiterate rural poor and refugee women, are the least likely to receive redress (Brysk 2002: 2-5).

Over 25 million people are international refugees, and an estimated similar number are economic migrants. Refugee camps can become sites of human rights violations, as in Rwanda, Lebanon, Guatemala, and Indonesia. In China alone, an estimated 100 million people are unregistered domestic migrant workers (Brysk 2002: 10).

Environmental restrictions are lax in many countries. Manufacturers move to places where people are desperate for jobs and where governments are slack on environmental controls. Developing countries often encourage the movement of polluters to their shores, increasing effluents of all kinds into the ecosystem (Turner 2006: 369).

Conditions That Promote Development

Turner (2006: 377-378) identifies several conditions that encourage development. They include a skilled population that can take advantage of capital investments; free markets connected to foreign markets, that can attract capital and technology and be used to export goods and services; a favorable political position that can draw key nations into political alliances; governments committed to economic development; and governments or economic actors that can thwart high levels of dependency on foreign nations for key technologies and capital, while being able to convert foreign investments into productive interests serving domestic markets.

However, Turner (2006: 378) fears that world-level poverty will persist and, indeed, increase. A few nations that meet the conditions listed above will grow wealthier. Overall, world inequality will increase and pose severe problems for globalization.

A consensus exists about the important elements necessary for human progress: open economic markets; lower income inequality; democracy and human rights; effective legal systems; literacy and public education; social programs and reasonable safety nets; family planning and environmental protection; and effective though limited government planning (Harper and Leicht 2007: 321).

Brysk (2002: 248-249) argues that transnational and intergovernmental mechanisms are needed to restrain repressive states. The need is to broaden accountability and effective citizenship. Interstate transactions should be shifted to more multilateral mechanisms. Social movements, democratization, and global governance of the market can expand human rights and rescue globalization.

Societies will need to become more inclusive, meaning the gains from increasing productivity will have to be more fairly shared. New technologies could be harnessed so capital widening and deepening take place simultaneously, and combined with a new mode of social regulation, with global dimensions, allowing gains from human ingenuity to be shared more widely. Another mode of social regulation is needed to bring about a more inclusive model of development on a global scale. Some form of global governance resting upon participatory forms of democracy would enable all to share in the fruits of freedom (Perrons 2004: 330).

A global civil society needs to emerge that joins local groups into regional ones, and regional ones into national and international networks of concerned people, organization, and movements. Development of international networks of workers' organizations that can prevent the abuse of workers in one nation to the benefit of those in another is needed. There are networks of people and groups working for democracy, human rights, and sustainable development, but with only limited influence to this point (Harper and Leicht 2007: 322).

As Zakaria (2008) suggests, if China, India, Russia, and Brazil all feel that they have a stake in the existing social order, there will be less danger of war, depression, panics, and breakdowns. There will be many problems and crises, but they will occur against a backdrop of systemic stability.

It is difficult to say if future changes will be progressive or regressive. There is a real need to overcome structures of exploitation and domination. Greater equality such as universal health care and equal opportunity in education is urgently needed. A new management-labor cooperation could increase productivity while providing fair wages and protecting job security. Global hotspots such as the Israeli-Palestinian conflict should be the main priority for international efforts. Issues of social justice involve progressive taxation and pay equity, and programs to guard against race and gender biases in such areas as employment and housing. Steps could be taken to reduce global warming and gain more control over toxic pollution.

Summary

Social change refers to significant modification in the organization or operation of social life. Recent generations have seen huge changes in the world and in this country. Innovation is the invention or discovery of something new, such as what has been seen in computers and telecommunications.

Industrialization and modernization brought important changes to the world. Weber showed how changes from a tradition-oriented society to a modern, rational one affected the world. Durkheim thought that older societies were held together by their common bonds, but the modern society is held together by interdependence. Conflict is both a consequence and cause of change. Marx thought capitalism had brought about important changes, but eventually would give way to revolutionary social change.

Today there is no one dominant family form. Single parent households, blended families, and families headed by gays are only some of the family types present. Despite changes in family life, the core of romantic freedom remains. The role of women has changed but women have not achieved dramatic equality.

While world population may grow to about nine billion, many countries are losing population. The aging of many countries will bring about different political and economic choices. Immigration will be seen as an increasing problem by some, but most scholars believe that, in the long run, it is a good investment for society.

Faith in the government has weakened, partly because of misadventures in Vietnam and Iraq, and partly because the reduction in resources makes it less likely to solve some of our major social problems.

Enormous changes in China include a booming economy and a growing middle class. A huge number of American products are made in China. Yet there are serious problems in pollution, automobile accidents, widespread poverty in rural areas, and a sense of unease in facing these changes.

Social movements occur when people organize to change some area of society; examples include the environmental movement, the women's movement, and civil rights. Individuals can do little to effect social change, but social trends can. Change is most likely when the social situation favors it.

Globalization is the growing interdependence between countries. It can increase employment, spread technology, especially through new information and communications, and promote cultural understanding. Critics claim it outsources jobs, is unfair to poorer countries, tends to make poorer countries dependent on the rich ones, endangers human rights, and encourages corruption.

Conditions that encourage development are reviewed, and possible future trends are discussed.

References

Chang, Leslie T. 2008. "Gilded Age, Gilded Cage" (**National Geographic**, May).

Charon, Joel. 2007. **Ten Questions: A Sociological Perspective**, sixth edition (Belmont, California: Thomson Wadsworth).

Eitzen, D. Stanley, and Maxine Baca Zinn. 2007. **In Conflict and Order: Understanding Society**, eleventh edition (Boston: Allyn and Bacon).

Ferrante, Joan. 2006. **Sociology: A Global Perspective**, sixth edition (Belmont, California: Thomson/Wadsworth).

Fischer, Karin. 2008. "Economic Competitiveness: A Campaign Primer, **The Chronicle Review** (April 25, p. B15).

Franklin, V. P. 2003. "Commentary: U. S. African Americans, Africans, and Globalization" (**The Journal of African-American History,** Vol. 88).

Gray, John. 2004. 'An Illusion With a Future" (**Daedalus,** Vol. 133).

Galvin, Kathleen. 2004. "The Family of the Future: What do we Face?," pp. 675-696 in **The Handbook of Family Communications** (Mahwah, New Jersey: Lawrence Erbaum).

Grimmond, Sue. 2007. "Urbanization and Global Environmental change: Local Effects of Urban Warming" (**The Geographical Journal**, Vol. 173).

Harper, Charles L., and Kevin T. Leicht. 2007. **Exploring Social Change: America and the World**, fifth edition (Upper Saddle River, New Jersey: Pearson).

Held, David, 2005. "Toward a New Consensus: Answering the Dangers of Globalization" (**Harvard International Research**, Vol. 27).

Hessler, Peter. 2008. "Inside the Dragon" (**National Geographic,** May, p. 42).

Katz, Susan Roberta, and Cecilia Elizabeth O'Leary. 2002. "Overview of new pedagogies for social change" (**Social Justice,** Vol. 29).

Koppel, Ted. 2008. "The People's Republic of Capitalism," TNT (July 12).

Laipson, Ellen. 2002. "The Middle East's Demographic Transition: What Does it Mean?" (**Journal of International Affairs**, Vol. 56).

Macionis, John J. 2004. **Society: The Basics,** seventh edition (Upper Saddle River, New Jersey: Prentice Hall).

Martin, Paige D., Don Martin, and Maggie Martin. 2004. "Redefining the American Family" (**Annals of the American Psychotherapy Association**, Vol. 7).

Mohrman, Kathryn. 2006. "Education and Social Change in China: Inequality in a Market Economy" (**Pacific American,** Vol. 79).

N. A. 2006. "Universities Branch Out: From Their Student Bodies to Their Research Practices: Universities are Becoming More Global" (**International Journal of Humanities and Peace**, Vol. 22).

National Geographic. 2008. "China: Inside the Dragon" (May).

Perrons, Diane. 2004. **Globalization and Social Change, People and Places in a Divided World** (London: Routledge).

Perrow, Charles. 2002. **Organizing America: Wealth, Power, and the Origins of Corporate Capitalism** (Princeton, New Jersey: Princeton University Press).

Peterson, Peter G. 2002. "The shape of things to come: global aging in the 21st century" (**Journal of International Affairs**, Vol. 56)

Richter, Rudolf. 2005. "Should We Worry about Family Change?" (**Journal of Comparative Family Studies**, Vol. 36).

Rubin, Beth. 1996. **Shifts in the Social Contract: Understanding Change in American Society** (Thousand Oaks, California: Pine Forge Press).

Samuelson, Robert J. 2008. "Globalization's Achilles Heel," **Newsweek** (July 21).

Singleton, Andrew, Jane Maree Maher. 2004. "The 'NewMan' is in the House: Young Men, Social Change, and Housework" (**The Journal of Men's Studies**, Vol. 12).

Therborn, Goran. 2004. **Sex and Power: Family in the World, 1900-2000** (London: Routledge).

Turner, Jonathan H. 2006. **Sociology** (Upper Saddle River, New Jersey: Prentice Hall).

Ungar, Sheldon. 2007. "Robert K. Schaeffer, Understanding Globalization: The Social Consequences of Political, Economic, and Environmental Change" (**Canadian Journal of Sociology**, Vol. 32).

Zakaria, Fareed. 2008. "The Rise of the Rest" (**Newsweek**, May 12).

GLOSSARY
(*--indicates an extremely important term)

achieved status: a voluntary status that is earned or accomplished.

active adaptation: According to Piaget, biologically based tendency to adjust to and resolve environmental challenges.

actor: one who engages in behavior seen or heard by others.

affirmative action: programs intended to open educational and job programs to minorities.

agents of socialization:* people or groups that affect the individual's self-concept, attitudes, or behaviors.

applied research: specific research projects with policy implications.

applied sociology: the use of sociology to solve social problems.

alienation:* term by Marx meaning a sense of separation from the surrounding society, or a feeling of powerlessness.

anomie: a detachment from the usual norms that guide behavior.

arranged marriage: alliances between two extended families of similar social standing.

ascribed status: a status that is involuntary, either inherited or conferred later in life.

assimilation:* the process by which ethnic and racial distinctions between groups disappear or at least become minimal.

audience: the people viewing or listening to an actor.

authoritarianism: a political system that denies popular participation in government.

authority: legitimate power considered just and proper.

back stage: private places out of sight of the audience.

beliefs: conceptions or shared ideas people accept as true.

blended family: a family whose members were once part of other families.

bourgeoisie: For Marx, capitalists who own or control most things.

Brahman: in Hindu thought, the God above all gods.

bureaucracy:* a government or organization characterized by specialization of function, adherence to fixed rules, and a hierarchy of authority.

capitalism:* an economic system in which natural resources and means of producing goods and services are privately owned.

case study: an intensive examination of a single individual or a small unit.

caste system: a stratification system that is determined at birth and is completely closed.

class consciousness: Marxist term meaning awareness of one's social class position.

classical economics: stresses the individual, profit, and free choice; assumes that consumption is the end of all economic activity. Also known as orthodox economics.

class system:* a stratification system that is relatively open.

cognitive: thinking or reasoning. Cognitive development in children was developed by Jean Piaget.

cohabitation: couples living together before or instead of marriage.

common crime: street crimes, either violent crimes or crimes against property.

community:* a physical place where people settle and where basic institutional activities take place.

comparative studies: a research method of comparing behavior in different cultures.

conflict:* the struggle between major groups in a society. Conflict leads to social change.

conflict perspective:* a point of view that emphasizes the tensions and struggle among different groups in a society.

conglomerates: giant corporations composed of many small ones.

connotation: a word or set of words that implies certain assumptions beyond their literal meaning.

control group: in a classical experiment, the group very much like the experimental group but one that does not receive the stimulus (or variable) being studied.

control theory: the claim that deviants lack strong attachments to those who reject deviance.

corporate crime: the violation of the law by a corporation or on behalf of a corporation.

correlation:* a relationship between two or more variables. It exists if one variable is more (or less) likely to occur when the other occurs.

cosmopolitan: awareness of the larger national and international world.

crime:* the violation of rules that have been written into law; a form of deviance.

crimes without victims: a willing exchange among adults of widely desired but illegal goods and services.

critical theory: a form of conflict theory that favors emancipating people from oppression.

cultural change: a shift in ideas and behaviors in a given society.

cultural diffusion: borrowing of ideas, products, and other things from other societies.

cultural lag: failure of the nonmaterial culture to keep up with material culture (Ogburn).

cultural relativism: examination of other cultures in terms of that society's own values.

cultural transmissions: the process by which one generation passes culture to the next.

cultural universals: values or norms found in every society.

culture:* a distinctive way of life of a group of people; their shared customs and practices.

culture shock: the disorientation and stress found in an unfamiliar cultural setting.

data:* recorded information, often in quantified form.

definition of the situation: the interpretation of a particular situation people find themselves in. See social construction of reality.

democracy:* a system of government that vests power in the people and gives citizens a voice in the decision-making process.

dependency theory: the claim that because of globalization, poor countries become dependent on richer ones.

detached observation: observations of people's behavior without being a part of the group. Also known as nonparticipant observation.

deviance:* behavior that does not conform to social expectations, or the violation of norms.

differential association: a theory of crime by Edwin Sutherland. Individuals learn techniques of crime from close association with those who engage in it.

discrimination:* a behavior that denies valued goals to minority groups.

division of labor: a specialization of economic roles.

dramaturgy: the view that compares social life to the theater or a play (Goffman).

dysfunctions: the negative impact on the society when something is not functioning well.

economic conflict: a struggle between those with large resources and power and those economically deprived.

economics:* the way a society deals with the production and distribution of goods and services. A social institution.

ecumenical: the attempt to promote cooperation, if not merger, among denominations.

egalitarian: authority roughly divided between two groups, especially with reference to race or gender.

endogamy: the norm that people marry someone similar to themselves.

ego: Freudian term for the conscious, rational part of the self that seeks to reconcile the id and the superego.

empirical:* use of the real world for doing research.

environmental racism: the disproportionate exposure of some racial groups to toxic substances.

ethnic group:* a group that shares a common national origin and/or a common culture.

ethnocentrism:* using one's own culture as the standard for judging the worth of foreign ways.

existing data: a form of research that utilizes data that has already been gathered. Same as secondary analysis.

exogamy: the norm that encourages marriage to someone of a different social category.

experiment:* an investigation to untangle cause from effect.

experimental group: In a classical experiment, the group that receives the stimulus (or variable) being tested.

exploitation: use of other human beings as a means to one's own ends (Marx).

exploitation theory: prejudice against minority groups is seen as an extension of the inequality faced by the entire lower class.

extended family: a family unit that includes not only parents and children but other kin.

exurbia: communities located some distance from suburbs.

family:* a group or social network linked by blood, marriage, or adoption. Or, living arrangements recognized under law as constituting a family.

folkways: less salient norms that apply to mundane aspects of daily life.

folk society: a rural lifestyle handed down from the past.

front stage: the public arena in which people perform their roles.

functionalist perspective:* the view that views society as composed of various parts, each with a function that contributes to the stability of the society.

functions: benefits accruing to society. See manifest and latent functions.

fundamentalism: a movement in religion that values revealed truth, rejects modernization, and emphasizes rigid discipline.

game stage: structured, organized activities with rules and a projected outcome (George Herbert Mead).

generalization: the application of what one learns in one situation to similar situations.

generalized other: a system of expected behavior, meanings, and viewpoints that transcend those of the people participating (Mead).

gender roles: behavior and attitudes a society considers proper for its males and females.

genocide: the attempt to eliminate a hated or feared minority group.

global economy: the expanding of economic activity with little regard for national borders.

globalization:* the process of ever-increasing cross-border flows of goods, services, money, people, information, and culture.

goods: commodities such as food and computers. See economics.

group:* people who feel a sense of belonging and regularly interact directly or indirectly with one another.

hate crimes: crimes, especially assault, motivated by bias towards the victim's race or ethnicity, religion, sexual orientation, disability, or national origin.

heterogeneous:* a mixture of many different types of people.

hierarchy: an arrangement of people or things in order of their importance.

high culture: cultural patterns that distinguish a society's elite.

homogamy: the tendency of people to marry someone similar to themselves.

homogeneous:* a similarity among the population.

hypersegregation: extreme segregation where residents have little contact with people in the larger society.

hypothesis:* a statement of what one expects to find in a research project, or how variables are expected to be related to one another..

"I": term by George Herbert Mead referring to the spontaneous, creative self. See "me."

id: the base desires of the self, especially sexual (Freud).

ideal culture: that culture (and its goals) worth aspiring to. See real culture.

impression management: the process by which people manage their dress, words, and gestures to fit the impression or image they are trying to project.

incest taboo: norm forbidding sexual relations or marriage between certain relatives.

Industrial Revolution:* the historical shift from human and animal labor to machines.

Information Revolution: the change resulting from the impact of computers and technologies.

ingroup: a group to which people feel closely attached, particularly in opposition to another group. See outgroup.

innovation: the invention or discovery of something new.

innovator: in deviance, one who accepts the goals of society but rejects the means for fulfilling them.

instinct: the biological origin of behavior. See nature.

institutional discrimination: discrimination that is part of established practices or the customary ways that institutions behave.

institutions: see social institutions.

integration: uniting or bringing people together. See assimilation.

interaction: see social interaction.

interview: in a survey, questions asked of people, recorded by the researcher.

labeling: in deviance, the focus on the significance of labels (names, reputations) that people are given.

laboratory: a room used for research, such as an experiment.

latent functions: unintended, less obvious functions. See manifest functions.

liberation theology: a religious movement concerned about oppression of the poor and marginalized.

life chances: opportunities to live a full, healthy, and meaningful life.

looking-glass self: self-image based on how people think others see them (Charles Cooley).

macro approach: one that emphasizes large-scale patterns of society like urbanization.

manifest functions: obvious and intended functions of some institution.

mass media:* forms of communication widespread in the culture.

mass society: theory that the erosion of traditional societies has led to isolation.

"Me:" the social self that has learned appropriate behavior (Mead). See "I."

mechanical solidarity: as used by Durkheim, solidarity (cohesion) based on commonality or the similarity of the people.

megacities: cities with populations of over 10 million.

megalopolis: metropolitan areas that blend into each other.

melting-pot assimilation: a type of assimilation where groups accept new behaviors and values from each other, so that a blended cultural system emerges.

mestizos: physical type in Mexico combining European and Indian traits.

metropolitan area:* one or more cities and the relatively densely populated area surrounding it.

micro approach: emphasizes small-scale patterns of society.

minority group:* people singled out for unequal treatment and who regard themselves as objects of collective discrimination.

mobility:* movement to a different social class (upward or downward).

modernization:* the process of social change begun by industrialization.

monogamy: marriage that unites two partners.

monopoly: the domination of a market by a single producer.

mores: norms considered extremely important for a society.

multiculturalism: a policy that encourages ethnic differences. See pluralism.

multinational corporations:* enterprises that own or control production and service facilities in countries other than the one in which their headquarters are located.

nature: genetic makeup or biological inheritance of the individual.

Nirvana: in Buddhism, the cessation of suffering.

nonverbal communication: communication using body movements, gestures, and facial expression.

nuclear family:* a family consisting of one or two parents and their children.

nurture:* learning experiences or environmental influences on the individual. See socialization.

norms:* written or unwritten rules that specify behavior appropriate for a certain situation.

observation:* observing and recording people's behavior. See participant and detached observation.

oligopoly: control of the market by a few corporations.

organic solidarity: solidarity brought about by specialization among members of a society. See mechanical solidarity.

organizations: coordinating mechanisms created by people to achieve stated goals.

organized crime: groups that provide and profit from illegal goods and services, or who provide legitimate goods and services by illegal means.

outgroup: a group of individuals towards which an ingroup feels a sense of separation or opposition.

parochial: interests confined to the local scene.

participant observation: observing the behavior of others by engaging in the activities of those one is studying. Also known as fieldwork.

patriarchal: male-dominated, as in an organization or a society.

peer group: a social group whose members have interests, social position, and age in common.

personality: a fairly stable configuration of feeling, attitudes, ideas and behaviors that characterize a person.

perspective: a framework used to think about what is going on around us; a way of looking at society.

play stage: voluntary or spontaneous activity where the child takes the role of another (Mead).

pluralism: in race and ethnic studies, a state in which peoples of all races and ethnicities are distinct but have social parity.

pluralist model of power: the theory that power is dispersed among many different groups and interests. See power elite.

political system:* an institution that organizes and regulates the use of and access to the power necessary to realize local, regional, or international interests.

polygamy: the marriage of three or more people, usually one man and two or more women.

popular culture: cultural patterns that are widespread among a population.

population: the larger group of interest to the researcher.

postindustrial economy: a productive system based on service work and high technology.

postmodernism: the claim that modern technological society devitalizes life and robs humans of the dimensions of experience found in myth, art, ritual, and community.

power:* the ability to exert one's will over the opposition of others.

power elite:* the theory that power is concentrated among a relatively few people at the top.

prejudice: a rigid and usually unfavorable judgment about a minority group; an arbitrary belief or feeling.

preparatory stage: the early stage in childhood marked by imitation (Mead).

prestige: honor or recognition.

primary group:* an intimate group with face-to-face interaction that helps shape people's development.

profession: a prestigious, white-collar occupation that requires education and credentials to perform certain kinds of work.

professional crime: individuals who make their livelihood from crime.

proletariat: the mass of workers with little ownership (Marx).

props: items or objects that decorate or identify a person.

psychoanalytic theory: based on Sigmund Freud, the interpretation of human development in terms of intrinsic drives and motives, many of which are unconscious.

psychology: the study of behavior, especially thinking, learning, perception, emotion, and motives.

questionnaire: questions answered by the people in the sample being surveyed.

race:* a label used to describe perceived biological characteristics of socially defined groups.

racism: the belief that something in the makeup of a minority group explains and justifies their lower status. Also, a domination of one race by another.

rational society: one that gives thought to the most efficient ways to reach goals.

real culture: that which people actually follow.

rebel: in deviance, one who rejects conventional means and goals, but who would like to replace them with new means and/or goals.

recidivism: the repetitive nature of crime or other deviant act.

reference group: a group that people use as guides in developing their attitude and behavior.

religion:* human responses that give meaning to the ultimate problems of existence, or, belief in the sacred.

replication: the repetition of a research study.

research design: choosing one or more research methods.

research methods:* specific strategies used to gather and analyze data.

retreatist: in deviance, one who rejects both the goals and means of society.

resocialization: the process of learning new norms, attitudes, or behaviors, or being socialized all over again.

ritual: a patterned and stereotyped sequence of actions; in religion, these are directed towards the sacred.

ritualist: in deviance, one who rejects the goals of society but who accepts the means.

role:* behavior expected in a particular status. The part one plays.

role conflict: a tension between roles corresponding to two or more statuses.

role exit: the process by which people disengage from important social roles.

role performance: the emphasis or interpretation people themselves; their style.

role strain: a tension between roles connected to a single status.

role taking: imagining one's appearance to an outsider (Mead).

sacred: deep and absorbing sentiments of respect, mystery, and awe.

sample: the segment of a larger group (the population) that is questioned in a survey.

sanctions: socially imposed rewards for conformity and punishments for deviance; may be formal or informal.

secondary groups: those that people belong to but on a less intimate and more formal basis.

sect: a smaller church, usually one that has broken away from a denomination and holds certain distinctive beliefs.

secularization: the decline in importance of religious institutions in society and in the lives of individuals.

self:* an identity that arises as people see themselves as others see them.

self-employment: employed people who do not work for an organization.

segregation: a physical or social separation of racial and ethnic groups.

services: tasks performed by people. See economics.

social capital: advantages individuals possess by being connected to others.

social change:* any significant alternation or transformation in the organization and operation of social life.

social classes:* categories of people ranked in a hierarchy.

social conflict: see conflict.

social construction of reality: the creation by people in social relationships of what they regard as true. See definition of the situation.

social contract: the shared understandings that structure cooperation, such as in the workplace or in a marriage.

social control:* mechanisms that ensure conformity or punish deviance. See sanctions.

social economics: a perspective that focuses on the wholeness of social life, the good and just society.

social inequality: condition that exists when significant numbers of people have less resources than others.

social institutions:* established patterns of interaction and thought that organize social activities, such as education, economics, and politics.

social interaction:* the process by which people act and react in relation to others.

socialism: an economic system in which natural resources and the means of production are collectively owned.

socialization:* the lifelong process of learning the values and norms of one's culture.

social construction of reality: the process by which people creatively shape reality through social interaction.

social learning: imitation or modeling of others (Bandura).

social movements:* the organization of a substantial number of people to change (or resist change in) some aspect of society.

social networks: the social ties radiating outward from someone that link people together.

social patterns: themes or regularities in social interaction. They make possible a cooperative social order.

social sciences: the disciplines that study human behavior, usually sociology, anthropology, psychology, economics, and political science.

social stratification:* a system by which society ranks categories of people in a hierarchy.

social structure: the typical patterns consisting of relationships of people to one another, which gives direction and sets limits on behavior.

social trends: long-lasting, far-reaching, general developments that affect all the various social patterns in society.

social work: a profession for helping people.

society:* the people who interact in a defined territory and share a culture.

sociocultural theory: growth of knowledge and development in terms of the guidance and support provided by the society (Vygotsky).

sociological imagination: the realization that individual circumstances are linked to the structure of society.

sociology:* the systematic study of society and social interaction.

solidarity: cohesion, or the unity of people through shared values.

Standard Metropolitan Statistical Area (SMSA): one or more cities of at least 50,000 inhabitants, and the surrounding area that has a metropolitan character.

status:* a social position an individual occupies

status consistency: condition that exists when the measures of social class agree in placing an individual.

status inconsistency: condition that exists when two or more measures of social class disagree, as when a poor person has a college degree.

status symbols: signs that identify a status.

stereotypes: exaggerated generalizations about a group of people. See prejudice.

stigma: characteristics that discredit people.

structural strain: a theory of deviance that emphasizes the tension between the established goals of a society and the means for achieving them.

subcultures:* groups that possesses distinctive traits that set them off from the larger culture.

suburbs: smaller cities surrounding a large one.

superego: For Freud, the voice of society, formulated as conscience.

surveys:* polls which collect data by having people answer a series of questions.

symbolic interaction:* a perspective in sociology focusing on everyday interactions of people and how they are interpreted.

symbols: objects, words, or gestures people use to communicate with one another. "Significant" symbols are the more important ones in people's development.

technology: the information, techniques, and tools used by people to satisfy their various needs and desires.

theocracy: a government controlled by religious leaders.

theory: a set of related statements about how some parts of the world fit together and how they work.

Thomas theorem: a theory that holds that situations defined as real are real in their consequences.

totalitarianism: a system with centralized political power and an official ideology.

traditional society: one in which things were done because they had always been done that way.

underclass: the static poor trapped in their situation by restricted opportunities and other forces.

unobtrusive measures: a research method seeking information after the behavior has occurred.

urbanization: the process whereby an increasing proportion of the population lives in cities.

urban society: modern society held together by specialization and interdependence.

values: broad, abstract, shared standards of what is considered right and worthwhile.

variable: a trait or characteristic that can change from one person to another.

visual studies: research method using photographs and filmed material.

wealth: one's total assets, including income, property, etc.

welfare capitalism: market-based economy that also offers broad social welfare programs.

white-collar crime: violation of the law by middle and upper-class people in the course of their business and social lives.

About the Author

Charles Emory Burton is a retired sociologist living in Dallas, Texas. In addition to a seminary degree, he holds the Ph.D. in sociology from the University of Tennessee, Knoxville. He has taught at such schools as the University of Alabama in Huntsville and McMurry University, Abilene, Texas. He has also taught part-time at several community colleges and at the University of Texas at Dallas.

Dr. Burton is the author of two previous books, *The Poverty Debate* (Greenwood Press, 1992), a textbook on poverty in the United States, and *Preacher, Prophet, Poet, The Biography of Wallace E. Chappell* (AuthorHouse, 2004). He has written several book chapters and articles on such subjects as poverty in America, homelessness, and film. He is also an ordained minister of the United Methodist Church.